Cambridge Review

ARCO
Teach Yourself
the TOEFL*

in 24 Hours

2000 Edition

MACMILLAN • USA

*TOEFL is a registered trademark of the College Entrance Examination Board, which does not endorse this book.

Macmillan General Reference
A Pearson Education Macmillan Company
1633 Broadway
New York, NY 10019

Macmillan Publishing books may be purchased for business, education or sales promotional use. For information please write: Special Markets Department, Macmillan Publishing USA, 1633 Broadway, New York, NY 10019.

ISBN: 0-02-863240-0 (book only)
ISBN: 0-02-863241-9 (book with CD-ROM)

Library of Congress number:

99-63232 (book only)
99-63233 (book with CD-ROM)

Manufactured in the United States of America

01 00 99   10 9 8 7 6 5 4 3 2 1

Contents

Part IV Listening Questions   211

From the desk of David Waldherr
President, Cambridge Educational Services

Dear Teacher or School Administrator,

This Teach Yourself book has been designed by Cambridge Educational Services as a self-study program. However, as an educator, I know that many students need the structure of a course schedule and the discipline of a classroom environment in order to succeed on the TOEFL. Many families make a large financial sacrifice to enroll their children in expensive test-preparation courses, and indeed, studies have shown that such programs can be very effective.

Now your students don't have to choose between spending a fortune on test-prep coaching and perhaps risking rejection at a first-choice school or missing out on a scholarship.

Today, hundreds of schools in every state use materials that Cambridge has created to provide top-quality, in-school TOEFL preparation. These materials are designed especially for use by your teachers in your classrooms. Cambridge has more school partners than all of the expensive test preparation companies combined!

Cambridge makes it easy for you to establish and expand your own high-quality, affordable test prep programs. Here's what you get:

- **The finest teaching materials:** Affordable student textbooks, official diagnostic and final exams and explanations, classroom-tested programs, practice tests, remedial review, quizzes, skill-builders, and computer software.

- **First-rate teacher assistance:** Teacher training, toll-free 24-hour teacher assistance hot line, class formats and schedules, teacher guides, concept outlines and summary sheets, test-prep strategies, and local teacher training conferences.

- **Administrative convenience:** Administrator's handbook including sample brochures, evaluations, schedules, parent and student letters, teacher selection criteria, and detailed course outlines for intensive, premium, overlapping and revolving courses.

Your school will schedule classes and set course fees (if any), select and compensate the teachers you choose, and register your own students. Schedules are available for after-school, weekend, or semester-long credit and non-credit courses.

For more information about offering Cambridge courses at your school, and to obtain a free sample of our GRE, PSAT, SAT, ACT, PLAN, EXPLORE, GMAT, TOEFL, LSAT, MCAT, GED, NTE, PPST, ITBS, Standardized Test Math, or College Prep materials please call us at 847-299-2930 or visit our Web site at **www.cambridgereview.com**.

About This Book

Welcome to *ARCO Teach Yourself the TOEFL in 24 Hours*. The test-makers, otherwise known as ETS, would like you to believe that you can't beat the TOEFL. Well that's only half true. You can't study for the TOEFL, but you sure can prepare for it—and that's where this book comes in. As Cambridge teachers. we have examined the TOEFL question by question and answer choice by answer choice. We've literally taken each test apart, analyzed every component, and then put the pieces back together again. The result of all of our efforts is a proven plan. We call it the Cambridge Action Plan. It's the surefire method that works so well for students in our classes. And we're using many of these methods in this exciting new book.

By working your way through these pages, you'll get a structured course covering all the key points you need to know to raise your TOEFL score. In just 24 one-hour lessons, you'll review all of the topics and concepts that are tested on the TOEFL, and you will learn powerful strategies for answering every question type.

How to Use This TOEFL Book

This book has been designed as a 24-hour teach-yourself training course, complete with examples, workshops, quizzes, and full-length sample test sections. It is expected that you can complete each lesson in about one hour. However, you should work at your own rate. If you think you can complete a lesson in an hour, go for it! Also, if you think that you should spend more than one hour on a certain topic, spend as much time as you need.

Who Should Use This Book

- Students looking for a self-paced tutorial written by Cambridge Educational Services—the course used by over 500 educational institutions in the United States

- Students who are too busy to spend hundreds of hours in a classroom

- Students who cannot afford a private course costing thousands of dollars

- Students who want extended practice—you'll get extra drills at **www.CambridgeEd.com**

About the Authors

Who are we? We're the teachers at Cambridge Educational Services, the fastest growing new powerhouse in on-campus test-prep. On hundreds of high school and university campuses nationwide, we help students raise their test scores and get into the college or graduate school of their choice. We wrote this book to help you beat the TOEFL. We don't promise to raise your GPA or to get you on the honor roll. And we won't ask you to spend every night for the next six months chained to your desk, studying. What we do promise is that absolutely everything in this book has just one purpose: to help you earn the highest TOEFL score you can. And isn't that exactly what you want?

We're on your side, so count on us to make your college dreams come true!

—The Curriculum Committee
at Cambridge Educational Services

Acknowledgments

Many, many thanks to all of the hardworking teachers, authors, and educators who have helped make Cambridge Educational Services the largest campus-based test-prep in the United States. Ever since Cambridge was started in 1990, our mission has been to provide schools all across America with first-rate test-prep at an affordable price. And now teachers all over America are teaching their own students test-prep strategies. Over 3,000 teachers have put forth an extraordinary effort to make our mission come true.

My special thanks to Tom Martinson, Senior Cambridge author and Chair of the Cambridge Review Curriculum Committee; and to my wife, Kathy, for her extraordinary insight as a mathematics teacher. I also wish to thank my dedicated staff, especially Matthew and Sally.

And of course to the hundreds of high schools, colleges, and universities across America who chose Cambridge materials for their campus-based test-preparation programs—your devotion and loyalty have truly launched a test-prep revolution.

Thanks for being a part of Cambridge Educational Services!

David P. Waldherr
President

CAMBRIDGE *Review*™

Find out more about Cambridge!

Whether you are a student, parent, teacher or school administrator, you can get more information about our low-cost, top-quality TestPrep PLUS™ courses and study materials just by filling out this form below. Mail the information to River Road Office Center, 2720 River Road, Des Plaines, IL 60018. Or e-mail us at: testprep@cambridgereview.com.

Cambridge TestPrep PLUS™ Information Request Form

Attach or Staple Business Card or Label Here	Name: _____ Job Title (position): _____ School: _____ School Address: _____ City/State/Zip: _____ Phone: _____ Fax: _____ E-mail: _____

Total School Enrollment: _____

School Grade (circle all that apply):

K 1 2 3 4 5 6 7 8 9 10 11 12 College

Circle choices below to receive (fill in quantity) _____ complimentary sample(s) of Cambridge TestPrep™ materials for you, your school, or your district:

ACT	MCAT	EXPLORE	SAT
TOEFL	PLAN	PSAT	PRAXIS I PPST
COLLEGE PREP	GRE	PRAXIS II NTE	ITBS (Iowa)
GMAT	GED	LSAT	Standardized Test Math

OTHER (please specify)

Do you currently offer any test preparation programs?   ☐ Yes   ☐ No

If yes what material(s) do you use? _____

_____

If not, have you ever considered implementing a test preparation program at your school?   ☐ Yes   ☐ No

Would you coordinate your test preparation course programs?   ☐ Yes   ☐ Someone Else? _____

I am primarily interested in receiving Cambridge's free sample(s) for (circle all that apply):

Teaching our own course

Outside party teaches course

Student self-study course

Diagnostic assessment

Software preparation (take home)

Software preparation (school lab)

Semester-long course

After-school course

My school

My community

Myself

Son/daughter

Part I

Get to Know the TOEFL

Hour

Hour 1

Teach Yourself All About the TOEFL

What You'll Do This Hour

- What is the TOEFL?
- TOEFL Subjects
- TOEFL Strategies
- Q & A Session

Your Goals for This Hour

Today, you'll begin teaching yourself how to get a top score on the TOEFL. Here are your goals for this hour:

- Learn what the TOEFL is
- Learn what subjects are tested

- Learn TOEFL strategies
- Get answers to frequently asked questions

What Is the TOEFL?

"TOEFL" stands for the Test of English as a Foreign Language. The TOEFL is an English proficiency exam. Scores on the TOEFL are required by many colleges and universities of applicants whose native or first language is not English. If your native or first language is not English, you'll probably have to take the TOEFL; but before you do, you should contact the schools to which you will apply to determine whether or not you're required to take the TOEFL.

For many years, the TOEFL was exclusively a paper-and-pencil-based exam, that is, the kind where you work from a booklet containing test questions and indicate your answers by darkening ovals on a separate answer sheet with a No. 2 pencil. In some countries, the TOEFL is still a paper-and-pencil-based exam.

In other countries, the TOEFL is a computer-based test. You take the test while seated in a carrel at a computer center. Questions appear on the monitor screen, and you answer by pointing and clicking with a mouse. The computer keeps track of your responses, selects new questions from its data banks, and scores your results.

 NOTE Whether you will take the computer-based or the paper-based test depends entirely on where you take the exam. If the computer-based exam is available, you must take that format because the paper-based format is no longer an option in that area. The paper-based format is gradually being phased out.

When you are ready to take the test, you must register with the testing agency. To get more information about testing in your area, you should obtain a copy of the TOEFL *Information Bulletin*. The *Information Bulletin* is available at United States educational commissions and foundations, U.S. Information Service (USIS) offices, bi-national centers, and some private educational organizations. The *Information Bulletin* is available free of charge. You can also obtain information directly from the testing agency:

TOEFL
P.O. Box 6151
Princeton, NJ 08541-6151
USA
http://www.toefl.org

TOEFL SUBJECTS

Your TOEFL exam will include four subjects.

- Listening Comprehension
- Sentence Structure
- Reading Comprehension
- Essay

NOTE

The Essay, called Test of Written English (TWE), is an integral part of the computer-based TOEFL. The TWE is offered with only certain administrations of the paper-based format. Check the TOEFL registration materials for more information.

Listening

Listening involves listening to a recording of spoken English and answering questions on the content of what you've heard. For example:

You hear:

(a man) I'm hungry.

(a woman) Me too. We'd better hurry because the student cafeteria closes in 20 minutes.

(narrator) What will the man and the woman do?

      (A) Wait 20 minutes before going to the cafeteria.

      (B) Go immediately to the cafeteria to eat.

      (C) Eat out at a restaurant sometime later.

      (D) Buy groceries to prepare something to eat.

The correct answer is (B).

MAKE CONNECTIONS

This book includes recordings of practice Listening exercises and scripts of those recordings. See the instructions before each Listening exercise for advice on how to make the best use of these preparation resources.

Structure

The Structure section tests your ability to recognize standard written English. There are two kinds of structure questions.

Type I

DIRECTIONS: The sentence below is incomplete. Choose the word or phrase that best completes the sentence.

After breaking away from Miles Davis in 1959, John Coltrane —— his own musical instincts and had an important influence on the development of Jazz.

    (A) followed

    (B) following

    (C) to follow

    (D) he follows

The correct answer is (A). The sentence should read:

After breaking away from Miles Davis in 1959, John Coltrane followed his own musical instincts and had an important influence on the development of Jazz.

Type II

DIRECTIONS: The sentence below has four underlined parts. Choose the one that contains an error.

The court <u>ordered</u> the <u>pilots striking</u> to return to work <u>or</u> face a stiff fine and perhaps
         A   B   C

<u>even</u> jail.
 D

The correct answer is (B). The sentence should read:

The court ordered the striking pilots to return to work or face a stiff fine and perhaps even jail.

Reading

The Reading section tests your ability to comprehend written English. Here is an example:

DIRECTIONS: Following the passage below is a question with four answer choices. Choose the best answer based upon what is stated or implied in the passage.

The great Shawnee chief Tecumseh feared that contact between white and Indian civilizations would mean the eventual destruction of the Indian civilization. By 1794, he had become a charismatic leader with a well-deserved reputation as an able warrior and just leader. When the Delawares were pushed out of lands guaranteed to them by treaty, they turned to Tecumseh for leadership. Tecumseh attempted to block the advance of white settlers into the Old Northwest Territory by forming a federation of Indian tribes that reached all the way from Alabama to Minnesota. He traveled to many other tribes and addressed them in council. He explained that he hoped that the white settlers would withdraw peaceably; but if they did not, it was his plan to drive them out by using superior force.

According to the passage, Tecumseh was a

    (A) white settler

    (B) Shawnee

    (C) Delaware

    (D) Alabaman

The correct answer is (B).

In this passage, the word "federation" means

    (A) region

    (B) culture

    (C) battle

    (D) alliance

The correct answer is (D).

The Essay

In the Essay part, you'll be allowed 30 minutes to prepare an essay on an assigned topic. Here is a sample essay topic:

Read and think about the following statement:

Some people say that the purpose of a university education is to encourage students to become intellectually independent by teaching them to think on their own; others say that the purpose is to teach skills that will be useful in later life.

Do you agree or disagree? Write an essay stating your opinion and giving reasons to support your position.

There is no right or wrong answer to the essay question. Instead, you are graded on how well you write. But writing well for an essay question means a lot more than just avoiding grammatical mistakes. We'll cover everything you need to know about the Essay section in Hour 22.

Format

The number of questions and the amount of time to answer that you will receive depends on whether you take the paper-based version of the test or the computer-based version.

Paper-Based Version

PART	NUMBER OF QUESTIONS	TIME LIMIT
Listening	50	35 minutes
Structure	40	25 minutes
Reading	50	55 minutes
TWE*	1 Prompt	30 minutes

*Depending on whether this component is offered with your TOEFL administration.

Compter-Based Version

PART	NUMBER OF QUESTIONS	TIME LIMIT
Computer Tutorial	No Scored Questions	Untimed
Listening	30 to 50	40 to 60 minutes
Structure	20 to 25	15 to 25 minutes
BREAK		10 minutes
Reading	44 to 60	70 to 90 minutes
Essay	1 Prompt	30 minutes
Total Time: 4 to 4.5 hours		

1

Your TOEFL Scores

How your test is scored depends on whether you take the paper-based or the computer-based version of the TOEFL. We'll return to that question below. For right now, you can use the following tables to see what the ranges are. TOEFL scores are reported on artificial scales designed especially for the TOEFL; and when the computer-based version was developed, new scales were introduced so that there wouldn't be any confusion between the old version and the new version.

Paper-Based TOEFL Scores

PART	MINIMUM	MAXIMIM
Listening	31	68
Structure	31	68
Reading	31	67
Total	310	677
Essay	0	6

Computer-Based TOEFL Scores

PART	MINIMUM	MAXIMIM
Listening	0	30
Structure	0	30
Reading	0	30
Total	0	300
Essay	0	6

Because the scores for the two different formats are reported on different scales, admissions officers are given concordance (comparison) tables that permit them to compare a score on one format with a score on the other format.

 NOTE

According to the testing agency, scores on the two formats are comparable, so it should not matter which version you take. Even though scores on the paper-based scale seem to be higher (310 to 677) than those on the computer-based scale (0 to 300), there is really no difference, because admissions officers use conversion tables to make them comparable.

Here is a partial concordance table that permits you to compare scores on the pencil-and-paper version of the TOEFL with the computer-based version.

Concordance Table

LISTENING		STRUCTURE		READING		TOTAL SCORE	
PAPER	COMP.	PAPER	COMP.	PAPER	COMP.	PAPER	COMP.
68	30	68	30	67	30	677	300
65	28	65	28	65	28	650	280
60	25	60	25	60	25	600	250
55	21	55	22	55	21	550	213
50	16	50	18	50	17	500	173
45	11	45	14	45	13	450	133

TOEFL Strategies

In the lessons that follow, you'll learn strategies for each of the topics covered by the TOEFL. And this material is extremely valuable regardless of which TOEFL format you'll be taking—the computer-based or the paper-and-pencil version.

The paper-and-pencil version of the TOEFL and the computerized version of the exam are nearly identical in terms of content. They use the same question types, and they test the same concepts. In fact, the two versions are so similar that the testing agency maintains that scores on the two versions are comparable in spite of the fact that the scales used to produce those scores are dissimilar—provided that one uses the appropriate concordance tables.

Still, there are obvious differences in the way that the two tests are delivered. The paper-and-pencil version is delivered using the traditional format of a test booklet and a separate answer grid on which you enter your responses to the questions in the booklet. The computer-based version is administered by a computer. Consequently, the two versions differ in terms of the mechanics of testing.

You should read about both versions. That way, if you hear something from someone about "taking the TOEFL," you'll know whether it applies to you or not.

The Paper-and-Pencil TOEFL

The paper-and-pencil version is delivered in the form of a booklet accompanied by an answer sheet. You indicate your responses to the questions in the booklet by coding the appropriate oval or bubble on the answer sheet using a No. 2 pencil. You are responsible for bringing your own No. 2 pencils to the testing center. In fact, No. 2 pencils are the only items that you should bring to the examination center—aside from the identification that you need.

NOTE | According to the testing agency, scores on the two formats are comparable. The only thing you'll be allowed to bring into the examining room are your pencils. You'll not be allowed to have beverages, chewing gum, or tobacco; you'll not be allowed to have paper, highlighter pens, or reference guides; and you'll not be allowed to have a recording device, a pager, or a cell phone.

At the end of the test, the answer sheets are collected by the proctor (along with the booklets) and sent to a central processing location where they are machine-graded. After grading, a computer scores your test and generates a score report.

It's important that you code your answer sheet correctly. Make certain that each oval is completely dark and that you erase any stray marks before submitting your answer sheet, as a stray mark might be read as an intended response.

TIP | Darken your answer ovals from the inside out rather than vice versa. This method is quicker.

Each of the three sections of multiple-choice questions plus the Test of Written English is separately timed. You're permitted to work on only the section that is currently being administered. You're not permitted to go back to an earlier section on which time has already expired; and you're not permitted to skip ahead to a new section, even if you finish your work early on a section.

CAUTION | The sections in the testing material are clearly marked, so the proctor can observe anyone who is not working on the correct section.

You are, however, permitted to work on all the questions within a section during the time that section is being administered. This means that you can go back and check your work if you finish the section early—but you can check your work on that section only.

> **TIP** Bring a watch to the testing center. Keep track of the passing time. If you suspect that the proctor has not correctly administered the examination, lodge a complaint immediately.

Don't think in terms of "average time per question;" think more generally about milestones. When three-quarters of your time remains, you want to have finished the first one-fourth of the work on that section. At the halfway marker, you should be halfway through the questions . . . and so on.

> **TIP** Don't spend too much time on any one question. If you sense that you're not making any progress on an item, enter an answer choice and move along. Perhaps before time expires on that section, you'll have time to come back to that question.

One of the issues that always seems to come up with standardized multiple-choice tests like the TOEFL is the question of guessing: Should I guess or leave blank items that I can't answer? The short answer to this question is: Guess.

The TOEFL uses the "right answers only" method of scoring. In other words, you get credit for right answers but no adjustment is made for wrong answers; there is no penalty for guessing. So make sure that you enter an answer for every item.

> **TIP** While there is no penalty for guessing, "educated guessing" is better than "random guessing." Eliminate as many choices as you can before you make your guess.

The Computer-Based TOEFL

The first thing to note about the computer-based TOEFL is that the restrictions on what you are permitted to have with you in the testing room are similar to those for the paper-and-pencil version. (See above.) You, however, won't even need a No. 2 pencil. Everything is done by the computer, including your TWE response.

> **TIP**
>
> Even with the computer-based TOEFL, you're given the option of writing your essay in hand. If you're not comfortable composing at the keyboard, choose the handwriting option.

As the chart in the preceding section shows, your computerized testing session begins with an untimed tutorial. During this period, you will familiarize yourself with the hardware that is available (the monitor, the mouse and the keyboard) and the on-screen testing tools and procedures.

> **TIP**
>
> Take as much time as you need to complete the tutorials. Make certain that you're comfortable with the equipment that you will be using.

In addition to the hardware tutorial, the computer-based version of the TOEFL uses a number of on-screen testing tools. For example, you indicate your response to a question by using the mouse to position the cursor. You then press one of the buttons on the mouse to highlight your selection. At that point, you indicate to the computer that you've made your selection by choosing the arrow key on the toolbar to show that you wish to proceed. You then have to click on a second button labeled "Confirm."

These actions are more complicated to read about than to do. Just make sure that you spend the time with the tutorial to become comfortable with the procedure.

> **CAUTION**
>
> If you are staring at the screen and nothing is happening, then you've probably forgotten to confirm your response. Immediately click on the "Confirm" button.

At the beginning of each section, you'll see the directions displayed. You'll already be familiar with the directions from your work in this book, so don't bother to read them. Get right to work answering questions.

In order to get to work however, you must "Dismiss" the directions. This is accomplished by pointing to and clicking on the button entitled "Dismiss Directions."

If you're staring at the screen with the directions, then you've forgotten to dismiss the directions. Make it a practice to dismiss the directions immediately so this does not happen to you.

In the Listening part, you'll be given the opportunity to adjust the volume of the recording before the section begins. Take a few moments to experiment with the volume control and find a level that is comfortable—not too loud to be distracting but loud enough to be heard clearly.

 Once you begin the Listening section, you'll not be able to adjust the volume. You have to adjust the volume *before* the Listening section begins.

In the Reading section, you'll have to use the on-screen "scroll" function in order to read the entire reading passage. It's a peculiarity of the Reading section that the computer does not allow you to answer the first question until you have used the scroll function to review the entire passage.

 Begin each reading passage by automatically scrolling to the bottom of the passage—even before you read a word. This will return control of the mouse to you.

When you take the computerized version of the TOEFL, the computer keeps track of the passing time. On the toolbar, you'll see a clock icon that shows the passing time.

 You can suppress the time display. Simply click on the icon to suppress; click a second time to activate.

The computer-based version of the TOEFL gives you the option of entering your response to the TWE prompt by using the keyboard—that is—by typing or word-processing your answer. You may, if you choose, produce a handwritten response. It's your choice.

You'll be given an opportunity during the untimed tutorial at the beginning of the testing session to experiment with the keyboard. You'll find that the word processing program used to produce TWE responses is fairly primitive. It will not contain many of the functions that you may have grown accustomed to. You will be able to delete, insert, type, and cut-and-paste; you will not, however, have a spell-checker and other functions.

Experiment with the keyboard before you decide which method to use for the TWE.

NOTE

The keyboard at your testing center may or may not be in English or your native language. If not, then you should probably prefer to submit a handwritten response.

While the mechanics of testing are important, the most significant feature of the computer-based version of the TOEFL goes on behind the scenes. Two of the sections (Listening and Structure), are computer-adaptive—that is, the computer is actually constructing your test as you enter your answers. (The Reading section is still a linear or non-interactive section.)

Here's how it works. The computer has access to a database of items that are sorted according to the concept being tested and level of difficulty. The computer begins by giving a couple of items of average level difficulty. If you answer correctly, it moves you up the ladder of difficulty and gives you a couple of harder items; if you answer incorrectly, it moves you down the ladder of difficulty. The process continues—moving up a little and down a little—until the computer has determined what score represents your ability level.

TIP

Questions at the beginning of the interactive sections are worth more than questions at the end. So spend a little extra time on items at the beginning to make sure that you initially move up the ladder of difficulty and not down it.

Because the Listening and Structure are interactive, the computer does not allow you to proceed to the next item until you have entered an answer to the question that is on the screen. (Reading is a different matter; you can skip questions and go back if you want to.)

CAUTION

Even though you *can* skip a question in the Reading section, you should refrain from doing so, because in order to return to that question, you'll have to "page" back through every problem to get to it . . . and doing so is very time-consuming.

Insofar as the computerized TOEFL is concerned, guessing is a dead issue. There is no penalty for guessing on the Reading, and you have no choice in the matter for the other two sections: You can't get to the next question until you answer the one on the screen.

> **TIP**
>
> Keep an eye on the passing time and the number of questions remaining. Ideally, you want to finish the last question just as time expires because you don't get extra credit for finishing earlier and the more time you have the more accurate you'll be.

Q & A Session

Q: Are the questions that I study in this book the same ones that will be used on my TOEFL?

A: No. Each new edition of the TOEFL uses new questions. The questions in this book are representative of those that you will have on your test. If you can answer the questions in this book, then you can answer similar questions on your TOEFL.

Q: Do I have to know a lot about computers to take the computer-based TOEFL?

A: No. The test itself has virtually nothing to do with computers. The computer is just the delivery mechanism. And you're given an untimed period at the start of the test to practice manipulating the mouse. If you can play a video game, then you can take the computer-based TOEFL.

Q: When should I take the TOEFL?

A: That depends on the deadlines set by the programs to which you are applying. Just remember to allow yourself enough time to schedule the test, register to take it, receive your scores, and have your scores sent to the schools to which you're applying. In general, this takes longer if you register for the paper-and-pencil version of the TOEFL.

This Hour's Review

1

1. The TOEFL stands for Test of English as a Foreign Language. If English is not your first or native language, you'll probably be required to take the TOEFL—but check with the schools to which you're applying just to be sure.

2. The TOEFL is not given in two different forms: paper-and-pencil and computer-based. You'll have to take the one that's offered in your region.

3. Both versions of the TOEFL test the same subjects:

   Listening

   Structure

   Reading

   TWE (Not offered with all paper-and-pencil tests.)

4. Be sure you are familiar with the testing procedures for the version of the TOEFL that you'll be taking.

Hour 2

The TOEFL MiniTest

What You'll Do This Hour

- The TOEFL MiniTest
- The MiniTest Review
- Q & A Session

Your Goals for This Hour

The best way to get familiar with the TOEFL is to "jump right in." Today, you'll take the TOEFL MiniTest. You'll be using it to get familiar with the kinds of questions asked and the issues that are tested.

Here are your goals for this hour:

- Take the TOEFL MiniTest
- Review your work on the MiniTest
- Get answers to frequently asked questions

The MiniTest consists of three parts. Each part is separately timed. Set aside a half hour for the whole MiniTest during which you won't be disturbed. Be sure to have a watch or a clock available to time yourself. Mark your answers in your book.

> For Part I, have a friend read Script 1 to you. If that is not possible, then read Script 1 to yourself. You can find all the scripts used throughout this book in Appendix A.

> The MiniTest does not include an Essay part.

The TOEFL MiniTest

Part I

10 Questions • Time—10 minutes (approximately)

> Even though the directions say "On the recording, you will hear people speaking," there is no actual recording of the scripts in Appendix A. You can, however, use the accompanying CD-ROM to practice with the Listening section (as there are recorded scripts available on the CD-ROM, just not the scripts that match those you will read in the appendix). Again, you'll need a friend to read you the scripts, or you can read them yourself.
>
> We've left the instructions as they are, to represent how instructions will be presented on a real test.

DIRECTIONS: This is a test of Listening Comprehension. On the recording, you will hear people speaking. A narrator will ask you questions. The narrator's questions and answers to the questions appear below. Choose the <u>best</u> answer to each question.

The taped discussion is NOT repeated. Time for this part is over when you have answered the last question.

Begin listening now.

NOTE These questions reference Script 1 in Appendix A. Visit *www.cambridgereview.com* for audio transcripts.

2

Question 1

1. What does the woman imply?
   (A) She did not have to go to work last night.
   (B) Her telephone is often out of order.
   (C) She doesn't want to talk to the man.
   (D) The telephone company fixed her phone.

Question 2

2. What does the man mean?
   (A) He doesn't plan to go skiing again.
   (B) He doesn't need any new ski equipment.
   (C) The sale on ski equipment is over.
   (D) The store's merchandise is over-priced.

Question 3

3. What does the woman mean?
   (A) She did not borrow the man's calculus book.
   (B) The man is majoring in mathematics.
   (C) She did not attend junior high school.
   (D) She already returned the calculus book to the man.

Questions 4–5

4. What are the man and woman talking about?

   (A) Renting an apartment.
   (B) Finding a new job.
   (C) Doing library research.
   (D) Enrolling at another school.

5. What does the man imply?
   (A) He does not want a roommate.
   (B) He would like to share an apartment with the woman.
   (C) He does not have enough money for a new apartment.
   (D) His thesis is already finished.

Questions 6–10

6. What is the main focus of the passage?
   (A) Causes for the changing seasons
   (B) A ritual of ancient Egyptians
   (C) Rules of modern games
   (D) Ancient military battles

7. According to the professor, who was Set?
   (A) god of darkness
   (B) god of light
   (C) god of fertility
   (D) Egyptian pharaoh

8. Why did the mock combat take place in the spring?
   (A) The weather was mild.
   (B) People were not otherwise occupied.
   (C) Other cultures wished to participate.
   (D) Springtime marked the changing of the seasons.

9. According to the professor, what did the ball originally symbolize?

   (A) the head of a god
   (B) the earth
   (C) an egg
   (D) a piece of fruit

10. Why did the ancient Egyptians stage mock combat?

   (A) They believed that they could affect the changing of the seasons.
   (B) They used games to prepare physically for the growing season.
   (C) They wished to compete effectively with other ancient cultures.
   (D) They hoped to establish the rule of Horus and Set over Egypt.

Part II

15 Questions • Time—10 minutes

This part is a test of your ability to recognize standard written English.

Type I Questions

DIRECTIONS: Each item below is an incomplete sentence. Choose the answer that <u>best</u> completes the sentence.

1. The Everglades is —— marshy, low-lying tropical area of solidly packed muck, saw grass, and marsh hummocks.

   (A) a
   (B) at
   (C) then
   (D) some

2. Sir Edward Elgar was an English composer —— from 1857 to 1934 and is best known for his *Pomp and Circumstance* march.

   (A) who
   (B) that
   (C) who lived
   (D) what lived

3. An electrolyte is any electrical conductor such as a solution of salt in water in which the current is carried by ions —— free electrons.

   (A) as by
   (B) rather than
   (C) but for
   (D) when not

4. During World War II, over 300,000 Allied troops stranded at Dunkirk and cut off from land retreat by the Germans, —— British ships and boats.

   (A) were rescued by
   (B) rescued by
   (C) which rescued
   (D) by rescuing

5. Though dragonflies have elongated bodies that today may reach 5 inches, during the Permian period one species —— a wingspan of 2^1/$_2$ feet.

   (A) it had
   (B) having
   ✗(C) had
   (D) which had

Type II Questions

DIRECTIONS: Each of the sentences below has five underlined parts. Choose the part that contains an error.

6. The eagle, a large, predatory bird, is
   A   B
   solitude and believed to mate for life.
        C   D

7. The Embargo Act of 1807, which was in
                              A
   force until 1809, prohibits international
                      B
   shipping to and from all United States
         C   D
   ports.

8. The Chunnel, consisting of two railway
                  A
   tubes and a central service tube, runs
              B   C
   beneath the English Channel and connects
   D
   England and France.

9. Calling Aurora by the Romans, Eos was
   A   B   C
   the Greek goddess of dawn and the

   mother of the winds.
                 D

10. Enzymes are proteins that accelerate
            A   B
    chemical reactions in a cell that would

    otherwise proceed imperceptible or not
    C   D
    at all.

11. Since ancient times, days have arbitrarily
    A   B
    been inserted into calendars because the
         C
    year solar is not evenly divisible into
    D
    months and days.

12. The Hopi, a people of the Southwest
                        A
    United States, they resisted European
                   B
    influence more than other Pueblo tribes.
    C   D

13. Hokusai <u>was</u> a Japanese painter and wood
        A

    engraver <u>whose</u> prodigious output
              B

    <u>included</u> book illustrations, printed cards,
     C

    and <u>landscapings</u> in a variety of styles.
         D

14. Dramatic <u>theater</u> developed in ancient
           A

    Greece <u>where</u> religious rituals performed
         B

    in a <u>natural</u> amphitheater at the foot of
        C

    a <u>hill</u>.
    D

15. <u>Although</u> elected to national office,
     A

    <u>members</u> of the House of Representatives
     B

    are <u>typical</u> more attentive to local issues
        C

    <u>than to</u> national concerns.
    D

Part III

10 Questions • Time—10 minutes

DIRECTIONS: The passage below is followed by questions. Answer all questions based upon what is <u>stated</u> or <u>implied</u> in the passage.

    Silicon carbide is a highly promising material for many semiconductor applications, numbering among its advantages excellent physical stability and hardness, great
(5) strength at high temperatures, high thermal conductivity, and a low friction coefficient, all of which make it particularly useful for integrated circuits operating under extreme conditions. Unfortunately, silicon carbide
(10) is not in wide use because it is extremely difficult to work with.

    However, an elegant new technique for manufacturing silicon carbide microchips combines existing silicon technology with

(15) the unique way that C_{60} reacts with a heated silicon surface. Standard lithographic techniques are first used to deposit a controlled pattern of silicon dioxide to a thickness of about 1 micrometer on a silicon wafer.
(20) After the wafer is heated to 1100K (kelvin), it is exposed to a beam or flux of C_{60} vapor for about an hour. The carbon molecules stick to the bare silicon and bounce off the oxide. To remove the unwanted silicon di-
(25) oxide, the wafer is dipped in concentrated hydrofluoric acid. The end result is a silicon wafer with a silicon carbide microstructure in place.

Silicon carbide microcomponents can
(30) survive extreme mechanical and thermal
conditions. For example, they could be
used to detect flameouts in aircraft engines
by measuring pressure and temperature in
the engine quickly enough to stop and then
(35) restart the engine. Silicon carbide films
grown from C_{60} may, therefore, present
opportunities for application not previ-
ously considered.

1. What is the main focus of the passage?

(A) New uses for silicon carbide
(B) Different forms of pure carbon
(C) Designing electronic circuits
(D) Chemical properties of silicon
dioxide

2. The passage mentions all of the following as advantages of silicon carbide
EXCEPT:

(A) strength at high temperatures
(B) high thermal conductivity
(C) excellent physical stability
(D) relative ease of manipulation

3. In line 3, the word "numbering" most
nearly means

(A) including
(B) writing
(C) ignoring
(D) calculating ✗

4. According to the passage, silicon carbide
is not more widely used because

(A) it is very expensive
(B) silicon is fairly rare
✗ (C) it is difficult to work with
(D) it is carefully regulated

5. In line 12, the word "elegant" most nearly
means

(A) stylish
(B) effective
(C) expensive
(D) unproved

6. In line 16, the word "standard" most nearly
means

(A) widely used
(B) required
(C) innovative
(D) ineffective

7. Where could the following sentence be
most appropriately added to the passage?

The C_{60} molecule is the third member of
the pure carbon family that also includes
diamond and graphite.

(A) As the first sentence
(B) At the end of the first paragraph
(C) Between "surface" and "Standard"
in line 16
(D) Between "acid" and "The" in line
26

8. It can be inferred that silicon
carbide microcomponents may be
useful in aircraft engines because
such systems

(A) produce extreme conditions
(B) are relatively easy to build
(C) are protected from acid
(D) are recent innovations

9. The use of concentrated hydrofluoric acid (line 25) is like

(A) adding a new ingredient to a mixture to produce a new chemical
(B) breaking a mold to leave behind a product with a particular shape
(C) removing a naturally occurring impurity from raw ore during refining
(D) reconditioning a surface by scrubbing in order to remove contaminants

10. The author's attitude toward silicon carbide is

(A) qualified optimism
(B) fatalistic discouragement
(C) calculated indifference
(D) unrestrained enthusiasm

The MiniTest Review

Answer Key

Part I

1. D	4. A	7. A	10. A
2. B	5. A	8. D	
3. A	6. B	9. C	

Part II

1. A	5. C	9. A	13. D
2. C	6. C	10. D	14. B
3. B	7. B	11. D	15. C
4. A	8. C	12. B	

Part III

1. A	4. C	7. C	10. A
2. D	5. B	8. A	
3. A	6. A	9. B	

Later, for each question type you'll take a PreTest that you will score. See Hours 3, 9, and 16.

Part I

Review your answers to the Listening by reading through the script that you heard on the recording. Refer to Script 1 in Appendix A.

Part II

Here are the corrected sentences.

1. The Everglades is a marshy, low-lying tropical area of solidly packed muck, saw grass, and marsh hummocks.

2. Sir Edward Elgar was an English composer who lived from 1857 to 1934 and is best known for his *Pomp and Circumstance* march.

3. An electrolyte is any electrical conductor such as a solution of salt in water in which the current is carried by ions rather than free electrons.

4. During World War II, over 300,000 Allied troops stranded at Dunkirk and cut off from land retreat by the Germans, were rescued by British ships and boats.

5. Though dragonflies have elongated bodies that today may reach 5 inches, during the Permian period one species had a wingspan of 2½ feet.

Type II Questions

6. The eagle, a large, predatory bird, is <u>solitary</u> and believed to mate for life.

7. The Embargo Act of 1807, which was in force until 1809, <u>prohibited</u> international shipping to and from all United States ports.

8. The Chunnel, consisting of two railway tubes and a central service tube, <u>runs</u> beneath the English Channel and connects England and France.

9. <u>Called</u> Aurora by the Romans, Eos was the Greek goddess of dawn and the mother of the winds.

10. Enzymes are proteins that accelerate chemical reactions in a cell that would otherwise proceed <u>imperceptibly</u> or not at all.

11. Since ancient times, days have arbitrarily been inserted into calendars because the <u>solar year</u> is not evenly divisible into months and days.

12. The Hopi, a people of the Southwest United States, <u>resisted</u> European influence more than other Pueblo tribes.

13. Hokusai was a Japanese painter and wood engraver whose prodigious output included book illustrations, printed cards, and <u>landscapes</u> in a variety of styles.

14. Dramatic theater developed in ancient Greece <u>from</u> religious rituals performed in a natural amphitheater at the foot of a hill.

15. Although elected to national office, members of the House of Representatives are <u>typically</u> more attentive to local issues than to national concerns.

Part III

1. **(A)** The passage begins with an assessment of the new silicon carbide technology. Then it goes on to discuss how the technology works. In the last paragraph, the author discusses some possible uses for the technology. So the best description of the development is given by (A).

2. **(D)** In the first sentence, the passage mentions (A), (B), and (C). (D) is not mentioned; in fact, the material is hard to work with. (D) is correct, however, because the question stem asks for the idea that is NOT mentioned.

3. **(A)** The author says that the new technology "numbers" certain advantages and then lists those advantages. So the word must mean "include."

4. **(C)** In the last sentence of the first paragraph, the author says "unfortunately" and then goes on to explain why the new technology is not more widely used: it's hard to work with.

5. **(B)** The author calls the new technique "elegant" and then goes on to explain how it works. So the closest meaning is "effective."

6. **(A)** The "standard" technique refers to a technique that is already in widespread use.

7. **(C)** There is only one place in the passage that this sentence could go, and that has to be where the author mentions elemental carbon.

8. **(A)** In the last paragraph, the author says that silicon carbide microcomponents would be useful in "extreme conditions" and then suggests airplane engines. We can infer that an airplane engine produces these extreme conditions.

9. **(B)** The standard lithographic technique is used like a mold: it creates a pattern which the carbon fills in around. Then the outline of the pattern is washed away.

10. **(A)** The author has some good things to say about the new technology, but also says that it is difficult to work with.

Q & A Session

Q: Can I get a score based on the MiniTest?

A: No, there just aren't enough questions for a score. The purpose of the MiniTest was to let you get your feet wet. But each time you take up a new topic, you'll start with a PreTest that is scored. In fact, that's the very next hour: Hour 3: Test Your Knowledge of Structure.

Part II

Structure Questions

HOUR 3

Test Your Knowledge of Sentence Structure

What You'll Do This Hour

- Preview the Structure PreTest
- Take the Structure PreTest
- Evaluate Your Performance
- Review Your Work
- Q & A Session

Your Goals for This Hour

In this hour, you'll take the Structure PreTest. After you finish, you'll evaluate your performance and then review the correct answers for the PreTest.

Your goals for this hour are:

- Get ready to take the Structure PreTest
- Take the Structure PreTest under timed conditions
- Score the PreTest and evaluate your performance
- Review explanations for the correct answers

Preview the Structure PreTest

The Structure part of the TOEFL tests your ability to recognize standard written English. The phrase "standard written English" doesn't have a formal definition; it's an umbrella term that means grammatically correct, clear, and effective writing.

Structure questions test your ability to distinguish acceptable from unacceptable writing in areas such as word formation, word choice, word order, and agreement. In other words, Structure questions test many of the areas that you normally think of as "grammar."

 NOTE Structure questions do NOT test hyphens, apostrophes, capitalization or spelling.

The Structure part uses two different types of questions. One type uses a fill-in-the-blank format. Here is an example of a Type I Structure problem:

Type I Structure Problem

Every pharmaceutical company depends on its research and development division —— new drugs to maintain company sales.

(A) for creation

(B) by creation

ꭓ(C) to create

(D) create

The sentence should read, "Every pharmaceutical company depends on its research and development division to create new drugs to maintain company sales." So the correct answer is (C).

The other question type looks like this:

Type II Structure Problem

The New England aster <u>has</u> a long straight stalk and r<u>a</u>yed <u>flowers</u> that <u>varies</u> in
                                     A   B   C
<u>color</u> from deep purple to pale pink.
  D

The sentence should read, "The New England aster has a long straight stalk and rayed flowers that vary in color from deep purple to pale pink." So underlined part (C) contains an error, and you would choose (C) as the correct choice. With this type of question, you don't have to correct the error, just find it. In other words, the "incorrect" choice is the right answer because it's the one with the mistake in it. The rest of the sentence is correctly written.

NOTE

> This part of the TOEFL is sometimes called "Structure and Written Expression." "Structure" refers to the fill-in-the-blank questions, and "Written Expression" refers to the questions that have parts underlined. We'll use the current terminology, which is simply "Structure," to refer to both kinds of questions, and call the fill-in-the-blanks "Type I questions" and the other kind of questions "Type II questions."

The following Structure PreTest uses both Type I and Type II Structure questions.

Take the Structure PreTest

This section contains the Structure PreTest. Find a location where you can work undisturbed for approximately half an hour.

The time limit for the PreTest is 25 minutes, *including* the time you take to read the directions. Set your clock for 25 minutes and begin now.

1. Ⓐ Ⓑ Ⓒ Ⓓ   9. Ⓐ Ⓑ Ⓒ Ⓓ   17. Ⓐ Ⓑ Ⓒ Ⓓ   25. Ⓐ Ⓑ Ⓒ Ⓓ   33. Ⓐ Ⓑ Ⓒ Ⓓ

2. Ⓐ Ⓑ Ⓒ Ⓓ   10. Ⓐ Ⓑ Ⓒ Ⓓ   18. Ⓐ Ⓑ Ⓒ Ⓓ   26. Ⓐ Ⓑ Ⓒ Ⓓ   34. Ⓐ Ⓑ Ⓒ Ⓓ

3. Ⓐ Ⓑ Ⓒ Ⓓ   11. Ⓐ Ⓑ Ⓒ Ⓓ   19. Ⓐ Ⓑ Ⓒ Ⓓ   27. Ⓐ Ⓑ Ⓒ Ⓓ   35. Ⓐ Ⓑ Ⓒ Ⓓ

4. Ⓐ Ⓑ Ⓒ Ⓓ   12. Ⓐ Ⓑ Ⓒ Ⓓ   20. Ⓐ Ⓑ Ⓒ Ⓓ   28. Ⓐ Ⓑ Ⓒ Ⓓ   36. Ⓐ Ⓑ Ⓒ Ⓓ

5. Ⓐ Ⓑ Ⓒ Ⓓ   13. Ⓐ Ⓑ Ⓒ Ⓓ   21. Ⓐ Ⓑ Ⓒ Ⓓ   29. Ⓐ Ⓑ Ⓒ Ⓓ   37. Ⓐ Ⓑ Ⓒ Ⓓ

6. Ⓐ Ⓑ Ⓒ Ⓓ   14. Ⓐ Ⓑ Ⓒ Ⓓ   22. Ⓐ Ⓑ Ⓒ Ⓓ   30. Ⓐ Ⓑ Ⓒ Ⓓ   38. Ⓐ Ⓑ Ⓒ Ⓓ

7. Ⓐ Ⓑ Ⓒ Ⓓ   15. Ⓐ Ⓑ Ⓒ Ⓓ   23. Ⓐ Ⓑ Ⓒ Ⓓ   31. Ⓐ Ⓑ Ⓒ Ⓓ   39. Ⓐ Ⓑ Ⓒ Ⓓ

8. Ⓐ Ⓑ Ⓒ Ⓓ   16. Ⓐ Ⓑ Ⓒ Ⓓ   24. Ⓐ Ⓑ Ⓒ Ⓓ   32. Ⓐ Ⓑ Ⓒ Ⓓ   40. Ⓐ Ⓑ Ⓒ Ⓓ

DIRECTIONS: This PreTest is designed to measure your ability to recognize standard written English. There are two types of questions with special instructions for each.

Type I Questions

DIRECTIONS: Questions 1–15 are sentences with dashes to indicate that a part of the sentence has been omitted. Following each, you will see four lettered words or phrases. Choose the one that best completes the sentence and mark the corresponding space on your answer sheet.

Example

The city of St. Louis has been called the "Gateway to the West" —— it was the starting point for many of the trails used during the great westward migration.

    (A) due to

  ✗(B) because

    (C) regardless of

    (D) despite

The sentence should read, "The city of St. Louis has been called the "Gateway to the West" because it was the starting point for many of the trails used during the great westward migration." Therefore, you should choose (B).

Example

Recreational hot air ballooning is restricted to short day trips, so —— need for navigational instruments.

    (A) little is there

    (B) little is

  ✗(C) there is little

    (D) when there is little

The sentence should read, "Recreational hot air ballooning is restricted to short day trips, so there is little need for navigational instruments." Therefore, you should choose (C).

Now begin work.

1. Of all the factors that are used to predict future academic success, past success in school is the one —— the most important.

   ✗(A) admissions committees that it considers
   √(B) that admissions committees consider
   (C) admissions committees that it considers
   (D) why admissions committees consider it

2. —— of word origins is known as etymology.

   ✗(A) Studying
   (B) To study
   (C) That studying
   √(D) The study

3. New construction —— of all economic indicators of prosperity and growth in a given region.

   (A) the most is important
   √✗(B) is the most important
   (C) the most important is
   (D) that is the most important

4. The development of Web tools by scientists at the European Lab for Particle Physics made it —— easily over the Internet.

   (A) the possible communication
   (B) possibly to communicate
   (C) the possibility of communication
   √✗(D) possible to communicate

5. Human destruction of habitat is —— faced by animals on the endangered species list.

   (A) the usually greatest threat
   ✗(B) the greatest usual threat
   √(C) usually the greatest threat
   (D) usually the threat greatest

6. By observing the color shift of light, astronomers can determine the speed at which ——.

   (A) is a galaxy travelling
   √(B) a galaxy is travelling
   ✗(C) is travelling a galaxy
   (D) a travelling galaxy

7. Disintermediation, ——, occurs when interest rates offered by banks are not competitive with financial returns on other investments.

   √(A) the withdrawal of savings from banks
   ✗(B) withdraw savings from banks
   (C) which withdrawing savings from banks
   (D) savings from banks are withdrawn

8. During the 1970s, the Pittsburgh Steelers enjoyed success —— by other professional football teams of the modern era of the game.

   ✗(A) unmatched
   (B) was unmatched
   (C) is unmatched
   (D) the unmatched

9. ——, the Democrats and the Republicans, now dominate the political landscape of America.

   ✗(A) There are two political parties
   (B) That two political parties
   √(C) Two political parties
   (D) With two political parties

10. Ceremonial versions of the flag of the United States are trimmed with a decorative fringe, —— some oriental rugs.

(A) like that on
(B) because
(C) the way of
(D) similarly

11. A subsidiary of a large corporation that becomes an independent company may initially be less profitable because it must cover expenses of accounting and other services —— by the parent corporation.

(A) to be provided formerly
(B) formerly provide
(C) formerly providing
(D) formerly provided

12. In order to be effective as a team, —— oxen in a yoke must pull in the same direction with approximately equal force.

(A) and both
(B) both of
(C) the both
(D) both

13. Not only —— among the most versatile apples produced today, but they are also among the most widely cultivated.

(A) are Granny Smiths
(B) Granny Smiths
(C) some Granny Smiths
(D) they are Granny Smiths

14. Olives, when picked from the tree, are not edible and must first be cured in brine or lye —— eaten.

(A) as are they
(B) if to be
(C) that they are
(D) before they can be

15. Abraham Lincoln, largely on the strength of his performance in his debates against Douglas, became known as —— greatest orators in American history.

(A) the one who
(B) who the
(C) one of the
(D) who the

Type II Questions

DIRECTIONS: In questions 16–40, each sentence has four underlined words or phrases marked (A), (B), (C), and (D). Choose the one that contains an error. Then, mark the corresponding space on your answer sheet.

Example

Monkfish is sometimes <u>call</u> the "poor man's lobster" <u>because</u> the texture and taste of
                                    A   B

the fish <u>resemble</u> those of the <u>more</u> expensive crustacean.
              C   D

The sentence should read, "Monkfish is sometimes called the "poor man's lobster" because the texture and taste of the fish resemble those of the more expensive crustacean.

Example

After <u>winning</u> several crucial <u>battle</u> during the early part of the war, General
            A   B

Whitcomb <u>was</u> appointed commander <u>of</u> the entire combined armed forces.
                C   D

The sentence should read, "After winning several crucial battles during the early part of the war, General Whitcomb was appointed commander of the entire combined armed forces." Therefore, you should choose (B).

Now begin work on the questions.

16. The Magna Carta, <u>signed</u> by King John
                              A

in 1215, is <u>a</u> important <u>document</u> in the
                  B   C

<u>political</u> history of England.
      D

17. In 1970 the United States <u>passed</u> a law
                                          A

<u>requiring</u> all young <u>men</u> eighteen years
      B   C

<u>of old</u> to register with the Selective
      D

Service System.

18. During the so-called Golden Age of the

City College of New York, seven out of

every ten students <u>enrolled</u> at the <u>school</u>
                              A   B

<u>was</u> not born <u>in</u> the United States.
    C   D

19. George   Gershwin   <u>he   composed</u>
                                    A

soundtracks for several <u>films, including</u>
                                  B   C

Shall We Dance, <u>for which</u> his brother, Ira,
D
wrote the lyrics.

20. Law schools often <u>encourage</u> students to
A
concentrate on theoretical <u>issues</u> of
B
jurisprudence rather than on <u>practically</u>
C
matters of representing <u>clients</u>.
D

21. The State of the Union address required
<u>by</u> the Constitution <u>providing</u> a platform
A   B
<u>for</u> the President to <u>announce</u> major
C   D
legislative and political initiatives.

22. Food, <u>what</u> has been called the universal
A
mood-altering substance, <u>affects</u> how one
B
<u>feels</u> emotionally <u>as well as</u> physically.
C   D

23. The duckbill platypus, unlike other
<u>mammals</u> <u>does</u> not bear live young but
A   B
instead <u>reproduces</u> by <u>laying</u> eggs.
C   D

24. The Romantic poets <u>are</u> known generally
A
for creating <u>literary</u> works <u>that</u> are rich in
B   C
classical allusion and subtle <u>symbolic</u>.
D

25. The modern jet plane could not have been
<u>built</u> without aluminum, a metal <u>lightly</u> in
A   B
weight, remarkably <u>strong</u>, and relatively
C
inexpensive <u>to produce</u>.
D

26. The writings of Jules Romains <u>were</u> char-
A
acterized <u>by</u> a philosophy that maintained
B
that the adventure of humanity <u>is</u> essentially
C
<u>a</u> adventure of groups.
D

27. Following the announcement of <u>successful</u>
A
cold fusion in the lab, there was much
<u>interesting</u> in the popular press about the
B
<u>possibility</u> of free and <u>unlimited</u> energy.
C   D

28. <u>Although</u> gelatin <u>itself</u> is fairly neutral
A   B
in taste, <u>it</u> can be infused with various
C
<u>flavor</u> such as lemon, orange, and cherry.
D

29. Disagreements among various social
groups is less <u>obviously</u> during times of
A
economic expansion when <u>a</u> growing
B

economy <u>produces</u> enough to satisfy
                  C
rising <u>expectations</u>.
                D

30. Many <u>deserving</u> students have benefited
                A
of various government <u>programs</u> that
B   C
offer tuition assistance for <u>college</u> study.
                              D

31. Fusion cuisine is a West Coast style of

cooking <u>that</u> <u>combines</u> elements of
        A   B
Asian cooking <u>with</u> <u>them</u> of traditional
              C   D
American fare.

32. A difficulty facing modern dance compa-

nies <u>during</u> the 1970s until the present <u>is</u>
     A   B
<u>their</u> failure to attract the kind of financial
C
support <u>given</u> to ballet troupes.
        D

33. <u>Some</u> skyscrapers are <u>very</u> tall that they
    A   B
actually sway in the wind, <u>moving</u> as
                            C
much as two feet in each <u>direction</u> during
                          D
violent weather.

34. The <u>restructure</u> of the <u>traditional</u> classroom
        A   B
began in the British infant school prior <u>to</u>
                                          C

World War II and was later adopted by

educational <u>reformers</u> in the United States.
            D

35. During the summer months, plants <u>are</u>
                                      A
<u>plenty</u>, providing the deer population <u>with</u>
B   C
<u>abundant</u> food before the long hard winter.
D

36. Today's laptop computer <u>can</u> perform as
                            A
<u>much</u> calculations per microsecond as it
B
took a computer the size of railroad car to

do <u>when</u> computers were <u>invented</u>.
   C   D

37. <u>Despite</u> advances have been made in
    A
diagnosing and treating many <u>forms</u> of
                              B
cancer, <u>many</u> people die <u>unnecessarily</u> due
        C   D
to lack of screening.

38. Marianne Moore's poetry <u>is characterized</u>
                            A
by precisely crafted rhythms, by <u>rich of</u>
                                 B
imagery, and <u>by</u> subtle descriptions of
             C
<u>feelings</u> and events.
D

39. Roberto Clemente, <u>who</u> died in an aircrash
                     A
<u>while</u> on a relief mission to Nicaragua,
B

greatly <u>impression</u> everyone who knew
    C

<u>him</u>.
 D

sculptures <u>using</u> construction debris
     C

and <u>from parts</u> junked automobiles.
    D

40. <u>Some</u> modern artists have <u>created</u>
  A   B

Evaluate Your Performance

Check your answers against the key, and then assess your performance using the graph below.

1. B	11. D	21. B	31. D
2. D	12. D	22. A	32. A
3. B	13. A	23. A	33. B
4. D	14. D	24. D	34. A
5. C	15. C	25. B	35. B
6. B	16. B	26. D	36. B
7. A	17. D	27. B	37. A
8. A	18. C	28. D	38. B
9. C	19. A	29. A	39. C
10. A	20. C	30. B	40. D

Review Your Work

Here are the corrected sentences.

1. Of all the factors that are used to predict future academic success, past success in school is the one <u>that admissions committees consider</u> the most important.

2. <u>The study</u> of word origins is known as *etymology*.

3. New construction <u>is the most important</u> of all economic indicators of prosperity and growth in a given region.

4. The development of web tools by scientists at the European Lab for Particle Physics made it <u>possible to communicate</u> easily over the internet.

5. Human destruction of habitat is <u>usually the greatest threat</u> faced by animals on the endangered species list.

6. By observing the color shift of light, astronomers can determine the speed at which <u>a galaxy is traveling</u>.

7. Disintermediation, <u>the withdrawal of savings from banks</u>, occurs when interest rates offered by banks are not competitive with financial returns on other investments.

8. During the 1970s, the Pittsburgh Steelers enjoyed success <u>unmatched</u> by other professional football teams of the modern era of the game.

9. <u>Two political parties</u>, the Democrats and the Republicans, now dominate the political landscape of America.

10. Ceremonial versions of the flag of the United States are trimmed with a decorative fringe, <u>like that on</u> some oriental rugs.

11. A subsidiary of a large corporation that becomes an independent company may initially be less profitable because it must cover expenses of accounting and other services <u>formerly provided</u> by the parent corporation.

12. In order to be effective as a team, <u>both</u> oxen in a yoke must pull in the same direction with approximately equal force.

13. Not only <u>are Granny Smiths</u> among the most versatile apples produced today, but they are also among the most widely cultivated.

14. Olives, when picked from the tree, are not edible and must first be cured in brine or lye <u>before they can be</u> eaten.

15. Abraham Lincoln, largely on the strength of his performance in his debates against Douglas, became known as <u>one of the</u> greatest orators in American history.

16. The Magna Carta, signed by King John in 1215, is <u>an</u> important document in the political history of England.

17. In 1970 the United States passed a law requiring all young men eighteen years <u>of age</u> to register with the Selective Service System.

18. During the so-called Golden Age of the City College of New York, seven out of every ten students enrolled at the school <u>were</u> not born in the United States.

19. George Gershwin <u>composed</u> soundtracks for several films, including *Shall We Dance*, for which his brother, Ira, wrote the lyrics.

20. Law schools often encourage students to concentrate on theoretical issues of jurisprudence rather than on <u>practical</u> matters of representing clients.

21. The State of the Union address required by the Constitution <u>provides</u> a platform for the President to announce major legislative and political initiatives.

22. Food, <u>which</u> has been called the universal mood-altering substance, affects how one feels emotionally as well as physically.

23. The duckbill platypus, unlike other <u>mammals</u>, does not bear live young but instead reproduces by laying eggs.

24. The Romantic poets are known generally for creating literary works that are rich in classical allusion and subtle <u>symbolism</u>.

25. The modern jet plane could not have been built without aluminum, a metal <u>light</u> in weight, remarkably strong, and relatively inexpensive to produce.

26. The writings of Jules Romains were characterized by a philosophy that maintained that the adventure of humanity is essentially <u>an</u> adventure of groups.

27. Following the announcement of successful cold fusion in the lab, there was much <u>interest</u> in the popular press about the possibility of free and unlimited energy.

28. Although gelatin itself is fairly neutral in taste, it can be infused with various <u>flavors</u> such as lemon, orange, and cherry.

29. Disagreements among various social groups is less <u>obvious</u> during times of economic expansion when a growing economy produces enough to satisfy rising expectations.

30. Many deserving students have benefited <u>from</u> various government programs that offer tuition assistance for college study.

31. Fusion cuisine is a West Coast style of cooking that combines elements of Asian cooking with <u>those</u> of traditional American fare.

32. A difficulty facing modern dance companies <u>from</u> the 1970s until the present is their failure to attract the kind of financial support given to ballet troupes.

33. Some skyscrapers are <u>so</u> tall that they actually sway in the wind, moving as much as two feet in each direction during violent weather.

34. The <u>restructuring</u> of the traditional classroom began in the British infant school prior to World War II and was later adopted by educational reformers in the United States.

35. During the summer months, plants are <u>plentiful</u>, providing the deer population with abundant food before the long hard winter.

36. Today's laptop computer can perform as <u>many</u> calculations per microsecond as it took a computer the size of railroad car to do when computers were invented.

37. <u>Although</u> advances have been made in diagnosing and treating many forms of cancer, many people die unnecessarily due to lack of screening.

38. Marianne Moore's poetry is characterized by precisely crafted rhythms, by <u>richness of</u> imagery, and by subtle descriptions of feelings and events.

39. Roberto Clemente, who died in an aircrash while on a relief mission to Nicaragua, greatly <u>impressed</u> everyone who knew him.

40. Some modern artists have created sculptures using construction debris and <u>parts from</u> junked automobiles.

Q & A Session

Q: Do I need to know a lot of technical jargon about English grammar?

A: No. The TOEFL tests your ability to <u>use</u> English, not your abilty to <u>discuss</u> English. Some technical terminology will be used in this book simply because we have to talk about "subject," "agreement," "parallelism," and so on. But you will not be tested on your knowledge of those terms.

Q: Do I need to review the really obscure points of English like the use of the subjunctive?

A: Probably not. In the first place, the TOEFL tests really fundamental concepts like agreement between subject and verb and word order. The subjunctive and other such topics just don't arise; and if an obscure issue should come up, it would be only one question out of many and so not worth your investing weeks drilling on a minor point. Second, the TOEFL steers clear of areas where English is changing, and the subjunctive and other notoriously hard topics tend to fall into the area of shifting usage. So again, those points just aren't tested.

HOUR 4

Teach Yourself Grammar (I)

What You'll Do This Hour

- The Parts of Speech
- Errors with Nouns
- Errors with Verbs
- Workshop
- Q & A Session

Your Goals for This Hour

In this hour, you'll review TOEFL problems that involve nouns and verbs. Your goals for this hour are:

- Review parts of speech
- Review errors with nouns
- Review errors with verbs
- Get answers to frequently asked questions

The title of this book, *Teach Yourself the TOEFL in 24 Hours*, tells you how you should approach your study of Structure questions. English is a large language, and you can't expect to do a comprehensive review of *everything* that you've studied in even 24 weeks, let alone 24 hours. So don't try.

Fortunately, you don't need to. The TOEFL is a fairly predictable exam. By that, we mean that the same kinds of questions have been appearing in the Structure part for years. (This is one of the things the test-writers do to keep test forms comparable over time.) We have prepared a checklist of common errors for you to use. This checklist accounts for almost all of the concepts tested in the Structure part. If you can answer correctly on the items that test these concepts, you'll almost surely get a top score on Structure.

In this hour and the next, you'll review errors in the use of different kinds of words. To get started, you'll quickly review the eight basic categories of words or parts of speech in English. Then you'll start to work on your checklist.

The Parts of Speech

There are eight classes of words in English. These are most commonly called the *eight parts of speech.*

PART OF SPEECH	DEFINING CHARACTERISTICS	FUNCTION IN A SENTENCE
Noun	Names a concrete entity such as a person, place or thing—or names an abstract concept or idea such as sisterhood, happiness, or life	Subject, object, complement, appositive
Verb	Shows a concrete action such as running, burning, or reading, existence (*is*, *are*), or state of being such as *lives* or *rests*	Predicate (conjugated verb), auxiliary verb (modals such as *can* and *should*), subject and complement (gerund and infinitive), modifier (participle form)
Pronoun	Substitutes for a noun	Subject, object, possessive
Adjective	Modifies or qualifies a noun or pronoun	Modifier
Adverb	Modifies or qualifies a verb, adjective, or another adverb	Modifier

Preposition	Shows the relationship between its object and some other word in a sentence	Connector
Conjunction	Joins sentence elements	Connector
Interjection	Shows surprise or other feeling	Exclamation

Here are examples of the parts of speech:

- Nouns

Susan B. Anthony, Martin Luther King, Jr., Beethoven, Picasso, teacher, clerk, captain, minister, Paris, Cairo, park, city, kitchen, team, book, fork, virtue, joy

- Verbs

speak, eat, paint, build, drive, cook, understand, feel, reside, are

- Pronouns

we, you, they, her, them, ourselves, their, those, us, which, that, who

- Adjectives

red, cold, tall, generous, unreliable, timid, graceful, young, delicious, careful

- Adverbs

slowly, carefully, sincerely, coincidentally, maliciously, frequently, firmly, courageously

- Prepositions

by, into, on, upon, off, around, to, for, with, between, before, after, beside

- Conjunctions

and, but, or, although, because, if, since, when, where, while, yet

And here are the various parts of speech as they are used in sentences:

- Nouns

Susan gave the *trophy* to the *winner*.

The *professor* explained the *lesson* to the *students*.

The *student* wrote the *university* a *letter* to explain his *absence*.

- Verbs

My nephew *hopes* that he *will be accepted* by the university.

The field *was* a sea of colorful wildflowers.

The conductor *tapped* her baton on the podium, and the musicians *raised* their instruments and began to *play*.

- Pronouns

We cheered *ourselves* hoarse after *our* team won the game.

Professor Smith was not in *her* office, so *I* left the paper on the desk.

The car *that* caused the accident was not damaged.

- Adjectives

A *powerful* explosion rocked the *quiet* neighborhood.

A *blue* haze hung over the *still* waters of the lake.

Irate demonstrators tossed *large* rocks at the military tanks.

- Adverbs

The students listened *intently* to the speaker who *repeatedly* stressed that new adventures awaited them.

The train rolled *slowly* into the station as the waiting passengers stood *patiently* at the doors.

The artist painted *quickly*, *boldly* applying splashes of color to the huge canvas.

- Prepositions

The water flowed *over* the rocks.

The children sprinkled flower petals *on* and *around* the memorial.

During rush hour, workers carrying briefcases *in* their hands pushed *through* the revolving doors *at* an astonishing rate.

Errors with Nouns

There are only two errors in the use of nouns that you have to be concerned about. The first involves the distinction between singular and plural nouns; the second occurs in the formation of nouns.

Nouns of the Wrong Number

First, nouns are divided into two groups: count nouns and noncount nouns. Count nouns are words that represent individual items such as *pencil*, *child*, and *brick*. They are called count nouns because the items they refer to can be quantified or counted: *two pencils*, *several children*, *a few bricks*. Noncount nouns are mass nouns or group nouns such as *sand*, *water*, and *furniture*. Except in some unusual cases (not likely to show up on the TOEFL), the items referred to by noncount nouns cannot be quantified or counted individually, only overall. You would not say, for example, *three sands*, *four waters*, or *many furnitures*—though you could say *a pile of sand*, *a bucket of water*, or *much furniture* and you could also say *three grains of sand*, *a molecule of water*, or *two pieces of furniture*.

NOTE

Noncount nouns are sometimes called "uncountable nouns" and sometimes called "mass nouns." Regardless of terminology, words in this group don't exhibit the plural/singular distinction.

An error in number occurs when the sense of the sentence clearly requires the plural form of a count noun but uses the singular form or vice versa. The following sentences illustrate this kind of mistake:

Edwin <u>was</u> one of three <u>finalist</u> being <u>considered</u> for <u>the</u> assistantship.
      A   B   C   D

The sense of the sentence is that there are three people still being considered for the position, so the sentence requires the plural form of the noun:

Edwin was one of three <u>finalists</u> being considered for the assistantship.

Here is another example:

Fitzsimmons <u>was</u> the first in a series of moderate <u>leader</u> <u>who</u> moved the country <u>closer</u>
            A   B   C   D
to neutrality.

Again, the sense of the sentence is that there were several moderate leaders in succession, so the sentence needs the plural form of the noun:

Fitzsimmons was the first in a series of moderate <u>leaders</u> who moved the country closer to neutrality.

4

And here is an example in which a noncount noun is incorrectly treated as a count noun:

> <u>Many</u> of the furniture <u>designed</u> by Thomas Chippendale added Chinese, Gothic, and
>   A   B
> Rococo <u>motifs</u> to the sober design of the Queen Anne and Georgian <u>styles</u>.
>   C   D

"Many" can only be used to modify a count noun, e.g., *many children*, *many stars*, or *many airplanes*. The sentence can be corrected by using "much":

> <u>Much</u> of the furniture designed by Thomas Chippendale added Chinese, Gothic, and
> Rococo motifs to the sober design of the Queen Anne and Georgian styles.

CAUTION   An error of noun number is made harder to find when other modifiers separate the noun from the quantifier, e.g, *several [bloody and inconclusive] battle*—should be *battles*.

Modifier Where a Noun Is Needed

The second error of noun usage to look for in Structure questions is the use of a related adjective or verb where the noun form is required. Here is an example:

> The exquisite <u>beautiful</u> of Da Vinci's masterpiece *The Mona Lisa* takes away the breath
>   A
> of <u>viewers</u> as <u>they</u> enter the gallery where <u>it</u> is displayed.
>   B   C   D

"Beautiful" is intended as the subject of this sentence, but "beautiful" is an adjective, not a noun. The sentence should read:

The exquisite <u>beauty</u> of Da Vinci's masterpiece *The Mona Lisa* takes away the breath of viewers as they enter the gallery where it is displayed.

Here is another example of this type of error:

> Henry David Thoreau, <u>an</u> American writer of the mid-nineteenth century, <u>wrote</u> about
>   A   B
> the <u>solitary</u> of <u>his</u> cabin on Walden Pond.
>   C   D

The error here is that "solitary" seems to be the object of the preposition "about," but for that job you need a noun. The sentence can be correct by using the related noun form:

Henry David Thoreau, an American writer of the mid-nineteenth century, wrote about the <u>solitude</u> of life in his cabin on Walden Pond.

CAUTION | Many English nouns have related forms that belong to different parts of speech, e.g., *distinction* (n.) and *distinguished* (adj.), *cowardice* (n.) and *cowardly* (adj.), *value* (n.) and *valuable* (adj.). Watch out for the possibility that an underlined part uses the wrong form.

The mirror image of the error we've just been discussing occurs when a noun is used where an adjective or adverb is required. Here is an example of this variation:

<u>During</u> the second half of the twentieth century, the Congo <u>was</u> the scene of <u>many</u>
   A   B   C
struggles involving various military, <u>politics</u>, and ethnic factions.
                                        D

"Politics" is a noun, but what is needed is an adjective that, along with "military" and "ethnic," modifies "factions":

During the second half of the twentieth century, the Congo was the scene of many struggles involving various military, <u>political</u>, and ethnic factions.

And here is another example of this variation:

<u>The</u> secret to a truly <u>great</u> Beef Wellington is to sear in the juices and then <u>finish</u> the
  A   B   C
cooking in a very <u>heat</u> oven.
                    D

"Heat" is a noun, but what is needed is the adjective "hot" to modify the word "oven." Here is the corrected sentence:

The secret to a truly great Beef Wellington is to sear in the juices and then finish the cooking in a very <u>hot</u> oven.

TIP | Look for noun formation errors in any series of parallel elements. For example: *The benefits of regular exercise include weight loss, improved healthy, and better energy.* The TOEFL writers like this pattern because it makes the error harder to find.

4

Errors with Verbs

Structure questions frequently test the correct use of verbs. So another important group of errors is one involving the uses of verbs. You'll need a checklist of these errors as well.

> The TOEFL does not test many of the verb topics that you might associate with English grammar. For example, we've never seen a problem that tests the formation of the past tense of an irregular verb such as *drink*, *drank*, *drunk*. Reviewing lists of principal parts of verbs, therefore, is not likely to improve your TOEFL score.

Subject-Verb Agreement

A verb must agree with its subject in number, so a singular subject takes a singular verb and a plural subject takes a plural verb. Here are two TOEFL problems that illustrate this point:

The <u>major</u> essays <u>of</u> Charles Sanders Peirce <u>was</u> published posthumously in a volume
     A   B   C
<u>entitled</u> *Chance, Love, and Logic.*
   D

The subject of the sentence is the plural noun "essays," so the verb should also be plural:

> The major essays of Charles Sanders Peirce <u>were</u> published posthumously in a volume entitled *Chance, Love, and Logic.*

And:

> The Pekingese, a <u>toy</u> dog that <u>stands</u> 6 to 9 inches at the shoulders, <u>were</u> kept by
>   A   B   C
> Chinese emperors as early <u>as</u> the 8th century.
>   D

In this case, the subject of the sentence is the singular "Pekingese," so the verb must also be singular:

> The Pekingese, a toy dog that stands 6 to 9 inches at the shoulders, <u>was</u> kept by Chinese emperors as early as the 8th century.

The basic rule regarding subject-verb agreement is not difficult to understand, but sometimes it's difficult to apply. In fact, things can be quite tricky when the subject and the verb are separated from each other by other elements of the sentence. The following example illustrates the difficulty:

> Druidic ceremonies, <u>usually</u> held in an oak grove or at the source of a river, <u>was</u> often
>   A   B
> associated with <u>animal</u> and sometimes <u>human</u> sacrifice.
>   C   D

The subject of this sentence is the plural noun "ceremonies," so the verb should be plural:

> Druidic ceremonies, usually held in an oak grove or at the source of a river, <u>were</u> often associated with animal and sometimes human sacrifice.

The item is tricky because the subject and verb are separated by the modifier "usually held in an oak grove or at the source of a river." It's easy to lose track of the subject and mistakenly assume that the noun closest to the verb (in this case "river") is the subject.

TIP

> To determine whether or not you have a problem with subject-verb agreement in a sentence, mentally drop out any material that separates the verb from the subject and read the subject-verb to yourself in isolation. For example: *Professor Harmon, whose office is on the third floor, teaches English.*

4

A variation on the theme of agreement of subject-verb agreement is a subject that consist of two or more elements joined by "and":

> Energy and matter <u>is</u> permanently trapped <u>by</u> the <u>powerful</u> gravitational pull of <u>a</u> black hole.
>   A   B   C   D

A subject that consists of two or more elements joined by "and," as in this sentence, is considered a plural subject and must have a plural verb. So the sentence should read:

> Energy and matter <u>are</u> permanently trapped by the powerful gravitational pull of a black hole.

CAUTION

> A plural subject with multiple elements can look like it is singular when the element closest to the verb is singular, e.g., *various forms of resuscitation and the Heimlich maneuver are* (not *is* because the "and" creates a plural subject).

Logical Choice of Tense

When you first began studying English, you probably spent a lot of time memorizing verb conjugations and learning when to use the various tenses. Fortunately, there is only one thing regarding tense that is important for the TOEFL: Do the verb tenses logically reflect the sequence of events? In other words, about the most complicated that things could get would be to choose a tense for one verb in a sentence, making sure that the tense correctly places the event in the sequence. Here is an example:

> When he <u>retires</u> from professional soccer in 1977, Pelé, perhaps <u>the greatest</u> soccer
>   A   B
> player <u>ever</u>, had scored 1,281 career goals and led <u>his</u> team to three world titles.
>   C   D

The mistake in this sentence is in part (A). "Retires" is in the present tense, so the sentence implies that Pelé's retirement is an event that occurs in the present, but the date in the sentence makes it clear that the event occurred over 20 years ago. The sentence is easily corrected by putting the description of the event into the past tense:

> When he <u>retired</u> from professional soccer in 1977, Pelé, perhaps the greatest soccer player ever, had scored 1,281 career goals and led his team to three world titles.

TIP

> Don't go looking for trouble. You won't find problems on the TOEFL that involve exotic verb tenses like the Future Perfect Subjunctive. Unless there is an obvious reason to wonder whether the tense used is correct, assume that it is correct and look for a different kind of error.

Infinitives and Gerunds

Infinitives and gerunds, which are sometimes called *verbals*, are verb forms that usually function as nouns. The infinitive is the "to" form (*to go*, *to eat*, *to read*, etc.). And the gerund is the -ing form (*going*, *eating*, *reading*, etc.).

The use that you will most likely encounter on the TOEFL is as an object. For example:

> Bert wanted *to eat* at the new restaurant.

> The staff thanked us for *helping* with the project.

The first rule to keep in mind about infinitives and gerunds is that you cannot mix the *to* and the *-ing* forms. The following example illustrates this mistake:

George Sand, the French novelist <u>who</u> supported <u>herself</u> and her two children by her
AB

writing, adopted male attire <u>to protesting</u> the <u>unequal</u> treatment accorded to women.
CD

"To -ing" is never an acceptable English structure. The problem here can be easily
corrected by using the infinitive:

George Sand, the French novelist who supported herself and her two children by her
writing, adopted male attire <u>to protest</u> the unequal treatment accorded to women.

> **TIP**
>
> Some verbs usually take one verbal form rather than the other.
>
> These common verbs are followed by an infinitive: *agree, appear, ask, decide, desire, expect, intend, hope, need, plan, prepare, pretend, promise, refuse, request, want, was allowed.*
>
> These common verbs are followed by a gerund: *allow, appreciate, avoid, consider, delay, dislike, discuss, enjoy, finish, keep (on), like, mention, mind, prefer, propose, postpone, put off, suggest.*

Parallelism

A series of verb elements that have a similar function should also have a similar form.
This is called *parallelism*. Here is an example:

<u>While</u> Alabama is often associated <u>with</u> the <u>cultivation</u> of cotton, the state's economy
ABC

also includes significant fishing, <u>manufacture</u>, and lumbering.
D

In this sentence, you have a series of verb elements that are the objects of the verb
"includes." Since they all have the same function and are presented in a series, they should
all have the same form:

While Alabama is often associated with the cultivation of cotton, the state's economy
also includes significant fishing, <u>manufacturing</u>, and lumbering.

Here is another example:

Alabaster is <u>a</u> fine-grained, translucent mineral <u>that</u> is <u>easily</u> carved but also easily
ABC

soiled, <u>scratch</u>, and fractured.
D

Again, you have a series of verb elements: soiled, scratch, and fractured. But each element in the series should have the same form in order to ensure the parallelism of the series:

> Alabaster is a fine-grained, translucent mineral that is easily carved but also easily soiled, <u>scratched</u>, and fractured.

 MAKE CONNECTIONS | Parallelism is a general requirement in English that was also discussed above in connection with noun usage.

Workshop

The sentences in the Drill portion of this workshop contain errors involving nouns and verbs. There is no time limit. After you have finished, check your work.

Drill

DIRECTIONS: For each sentence below, select the underlined part that contains an error and enter the letter of your choice in the space provided. Next to the letter of your choice, write down the word or phrase that will correct the error.

Example

<u>In</u> fission, a nucleus absorbs a neutron, becomes unstable, and <u>division</u> into two
A   B
<u>nearly equal</u> nuclei, <u>releasing</u> the difference in total mass in the form of energy.
          C   D

Answer: **(B)** dividing

1. Khartoum, the <u>capital</u> of Sudan, <u>is</u>
                          A   B
   situated <u>at</u> the confluence of the Blue Nile
              C
   and White Nile <u>river.</u> S
                        D

2. Hieroglyphics and the alphabet <u>is</u> both   *are*
                                                    A
   forms of writing <u>that</u> date to the Middle
                          B
   Kingdom of Egypt, <u>though</u> the first was
                              C
   fading from use while the second was

   <u>only being</u> developed.
        D

3. Several of the <u>most influential</u> <u>economists</u>
                  A   B

   in the United States are <u>graduates</u> of or
                           C

   teachers <u>at</u> the University of Chicago.
            D

4. <u>During</u> his first and <u>only</u> trip to Pennsyl-
    A   B

   vania, William Penn, Quaker leader and

   founder of the colony, drew up a liberal

   Frame of Government and <u>establishes</u>
                         C

   friendly relations <u>with</u> the indigenous
                 D

   people.

5. Dynamite, an explosive <u>made</u> from
                  A

   nitroclycerine and various inert fillers,

   was
   <u>were</u> invented by Alfred Nobel, <u>the</u>
    B   C

   Swedish chemist <u>who</u> endowed the
                 D

   Nobel prizes.

6. Khachaturian, <u>a</u> Russian composer of
               A

   Armenian <u>heritage</u>, blended Armenian and
           B

   Asian folk <u>element</u> in <u>his</u> music.
            C   D

7. A considerable <u>improvement</u> over the
                A

   Bessemer Process, the open-hearth process

   of <u>producing</u> steel can use up to 100 per-
        B

   cent scrap metal, refine pig iron with a <u>high</u>
                    produce C

   phosphorus content, and <u>production of</u> less
                         D

   brittle steels.

8. <u>Usually</u> nocturnal and feeding on small
    A

   animals such as <u>insects</u> the salamander
               B

   <u>is found</u> in <u>damp</u> regions of the northern
     C   D

   temperate zone.

9. The first of Kepler's <u>law</u> states <u>that</u> the
                A   B

   shape of <u>each</u> planet's orbit <u>is</u> an ellipse
          C   D

   with the sun at one focus.

10. A <u>properly</u> designed forest management
      A

   program <u>cuts</u> mature <u>trees</u> so that <u>younger</u>
          B   C   D

   ones have room to grow.

11. <u>In rowing</u>, the direction and speed of the
     A   *are*

   boat or shell <u>is</u> controlled by the coxswain,
            B

   <u>who</u> also calls the rhythms of the rowers'
    C

   <u>strokes</u>.
     D

4

12. <u>Rayon</u>, one of the oldest synthetic <u>fiber</u>s
      A   B

    is made <u>from</u> cellulose, <u>chiefly</u> derived
            C   D

    from wood pulp.

13. George Bernard Shaw, the Irish playwright

    and critic, was a <u>popular</u> speaker <u>who</u>
                    A   B

    <u>writes</u> five novels before becoming a
      C

    <u>music</u> critic for a London newspaper in
       D

    the late 1890s.

14. In the 1760s, Adam Smith <u>traveled</u> in
                            A

    France <u>where</u> he met some of the
           B

    <u>Physiocrats</u> and started <u>to writing</u> his
        C   D

    masterpiece, *The Wealth of Nations.*

15. In order <u>to guiding</u> a smart bomb, an
               A

    aircraft pilot <u>aims</u> a laser beam at the
                  B

    target, <u>which</u> then reflects the beam back
            C

    to a computer in the weapon <u>itself</u>.
                               D

16. Chivalry was the system of ethical <u>ideal</u>s
                                A

    that grew <u>out of</u> feudalism and reached <u>its</u>
            B   C

    high point in the 12th and 13th <u>centuries</u>.
                                D

17. The area <u>that</u> is now Portugal was added
              A

    <u>to</u> the Roman Empire <u>around</u> 5 A.D.,
      B   C

    later overrun by Germanic tribes in the

    5th century, and finally <u>conquest</u> by the
                              D

    Moors in 711.

18. Valedictorian of his Rutgers class,

    <u>an</u> Olympic gold medalist, and an
    A

    <u>internationally</u> renowned singer, Paul
            B

    Robeson <u>was</u> a man of diverse <u>ability</u>.
             C   D

19. The cavities of the internal nose, <u>which</u>
                                A

    are lined with a mucous membrane,

    <u>is covered</u> with fine hairs that help <u>to</u>
        B   C

    filter dust and impurities <u>from</u> the air.
                         D

20. It has been noted that <u>when</u> one of the
                        A

    senses, such as sight, <u>hear,</u> or smell, is
                        B

    <u>seriously</u> degraded, the other two become
        C

    <u>more</u> acute.
      D

Review

1. **(D)** . . . the Blue Nile and White Nile rivers.

2. **(A)** . . . Hieroglyphics and the alphabet are both forms . . .

3. **(B)** Several of the most influential economists . . .

4. **(C)** Penn . . . drew up . . . and established . . .

5. **(B)** Dynamite . . . was invented by . . .

6. **(C)** . . . blends Armenian and Asian folk elements . . .

7. **(D)** . . . can use . . . , refine . . . , and produce . . .

8. **(B)** . . . on small animals such as insects, . . .

9. **(A)** The first of Kepler's laws . . .

10. **(C)** . . . cuts mature trees . . .

11. **(B)** . . . the direction and speed . . . are controlled . . .

12. **(B)** . . . one of the oldest synthetic fibers . . .

13. **(C)** . . . was a popular speaker who wrote . . .

14. **(D)** . . . started to write . . .

15. **(A)** In order to guide . . .

16. **(A)** . . . the system of ethical ideals . . .

17. **(D)** . . . added to . . . , later overrun . . . , and finally conquered . . .

18. **(D)** . . . a man of diverse abilities.

19. **(B)** The cavities . . . are covered . . .

20. **(B)** . . . sight, hearing, or smell . . .

4

Q & A Session

Q: Aren't there more lists that need to be memorized?

A: Not unless you really want to. The TOEFL is a high-focused exam that is designed to test a certain proficiency with English. The TOEFL is not a comprehensive test of all of English. Therefore, you need to stay focused.

Q: What about avoiding sentence fragments—a subject that my teachers spent so much time on?

A: Fragments are an important part of the TOEFL, but a sentence fragment is not really an error in the use of a particular word—even though it can usually be corrected by changing a verb form. Rather, a fragment is an error that is symptomatic of an underlying structural problem in a sentence. You'll take up those errors in Hour 5.

This Hour's Review

1. In English there are eight parts of speech:

   Nouns, verbs, pronouns, adjectives, adverbs, prepositions, conjunctions, and interjections

   Interjections are not tested by the TOEFL.

2. You only have to worry about two kinds of mistakes involving nouns:

   Number

   Word Formation

3. The verb errors that you need to be alert for are:

   Subject-Verb Agreement

   Logical Choice of Tense

   Infinitives and Gerunds

   Parallelism

HOUR 5

Teach Yourself Grammar (II)

What You'll Do This Hour

- Errors with Pronouns
- Errors with Adjectives and Adverbs
- Errors with Subject-Verbs
- Workshop
- Q & A Session

Your Goals for This Hour

In this hour, you'll continue to review the basic building blocks of English. Your goals for this hour are:

- Review errors with pronouns
- Review errors with adjectives and adverbs
- Review errors with subject-verbs
- Get answers to frequently asked questions

Errors with Pronouns

Insofar as pronoun usage is concerned, the TOEFL concentrates on two of the seven groups of pronouns: the personal pronouns and the relative pronouns.

> **NOTE** The TOEFL rarely, if ever, tests your knowledge of indefinite, intensive, reflexive, demonstrative, or interrogative pronouns, so there is no point in looking for those kinds of errors.

Personal Pronouns

The personal pronouns are those found in the following table:

	SINGULAR	PLURAL
Subjective	I	we
	you	you
	he, she, it	they
Possessive	my, mine	our, ours
	your, yours	your, yours
	his, her, its	their, theirs
Objective	me	us
	you	you
	him, her, it	them

Generally speaking, personal pronouns have three important characteristics: person, number, and case. *Person* refers to the distinction between I, you, and he, she, it, and the other variations are shown in the table above. *Number* refers to whether the pronoun is singular or plural. And *case* determines the function of a pronoun in a sentence.

As it turns out, person and case are not topics that have been tested by the TOEFL with any frequency, probably because such errors are too obvious. Consider this example:

Churchill <u>was</u> first lord of the admiralty <u>but</u> was discredited by the <u>failure</u> of the
           A   B   C
Dardanelles campaign, which <u>him</u> had championed.
                               D

There's a mistake in the sentence, an obvious mistake: (D). In fact, the mistake is so obvious that is almost impossible to overlook. Consequently, an item like this wouldn't serve any useful purpose on TOEFL; it's just too crude. So, as a matter of test-taking, you can pretty much forget about both case and person.

There is one possible exception to this universal rule, and it is illustrated by the following example:

> Victoria Woodhull <u>was</u> an American journalist, and <u>most</u> of <u>hers</u> writing <u>dealt with</u>
>   A   B   C   D
> controversial topics such as women's suffrage, free love, and socialism.

As first glance, this might seem to be an exception to our general rule that case is not relevant on the TOEFL, but "hers" is not even a personal pronoun. (See the table above.) Instead, the item is really just a matter of bad diction (wrong word choice), and the only reason that "hers" would be tested in this way is that it bears a resemblance to the possessive form of many nouns.

So, the only thing left to worry about with respect to personal pronouns is number, and number is important. Number is important because it is a principle of correct pronoun usage that a pronoun must agree in number with its antecedent (referent): if the noun is singular, the pronoun must be singular; if the noun is plural, the pronoun must be plural. Here's the kind of personal pronoun error you should be looking for on your TOEFL:

> The circulatory system <u>is</u> a group of organs <u>that</u> transports blood and the substances
>   A   B
> <u>they carry</u> to and from all <u>parts</u> of the body.
>   C   D

The error in this sentence is in (C). The pronoun "they" refers to "blood" (the blood does the carrying), but "blood" is a singular noun and "they" is a plural pronoun. The sentence should read:

> The circulatory system is a group of organs that transports blood and the substances <u>it</u> <u>carries</u> to and from all parts of the body.

This error is called a "failure of agreement between the pronoun and its antecedent (or referent)."

Here is another example to illustrate the point:

> Virginia Woolf's novels, <u>including</u> *A Room of One's Own* and *The Waves*, are
>   A
> <u>especially</u> well-known for <u>its</u> use of musical and visual <u>symbolism</u>.
>   B   C   D

5

The mistake occurs in (C). "Its" refers to "novels," but "its" is singular and "novels" is plural. The sentence should read:

> Virginia Woolf's novels, including *A Room of One's Own* and *The Waves*, are especially well-known for <u>their</u> use of musical and visual symbolism.

 TIP

> If you find a Structure item in which "it," "its," "they," or "theirs" is underlined, find its antecedent (referent) in the sentence and check for agreement of number.

Relative Pronouns

While the use of personal pronouns is not tested with any frequency, relative pronouns are very important. The important relative pronouns are:

	Singular or Plural
Subjective	who, which, that
Possessive	whose
Objective	whom, which, that

From the table, you can see that the choice of relative pronouns is fairly limited. There are only three subjective- and three objective-case relative pronouns, and there is no distinction for *which* and *that* in the two cases.

Relative pronouns are used to introduce adjective clauses. Here is an example of the correct use of a relative pronoun:

> Insider trading, which has been illegal since 1934, refers to stock market transactions made with knowledge of nonpublic information about corporate activity.

The relative pronoun "which" refers to "insider trading" and functions as the subject of the clause that it introduces. So a relative pronoun has two jobs. One, it relates one idea in a sentence to another idea by referring to its antecedent (referent); two, it functions as the subject of the clause that it introduces. Both aspects are tested by the TOEFL.

The relative pronoun must be the right one, and there are three things to be alert for:

- People take the *who* relative pronoun.
- *What* is not a relative pronoun.
- *That* is used for essential clauses; *which* for nonessential clauses.

Let's look at sentences that illustrate the three errors. First, the relative pronoun *who* should be used when referring to people:

John Burgoyne, <u>which</u> was a hero of the Seven Years War, <u>led</u> a poorly <u>equipped</u> army
               A   B   C
in the Battle of Saratoga and, <u>badly</u> outpositioned, was forced to surrender.
                                      C

The error occurs in (A). The relative pronoun *which* refers to Burgoyne, but John Burgoyne is a person, so the relative pronoun *who* is needed:

John Burgoyne, <u>who</u> was a hero of the Seven Years War, led a poorly equipped army in the Battle of Saratoga and, badly outpositioned, was forced to surrender.

TIP

Which cannot refer to people.

The second point is equally simple: *what* is not a relative pronoun. Here is an example of this mistake:

Camomile, <u>what</u> grows wild along the roadside in <u>many</u> areas of the United States, <u>is</u>
               A   B   C
an herb that is used <u>to make</u> tea.
                      D

The error is in (A). *What* is not a relative pronoun and cannot substitute for *which* or *that*. The sentence should read:

Camomile, <u>which</u> grows wild along the roadside in many areas of the United States, is an herb that is used to make tea.

TIP

What cannot be used to introduce a relative clause.

5

The third point is a little more complicated (though not much so) because it requires us to distinguish between essential and nonessential clauses. These are also called restrictive and nonrestrictive clauses, but we think the essential/nonessential terminology is easier to remember because it is self-explanatory. An essential clause is one that is essential to the meaning of the sentence; a nonessential clause is one that's not essential. Compare the following:

> The Erie Canal, *which* opened in 1825, joined Lake Erie and the Hudson River.
>
> The Erie Canal was the waterway *that* joined Lake Erie and the Hudson River.

Both sentences are properly constructed, and the difference between the two is that the information introduced by *that* in the second is essential: Which waterway? The one that joined Lake Erie and the Hudson River. The information provided by the relative clause in the first sentence (opened in 1825) is interesting but it is not essential to establish the identity of anything in the sentence.

Here's an example:

The tomato, —— is now considered a staple of Italian cooking, is a New World fruit that was not available in Europe until after the voyages of the European explorers.

> (A) that
>
> (B) what
>
> (C) which
>
> (D) who

The correct answer is (C). The blank must be completed by a relative pronoun that refers to "tomato" and introduces the relative clauses. "What" cannot be used since "what" is not a relative pronoun. "Who" cannot be used because a tomato is not a person. So the choice is between "which" and "that." "Which" is the correct pronoun because the relative clause is nonessential.

TIP

> If the relative clause is set off by commas, it's nonessential so use *which*; if the relative clause is not set off by commas, it's essential so use *that*.

The other thing you have to worry about with a relative pronoun is the clause that it introduces. Since the relative pronoun introduces a clause and functions as its subject, there will be a verb involved. And you know from Hour 4, that there must always be agreement between a verb and its subject. But since "that" and "which" are both singular and plural, what verb should you use? The answer is that the relative pronoun assumes the number of the noun to which it refers. For example:

the books that are on the shelf (plural)

the boat that is in the water (singular)

the flowers, which are on the table (plural)

the horse, which is in the pasture (singular)

You need to look to the antecedent of the relative pronoun to determine whether there is an error of agreement. Here is an example:

Falcons, ——typified by <u>notched </u>beaks, lay their <u>eggs</u> on the ground <u>or</u> on cliff ledges.

    (A) that are

    (B) which are

    (C) which is

    (D) who are

The correct answer is (B). Since the Falcon is an animal and not a person, and since the relative clause is set off by commas, the correct relative pronoun is "which." And "which" refers to "falcons," a plural noun that takes a plural verb.

TIP

> To determine whether the verb of a relative clause must be plural or singular, look to the antecedent of the relative pronoun. For example: *Our starting players, who* are the best in the league, were featured in this month's Sports News.

5

Errors with Adjectives and Adverbs

Adjectives and adverbs are modifiers, and there are three things that you need to be looking for:

- Confusion of adjectives and adverbs
- Misplaced adjectives
- Wrong or missing articles

First, as you learned from the review of the parts of speech in Hour 4, adjective and adverbs are modifiers, but they modify different things. In general, adjectives are used to modify nouns; while adverbs are used to modify verbs, adjectives, or other adverbs. An error that comes up on the TOEFL with some frequency violates this general rule. Here is an example:

Michael Faraday <u>developed</u> the first dynamo in <u>the</u> form of a copper disk rotated
A   B

<u>between</u> the poles of a <u>permanently</u> magnet.
C   D

The mistake in this sentence is in part (D). "Permanently" is an adverb, so it cannot be used to modify the noun "magnet." The sentence should read:

Michael Faraday developed the first dynamo in the form of a copper disk rotated between the poles of a <u>permanent</u> magnet.

And here is an example with an error that is the mirror image of the previous example:

Michael Faraday <u>developed</u> the first dynamo in <u>the</u> form of a copper disk rotated
A   B

<u>between</u> the poles of a <u>permanent</u> charged magnet.
C   D

Again, the error is in part (D). This time, "permanent" is not modifying "magnet"; instead, it modifies "charged," an adjective. And that means that "permanent" should have the adverb form rather than the adjective form. The sentence should read:

Michael Faraday developed the first dynamo in the form of a copper disk rotated between the poles of a <u>permanently</u> charged magnet.

TIP	Most adverbs have the characteristic -ly form. So an -ly word that is modifying a noun is probably wrong; conversely, a word without an -ly that modifies a verb is probably wrong.

The second thing to watch out for with adjectives is *order*. As a general rule, adjectives in English come before the noun they modify. (There are a few exceptions, particularly in poetry, but they don't show up on the TOEFL.) Here is an example of this kind of error:

The Federal Bureau of Investigation <u>is</u> the <u>agency federal</u> that is charged with <u>investigating</u>
A   B   C

espionage, sabotage, and other crimes <u>that</u> threaten the security of the nation.
D

The error is in part (B). The adjective "federal" should be placed in front of the noun "agency":

The Federal Bureau of Investigation is the <u>federal agency</u> that is charged with investigating espionage, sabotage, and other crimes that threaten the security of the nation.

> **TIP**   If the underlined part includes a noun <u>followed</u> by an adjective, that is probably an error.

A third modifier error involves the articles *a*, and *an*. There are two errors that you need to watch for. First, "an" rather than "a" must precede a consonant sound. Here is an example:

The Fenian <u>movement</u>, a secret revolutionary society <u>organized</u> around 1858 in Ireland,
            A   B
was <u>a</u> attempt to appeal <u>to</u> the nonagrarian population.
     C   D

The error in this sentence is in part (C). It should use "an" before the vowel sound of "attempt":

The Fenian movement a secret revolutionary society organized around 1858 in Ireland, was <u>an</u> attempt to appeal to the nonagrarian population.

Of course, you might find the mirror image of this error as well:

The Fenian <u>movement, an</u> secret revolutionary society <u>organized</u> around 1858 in
                  A   B   C
Ireland, was an attempt to appeal <u>to</u> the nonagrarian population.
                                D

And now the error is in (B). The consonant sound of "society" must be preceded by "a":

The Fenian movement, <u>a</u> secret revolutionary society organized around 1858 in Ireland, was an attempt to appeal to the nonagrarian population.

Second, the indefinite article "a" or "an" should be used with singular count nouns. Here is an example:

<u>For years, physicists</u> have attempted to <u>devise experiment</u> that <u>would prove</u> the
     A   B   C   D
existence of the so-called fifth force but so far have been unsuccessful.

The error is in part (C). The sentence could read:

5

For years, physicists have attempted to <u>devise an experiment</u> that would prove the existence of the so-called fifth force, but so far have been unsuccessful.

Or it could read:

For years, physicists have attempted to <u>devise experiments</u> that would prove the existence of the so-called fifth force, but so far have been unsuccessful.

Either would be correct. (Remember with this type of problem, you don't have to correct the error, just point out where it is.) The first sentence is acceptable because the "an" is used in front of the <u>singular</u> form of a count noun (you can count experiments—e.g., one experiment, two experiments, three experiments, etc.) And the second sentence is also acceptable: since the noun is plural, you don't need (and couldn't have) the article.

MAKE CONNECTIONS

> For more information about the distinction between count and noncount nouns, see Hour 4.

Errors with Subject-Verbs

Thus far, we've been concentrating on errors that are ordinarily associated with misusing a single word or phrase, e.g., using the wrong pronoun or using an adjective where there should be a noun. The TOEFL, however, also contains questions that test your sense of the overall structure of a sentence.

You know that in English a sentence begins with a word that is capitalized and ends with a punctuation mark. But this formal requirement is not really what makes a sentence a sentence. What really makes a sentence a sentence is the fact that the group of words expresses a <u>complete</u> thought or idea, and a complete thought requires both a subject and a verb:

Juan (not a complete idea)

told (not a complete idea)

Mary (not a complete idea)

a story (not a complete idea)

Juan told Mary a story. (a complete idea)

In the sentence above, *Juan* is the subject and *told* is the verb.

A group of words that begins with a capitalized word and ends with a punctuation mark that looks like a sentence but really isn't because it's missing the subject-verb element is called a *fragment*. It's called a fragment because fragment means *piece,* and a group of words without a proper verb is just a piece of a sentence. Compare the following examples:

The Professor announcing that there would be a test. (Fragment)

The Professor announced that there would be a test. (Complete sentence)

The train having pulled out of the station 30 minutes late. (Fragment)

The train pulled out of the station 30 minutes late. (Complete sentence)

To qualify as a main verb (for purposes of determining whether a sentence is complete or just a fragment), the verb must be a conjugated verb. Here is an example:

Charcoal, a non-volatile residue, —— by heating organic matter in the absence of air.

    (A) obtained

    (B) is obtained

    (C) obtaining

    (D) to obtain

The correct answer is (B). The subject of the sentence is "charcoal," but you need a verb. (D) is an infinitive, not a conjugated verb, so (D) is out of the question. (C) is a participle, not a conjugated verb, so (C) won't do the job. (A) and (B) are both conjugated verbs, but (A) would require an object. But the sentence doesn't include an object. So the best choice is (B).

This is not to say that a sentence cannot correctly use a nonconjugated verb; it can. But if a sentence includes a nonconjugated verb such as a participle, then the participle has to be used as an adjective and has to modify something. (Plus there still must be a conjugated verb elsewhere.) Here is an example of an acceptable use of a nonconjugated verb:

—— only 18 inches apart, the fir trees soon began to die because there wasn't enough moisture in the soil for all of them.

    (A) It planted

    (B) Planted

    (C) Planting

    (D) Was planted

The correct answer is (B). The past participle form, "planted," functions as an adjective that modifies "trees." But you should notice that there is still a subject and a main verb in the sentence: trees began to die.

NOTE

TOEFL sentences are declaratory sentences ending in periods. You don't have to worry about interrogatories (ending in question marks) or exclamations (ending in exclamation points).

5

Workshop

This workshop will give you practice on Type I Structure problems. There is no time limit for the Drill. Indicate your answers in your book. After you finish the Drill part, then check your work using the Review.

Drill

1. According to legend, Dr. Faust —— his soul to the devil in exchange for youth, knowledge, and magical powers.

    (A) selling
    (B) to sell
    (C) is sold
    (D) sold

2. St. Francis, the son of a wealthy merchant, —— permission by Pope Innocent III to form an order of friars.

    (A) he was given
    (B) was given
    (C) giving
    (D) to give

3. For their part, the revolutionaries —— as a way of ensuring the permanence of the revolution.

    (A) wanting an war
    (B) wanted a war
    (C) to want war
    (D) wanting war

4. —— many bronze sculptures because he did not destroy the molds from which the originals were made.

    (A) They are
    (B) There are
    (C) Are
    (D) The

5. —— in New York City, Henry James settled in London in 1876 and became a British citizen in 1915.

    (A) Was born
    (B) Born
    (C) To be born
    (D) To born

6. Not only —— widely distributed all through the North temperate zone, but many are important sources of oil and lumber.

    (A) are junipers
    (B) juniper
    (C) some junipers
    (D) they are junipers

7. —— occupational diseases, and although all can be debilitating, relatively few are ordinarily fatal.

    (A) Many
    (B) Where many
    (C) There are many
    (D) About many

8. Many orchids are native to North America, and these —— wild in bogs and moist woodlands.

    (A) grow
    (B) growing
    (C) they grow
    (D) to have grown

9. The male red-wing blackbird —— as though it is injured in order to lead a predator away from its nest.

    (A) flapping its wings
    (B) its wings flapping
    (C) flaps its wings
    (D) wings flap it

10. Although Edgar Allan Poe is best known as a writer of short stories, he also —— as a newspaper editor in Richmond, Philadelphia, and New York City.

    (A) working
    (B) to work
    (C) to working
    (D) worked

11. —— in 1961 to assist developing countries in training people for technical jobs, particularly in agriculture.

    (A) The Peace Corps established
    (B) The Peace Corps was established
    (C) Although the Peace Corps was established
    (D) When the Peace Corps was established

12. George Papadopoulos, —— through a coup d'etat by rightist army officers in 1967, was in turn overthrown by yet another military coup.

    (A) which came to power
    (B) that coming to power
    (C) power came to him
    (D) who came to power

13. The Great Lakes is a group of five connected waterways —— over 1,000 miles along the border between the United States and Canada.

    (A) what extends
    (B) that extends
    (C) who extend
    (D) which extending

14. The members of the Greenback Party —— farmers stricken by the Panic of 1873.

    (A) that were
    (B) which were
    (C) were
    (D) was

15. The primary function of guilds was —— by establishing local control over a profession or craft by setting quality standards and prices.

    (A) protect its membership
    (B) protecting its membership
    (C) to protect their membership
    (D) membership protecting

5

Review

1. D	5. B	9. C	13. B
2. B	6. A	10. D	14. C
3. B	7. C	11. B	15. C
4. B	8. A	12. D	

Q & A Session

Q: Why is it important to know what's NOT tested by the TOEFL?

A: There are two reasons. First, if you know what *not* to look for, then you can spend your time and energy looking for those things that *are* most likely to be tested. Second, if you find what you think is an error but you aren't sure, if you know that it's one of those things not ordinarily tested by the TOEFL, then you can eliminate that answer choice with some confidence and concentrate on the remaining choices.

Q: Should I review the distinction between who and whom?

A: You can if you want to, and it is a sign of someone who really has a good command of English to be able to use those forms properly. In the past, however, this distinction has not been particularly important on the TOEFL. And it is becoming increasingly less important in English itself, so it is even less likely that you would need that distinction on your test.

Q: You used commas to distinguish essential and nonessential clauses for the purposes of choosing the relative pronoun. Does that mean that punctuation is sometimes tested?

A: No. If you go back to those examples, you'll see that the punctuation did not change when we corrected the sentence. That means that the commas themselves were not part of the error that was tested. Instead, we suggested that you use the presence of commas as a tip-off that the clause is nonessential rather than essential. They're not part of the mistake, but they can help you find the mistake.

This Hour's Review

1. You should be alert for these pronoun errors:

   Failure of agreement

   Use of "which" or "that" to refer to people

   Use of "what" instead of a relative pronoun

   Use of "which" in an essential clause

2. You should be alert for these modifier errors:

   Improperly formed adjectives and adverbs

   Misplaced adjectives (behind noun)

   Wrong or missing articles (a, an)

3. Watch out for sentences that don't have main verbs:

   The main verb must be a conjugated verb

   A participle form must be used as a modifier

5

HOUR 6

Review the Structure PreTest

What You'll Do This Hour

- Review the Structure PreTest

Review the Structure PreTest

Now that you've reviewed some of the important grammar points tested by the TOEFL, we'll revisit the PreTest that you took in Hour 3 to talk about those items in greater detail and to add more entries to your checklist of grammar.

1. **(B)** The sentence has this structure:

SUBJECT	VERB	PREDICATE NOMINATIVE	RELATIVE CLAUSE
Success	is	one	that, which, or who

(B) completes the structure by using "that" to introduce a relative clause modifying "one." (The relative clause is essential to identifying "one," so "that" is the right choice.) And you'll notice that there are no commas setting off the relative clause.

(A) and (C) are wrong because they don't follow the word for a relative clause. The proper word order for a relative clause is like that of a main clause: subject-verb-etc.

(D) is wrong because "why" is not a relative pronoun.

 CAUTION | You cannot use "why" to introduce a relative clause.

2. **(D)** The sentence needs a subject, and that means a noun element. (C) is wrong because it is not a noun element. Sometimes "that" introduces a noun clause:

"That no lives were lost is a tribute to the skill of the flight crew."

But, as you can see, like other clauses it has a subject and a verb. (C) doesn't have these elements.

(A) and (B) are a bit more subtle since they are both noun forms. "Studying" is a gerund, and "to study" an infinitive. So why can't they be the subject here? Because they're not idiomatic. You probably don't like hearing that for an answer because it's not a rule that you can learn and apply in the future; but, unfortunately, it is the explanation. English is like other languages; there are some peculiarities that just can't be reduced to rules.

3. **(B)** The blank will have to introduce a verb for the subject "construction." All of the choices use the linking verb "is," but only (B) follows the right order for an English sentence. In this case, unless there is some element that modifies "construction," the verb needs to follow the subject directly. Compare the following acceptable writings:

New construction is the important indicator.

New construction of commercial property is the most important indicator.

New construction, as measured by residential housing starts, is the most important indicator.

New construction, which includes rehabilitation if it involves over 90 percent of the structure, is the most important indicator.

But the common theme for all of these variations is that the linking verb comes as close to the subject as possible.

TIP

> Eliminate choices that do not respect the accepted word order for English sentences.

4. **(D)** With this structure, you need an adjective to modify "it." As for (B), "possibly" is an adverb, not an adjective. In (C), "possibility" is a noun. And in (A), "possible," which is an adjective, modifies "communications."

5. **(C)** Here you have a mini-exercise in the use of adverbs and adjectives. First, "greatest," which is the superlative ("most") of "great," has to modify a noun. You can eliminate (B) because "greatest" seems to modify "usual," but one adjective cannot modify another adjective. In (D), "greatest" seems to modify "threat," but (D) doesn't respect the requirement that in English the adjective usually comes in front of the noun: "greatest threat" not "threat greatest." Second, "usually" is an adverb that must modify a verb or perhaps an adjective. (A) suggests that "usually" is meant to modify "greatest," but that is illogical: if something is *the* greatest threat, then there is not usual or unusual about it; it is one of a kind. So "usually" must modify "is" and explain the conditions under which this threat arises.

NOTE

> Adjectives have three degrees: simple, comparative, superlative. These are usually formed with the addition of -ier and -iest, though some use "more" and "most." The superlative refers to <u>one</u> member of the group: highest mountain, smartest pupil, most beautiful scene.

6

6. **(B)** The object of "at" is a clause, and the elements of the clause need to come in an acceptable order. Only (B) does this.

7. **(A)** Even without the material that will go into the blank, the sentence is a complete thought. So whatever you put into the blank must connect with some element of the

sentence without compromising the integrity of the existing structure. (A) does this. The technical description for (A) is "appositive." The noun "withdrawal" stands in "apposition" to the noun-subject "disintermediation." It's like:

John, my brother, is a student.

The Loeb Building, our student center, is on Park Street.

You can also build upon this structure:

John, my brother who is older than I am, is a student.

The Loeb Building, our student center noted for its great cafeteria food, is on Park Street.

But the noun has to be the anchor. Everything that is added must refer to the noun. The difficulty with the wrong choices in this problem is that they fail to respect this requirement. (B) uses the verb "withdraw," so (B) needs a subject; but there isn't one. (C) looks like the start of a relative clause, but there's no verb. (D) is a clause with a subject and verb, but it's not connected to anything in the rest of the sentence.

> **NOTE**
>
> An *appositive* is a noun that has the meaning of the noun it stands next to: *Hydrogen,* the *first element* on the chart, has one proton. An appositive is set off by commas and doesn't affect the structure of the rest of the sentence. You can think of an appositive as an echo.

8. **(A)** You could put a period after "success," and you'd have a complete sentence:

The Pittsburgh Steelers enjoyed success.

That means that anything added has to create a self-contained structure that is connected to something in this part but doesn't disrupt the flow of the sentence. (This is very similar to what is going on in #7.) (A) is correct because "unmatched" (a past participle) is an adjective that modifies "success." And the rest of the sentence then modifies "unmatched." So (A) connects the second part of the sentence to something in the first part, but doesn't disturb the structure of the first part.

(B) is wrong because introducing a verb like "was unmatched" makes the reader look for a subject, and the most likely candidate is "success." But we've already seen that "success" has a role in the sentence: the direct object of the verb "enjoyed." So (B) disrupts the logic of the first part of the sentence. And, of course, (C) makes the same mistake. Finally, (D) is wrong because the definite article "the" needs a noun, but "unmatched" is an adjective.

To simplify things, try reading the sentence without certain parts. If the sentence still makes sense, the element you dropped out is not essential to the sentence. It must be connected to the body of the sentence without interfering with the logic of the main part of the sentence.

9. **(C)** First, the material between the commas is an appositive. (See #7 above.) If you delete it, you'll see that the main sentence has this structure:

—— now dominate the political landscape.

So you need a subject to finish off the sentence. Only (C) provides a noun for the subject. (D) is a prepositional phrase, but a prepositional phrase is not a noun and can't be the subject of the sentence. (B) sounds like it should be a noun clause (which could be the subject of the sentence):

That two political parties are dominant is obvious.

But (B) doesn't have the verb needed to set up a clause. (B) actually contains both a subject and a verb. (The use of "there" creates an inverted structure in which the verb comes first and subject second, acceptable in English.) But since (B) has both a subject and a verb, the noun "parties" cannot also be the subject of the larger sentence.

10. **(A)** Everything down to the comma is a complete sentence. Everything that comes after must be connected with an element of the complete sentence. (A) does this by using the preposition "like" to join oriental rugs to "fringe." (B) is wrong because "because" is a conjunction, and conjunctions are used to introduce clauses. But what follows the blank is not a clause. (C) sounds a little like an appositive (see #7, above), but "way" doesn't mean the same thing as "fringe." So you have a word, "way," that doesn't connect to anything else. (D) is an adverb which would have to modify a verb, but there isn't a verb.

11. **(D)** Here you have a long sentence but a simple structure. For purposes of analyzing the sentence, you can bracket everything down to "profitable." Then, "because" introduces a subordinate clause with its own subject ("it") and a verb ("must cover"). That's followed by a direct object: "accounting and services." So whatever you put into the blank must modify one of these words. And (D) does: "providing" is a participle that modifies "services."(C) almost does the trick, but (C) is wrong because the services are no longer provided. ("Providing" suggests that the services are still being provided.) (B) is wrong because "provide" is a main or conjugated verb and cannot be used as an adjective. And (A) is not an adjective.

6

> **NOTE** Both the -ing and -ed forms of verbs can be used as adjectives, and they can imply whether the attribute of the noun modified was acquired in the past or is still being acquired, e.g., "the snow blowing against the window" and "the snow blown into huge drifts" or "the smell of chicken baking in the oven" and "the smell of chicken baked in the oven."

12. **(D)** The introductory phrase modifies "oxen," which is the subject of the sentence. So whatever goes into the blank has to leave that logic undisturbed. About the only thing that can go into the blank is an adjective, and that's why (D) is correct. (A) is wrong because "both" can be a pronoun, but here it won't work because the sentence already has a subject. (B) is wrong because you'd need the definite article: "both of the oxen must pull." And (C) is wrong because the "the" is out of place: "the both oxen."

13. **(A)** Here you have a sentence with two independent clauses, each with a subject and verb, joined in typical English fashion with an "and" and correctly punctuated with a comma. The second clause really doesn't affect our analysis. For the first clause, we need a subject and a verb. Neither (B) nor (C) include a verb, so we can eliminate them. (D) has a verb ("are") but it also assigns a subject to that verb, "they." So in (D) you've got two potential subjects, "they" and "Granny Smiths," but only one verb.

14. **(D)** If you put a period after "lye," you'll see that the sentence already has everything it needs. And that's the clue that whatever comes after has to be a self-contained unit: it must be connected with the main part of the sentence, but it can't interfere with anything that's already in place. One way of connecting would be to use "in order to be eaten," but that's not one of the choices. Another option would be to make the additional element into a clause, and that's what (D) does. "Before" is a conjunction that introduces a subordinate clause to modify "be cured," telling when the olives must be cured. (A) is wrong because "as," as a conjunction wouldn't have the right meaning; and, in any event, the words are in the wrong order. (B) would be okay if it actually introduced a clause: "if they are to be eaten." But (B) doesn't bring with it a verb like (D) does. As for (C), remember that "that" can be used to introduce a noun clause that can function as a subject. For example:

    That they are eaten by anyone is a great mystery.

    But a noun element, whether a simple noun word or a noun clause, would still have to be connected to something, and (C) doesn't do that.

15. **(C)** The structure "known as . . ." is going to require a noun element. (C) creates a noun phrase. The other choices try to create clauses, but they fail because they don't include verbs.

16. **(B)** You need "an" in front of a vowel sound: "an important document." (A) is correct because "signed" is a participle form used as an adjective to modify "Magna Carta." (C) is a predicate noun, and (D) is a perfectly good adjective that correctly modifies "history."

17. **(D)** (D) is just not idiomatic. It seems to be a confusion of two possibilities: eighteen years old or eighteen years of age. (A) is just a normal verb and is correctly used. (B) is a participle used as an adjective to modify "law" and to explain the content of the law. And (C) is a noun that is the object of "requiring."

18. **(C)** Here, you have a problem of subject-verb agreement: seven . . . was. You need the plural verb "were." (A) is a past participle form used as an adjective to modify "students." "School" is a noun that functions as the object of the preposition "at." And "in" is idiomatic, as in Bruce Springstein's "Born in the USA."

19. **(A)** This sentence commits the error of the superfluous subject: what is "he" doing in this sentence? It's not the subject of the sentence, because the subject of the sentence is "George Gershwin." It's not an object of any sort nor an appositive. "He" is just there doing nothing, so it's wrong. As for (B), "films" is the object of the proposition "for." (C) modifies "films" to provide further details. And (D) uses "which" to introduce a relative clause.

> **TIP**
>
> If a word doesn't have a clear role to play in a sentence, then it's superfluous and an error.

20. **(C)** An adverb, such as "practically," cannot be used to modify a noun, such as "matters." The adjective form of the word, "practical," must be used instead.

21. **(B)** The problem with the sentence is that it doesn't have a main verb. So the error is in (B). You can change "providing" to "provides" in order to produce a complete sentence.

22. **(A)** You can't use "what" to introduce a relative clause. You'd have to use "which." (B) is correct: "affects" is the singular verb for the singular subject "food." (C) is correct: "feels" is the singular verb for the singular subject "one" in the clause introduced by "how." And "as well as" is a conjunction that joins two like elements "emotionally" and "physically."

23. **(A)** "Other" has to modify a plural noun: other mammals. (B) is correct: "does" is a singular verb for "duckbill platypus." (C) is properly parallel to "does": does not bear but reproduces. And (D) is a gerund that functions as the object of the preposition "by."

6

24. **(D)** In this sentence, "allusion" and "symbolic" are supposed to be objects of the preposition "in." "Allusion" is a noun, and that's fine. But "symbolic" is an adjective, and an adjective cannot be an object. The sentence should read "in classical allusion and subtle symbolism." (A) is correct because the plural verb "are" agrees with its subject "poets." (B) is correct because "literary" is an adjective that properly modifies "works." "That" introduces an essential adjective clause that defines what kind of works are being discussed.

NOTE   Every rule has exceptions. The rules in this book are guidelines to help you make sense of the TOEFL. There may be exceptions to them that just aren't relevant to the TOEFL.

25. **(B)** "Lightly" is an adverb, but you need an adjective here: "light." Interestingly, this is one of those few times when you'll find an adjective that follows its noun, but notice that the wording is "a metal light in weight." This exception is just an unusual idiom. It would not be correct to say "a metal light." (A) is correct because it is a properly formed verb. (C) is fine because "strong" is an adjective modifying "metal." And (D) is fine because the phrase modifies "inexpensive."

26. **(D)** You need "an" in front of "adventure." (A) is correct because "were" is a plural verb that goes with its subject "writings." (B) is all right because "by" is an idiomatic preposition used to connect "philosophy" with "characterized." And (C) is acceptable because "is" is singular and "adventure" is singular.

27. **(B)** Here you have what is called an inverted sentence structure: "There is something." This is just a peculiar English structure in which the subject follows the verb. Here, however, "interesting" is supposed to be the subject, but it sounds like an adjective. You need the noun "interest." As for (A), "successful" is an adjective that modifies the noun "fusion." (C) is all right because "possibility" is a noun that is the object of "about." And (D) is acceptable because "unlimited" is an adjective that can modify "energy."

TIP   When a sentence is introduced by "there," the order of the subject and verb is reversed. The verb comes first and is probably the very first element after the "there."

28. **(D)** "Various" implies that there is more than one flavor, so you need a plural noun: various flavors. (A) is correct because "although" introduces a subordinate clause with "gelatin" as the subject and "is" as the verb. (B) is correct because "itself" is a reflexive pronoun added for emphasis. (Remember that the TOEFL really doesn't test reflexive pronouns, so this was not likely to be the correct answer in any event.) And (C) is acceptable because "it" functions as the subject of the main clause.

29. **(A)** "Obviously" is an adverb, but you need an adjective to modify "disagreements." The correct word would be "obvious." (B) is correct because this is an appropriate place for an indefinite article, and "a" is the right choice. (C) is correct because "produces" is a singular verb that agrees with "economy." And (D) is correct because "expectations" is a noun that functions as the object of "to satisfy."

30. **(B)** This is just a matter of idiomatic usage: "benefited from something." (A) is correct because "deserving" is an adjective form that modifies the noun "students." (C) is all right because "programs" is a noun that is the object of a preposition. (The correct one would be "for.") And (D) is okay because "college" can modify "study."

NOTE

> There are some nouns that behave like adjectives in certain contexts and modify other nouns, e.g., college student, office building, football team.

31. **(D)** This item doesn't fit neatly into any of the categories we've talked about. You need "those," which functions as a shorthand for "those elements." Otherwise, you have "them," which has nothing to refer to.

32. **(A)** This is just a matter of correctly using idioms. "During" is a preposition that refers to a time span that is self-defining. For example, "the 1970s," "the first century," "the month of May," "the semester break." All of these define their own time span. When you want to define a time span using two outside markers, you need to use the structure "from . . . to." For example, "from 1970 to 1979," "from the first year to the year 99," "from May 1ˢᵗ to May 31ˢᵗ," "from the time school gets out to the time it resumes."

33. **(B)** "Very" cannot substitute for "so." The other choices are correct.

34. **(A)** Here you need a subject for the verb "began," but "restructure" is a verb. "Restructuring," the gerund form, can be your subject. (B) is acceptable because "traditional" is an adjective modifying the noun "classroom." "Prior to" is idiomatic in this context. And "reformers" is a noun that is the object of the preposition "by."

6

35. **(B)** "Plenty" is a noun, but you need an adjective: "plentiful." (A) is correct, because "are" is a plural verb for the plural subject "plants." (C) is a preposition with the correct sense. And in (D), "abundant" is an adjective that modifies "food."

36. **(B)** Remember that "much" refers to noncount or mass nouns, while "many" modifies count nouns. Since calculations can be enumerated, you should use "many." (A) is correct because "can" is a modal verb that is properly followed by a simple form of "perform." (C) and (D) are correct because "when" is a conjunction that correctly introduces a clause with a subject ("computers") and a verb ("invented").

37. **(A)** "Despite" is a preposition, not a conjunction. But what follows "despite" is the subject-("advances") verb ("have been made") structure of a clause. You need to replace "despite" with a subordinating conjunction like "though" or "although." (B) is correct because "forms" is a noun that functions as the object of "diagnosing and treating." (C) is correct because "many" is used to modify the count noun "people." And (D) is correct because "unnecessarily" is an adverb that modifies "dies."

> **CAUTION**
>
> Do not mistake a preposition for a conjunction. Some prepositions that may be mistaken for conjunctions are: "because of" for "because," "despite" for "though," "due to" for "because," "except for" for "if (not)," "in spite of" for "although," "on account of" for "because."

38. **(B)** "By" is a preposition that requires a noun for its object, but "rich" is an adjective. You would use the word "richness." (A) is correct because "is characterized" is a singular verb that refers to "poetry." (C) is okay because "by" is a preposition that has "descriptions" as its object. And (D) is correct because the gerund "feelings" functions as the object of "of."

39. **(C)** "Roberto Clemente" is the subject of the sentence, so you need a verb. "Impression," however, is a noun. The sentence needs to read: "Roberto Clemente impressed . . ." (A) is correct because "who" is introducing a relative clause and correctly refers to "Roberto Clemente," a person. (B) is correct because "while on" is a prepositional phrase with the object "mission." And (D), "him," is the right case for an object.

40. **(D)** Either something is missing from (D), and the sentence should read: "from parts *of* junked automobiles." Or (D) is in the wrong order and should read: "parts from." Either would be correct, though their meanings are slightly different. That doesn't really matter, of course, because your job is to spot the error—not to correct it.

HOUR 7

The Structure WarmUp Test

What You'll Do This Hour

- Take the Structure WarmUp Test
- Evaluate Your Performance

Your Goals for This Hour

This hour, you'll take the Structure WarmUp Test. After you finish, you'll evaluate your performance.

Your goals for today are:

- Take the Structure WarmUp Test
- Score the WarmUp Test and evaluate your performance

Take the Structure WarmUp Test

This section contains the Structure WarmUp Test. Find a location where you can work undisturbed for approximately half an hour.

The time limit for the WarmUp Test is 25 minutes, *including* the time you take to read the directions. Set your clock for 25 minutes and begin now.

1. Ⓐ Ⓑ Ⓒ Ⓓ	9. Ⓐ Ⓑ Ⓒ Ⓓ	17. Ⓐ Ⓑ Ⓒ Ⓓ	25. Ⓐ Ⓑ Ⓒ Ⓓ	33. Ⓐ Ⓑ Ⓒ Ⓓ
2. Ⓐ Ⓑ Ⓒ Ⓓ	10. Ⓐ Ⓑ Ⓒ Ⓓ	18. Ⓐ Ⓑ Ⓒ Ⓓ	26. Ⓐ Ⓑ Ⓒ Ⓓ	34. Ⓐ Ⓑ Ⓒ Ⓓ
3. Ⓐ Ⓑ Ⓒ Ⓓ	11. Ⓐ Ⓑ Ⓒ Ⓓ	19. Ⓐ Ⓑ Ⓒ Ⓓ	27. Ⓐ Ⓑ Ⓒ Ⓓ	35. Ⓐ Ⓑ Ⓒ Ⓓ
4. Ⓐ Ⓑ Ⓒ Ⓓ	12. Ⓐ Ⓑ Ⓒ Ⓓ	20. Ⓐ Ⓑ Ⓒ Ⓓ	28. Ⓐ Ⓑ Ⓒ Ⓓ	36. Ⓐ Ⓑ Ⓒ Ⓓ
5. Ⓐ Ⓑ Ⓒ Ⓓ	13. Ⓐ Ⓑ Ⓒ Ⓓ	21. Ⓐ Ⓑ Ⓒ Ⓓ	29. Ⓐ Ⓑ Ⓒ Ⓓ	37. Ⓐ Ⓑ Ⓒ Ⓓ
6. Ⓐ Ⓑ Ⓒ Ⓓ	14. Ⓐ Ⓑ Ⓒ Ⓓ	22. Ⓐ Ⓑ Ⓒ Ⓓ	30. Ⓐ Ⓑ Ⓒ Ⓓ	38. Ⓐ Ⓑ Ⓒ Ⓓ
7. Ⓐ Ⓑ Ⓒ Ⓓ	15. Ⓐ Ⓑ Ⓒ Ⓓ	23. Ⓐ Ⓑ Ⓒ Ⓓ	31. Ⓐ Ⓑ Ⓒ Ⓓ	39. Ⓐ Ⓑ Ⓒ Ⓓ
8. Ⓐ Ⓑ Ⓒ Ⓓ	16. Ⓐ Ⓑ Ⓒ Ⓓ	24. Ⓐ Ⓑ Ⓒ Ⓓ	32. Ⓐ Ⓑ Ⓒ Ⓓ	40. Ⓐ Ⓑ Ⓒ Ⓓ

Type I Questions

Questions 1–15 are sentences with dashes to indicate that a part of the sentence has been omitted. Following each, you will see four lettered words or phrases. Choose the one that best completes the sentence and mark the corresponding space on your answer sheet.

Example

The city of St. Louis has been called the "Gateway to the West" —— it was the starting point for many of the trails used during the great westward migration.

    (A) due to

X(B) because

    (C) regardless of

    (D) despite

The sentence should read, "The city of St. Louis has been called the "Gateway to the West" because it was the starting point for many of the trails used during the great westward migration." Therefore, you should choose (B).

Example

Recreational hot air ballooning is restricted to short day trips, so —— need for navigational instruments.

    (A) little is there

    (B) little is

✗(C) there is little

    (D) when there is little

The sentence should read, "Recreational hot air ballooning is restricted to short day trips, so there is little need for navigational instruments." Therefore, you should choose (C).

Now begin work.

7

1. Arles, in the south of France, is —— the painter Van Gogh spent the last days of his life.

    (A) where
    (B) it where
    (C) where is
    (D) that is where

2. As new strains of bacteria emerge that have developed immunity to antibiotics, researchers are constantly challenged —— new treatments that will be effective.

    (A) the development of
    (B) to develop
    (C) develop
    (D) it develops

3. *The Screwtape Letters* is a small book by C. S. Lewis —— to be correspondence between Satan and an apprentice devil.

    (A) purports
    (B) that purports
    (C) that it purports
    (D) purports that which

4. Carbon monoxide, a potentially deadly gas, —— color or odor.

    (A) has no
    (B) which has no
    (C) not having
    (D) it does not have

5. The use of the steel skeleton, which made it —— modern skyscrapers, was pioneered by William Jenney in 1883.

    (A) the possible construction
    (B) possible to construct
    (C) the possibility of constructing
    (D) possibly constructed

6. —— complexities of the modern internal combution engine are impossible to explain in a single volume.

    (A) Though the
    (B) The
    (C) That the
    (D) Because of the

7. Interest rates —— of all economic indicators for predicting whether stock prices will rise or fall.

    (A) the most are reliable
    (B) are the most reliable
    (C) the most reliable are
    (D) that are the most reliable

8. Ancient Egyptian civilization appears ——, flourished, and passed into oblivion in three cycles called the Old Kingdom, the Middle Kingdom, and the New Kingdom.

    (A) was developed
    (B) having to develop
    (C) to have developed
    (D) have developed

9. ——, the billionaire Howard Hughes was a pilot who set several aviation records and a producer whose film credits include *The Front Page.*

    (A) A recluse who, eccentric
    (B) Eccentric a recluse
    (C) Is an eccentric recluse
    (D) An eccentric recluse

10. The temperature-humidity index gives a single numerical value —— as a measure of comfort or discomfort during warm weather.

    (A) that serves
    (B) when it serves
    (C) serving
    (D) it serving

11. New York University Law School, in part because of a substantial infusion of cash from the sale of its Meuller's stock, became —— premier law schools in the United States.

    (A) what the
    (B) one of the
    (C) which the
    (D) the one that

12. The town of New Amsterdam, —— later to become New York City, was founded by the Dutch as a trading post.

    (A) they
    (B) it
    (C) which was
    (D) what was

13. Inca engineers terraced and irrigated the difficult terrain of the empire, —— more fertile.

    (A) thereby making it
    (B) making them
    (C) makes it
    (D) which they make

14. Incense-tree —— the common name for several deciduous shrubs and trees found chiefly in tropical America and North East Africa.

    (A) which is
    (B) that is
    (C) is
    (D) being

15. —— concerns about the dangers of chemical insecticide residues in the ecosystem and in foodstuffs.

    (A) They are
    (B) There are
    (C) Of the
    (D) The

Type II Questions

DIRECTIONS: The sentence below has four underlined parts. Choose the one that contains an error.

Example

The court *ordered* (A) the *pilots striking* (B) to return to work *or* (C) face a stiff fine and perhaps *even* (D) jail.

The correct answer is (B). The sentence should read:

The court ordered the striking pilots to return to work or face a stiff fine and perhaps even jail.

7

16. The term "military-industrial complex"

    was coined <u>by</u> President Dwight
                  A
    Eisenhower in his <u>farewell</u> address to the
                         B
    nation, <u>which</u> he warned of the threat <u>it</u>
              C   D
    posed to democracy.

17. <u>Was invented</u> in 1948, the transistor <u>is</u>
       A   B
    a key component of radio <u>receivers</u>,
                                C
    electronic computers, and <u>automatic</u>
                                  D
    control instrumentation.

18. Shorthand, <u>any</u> rapid system of writing
                   A
    used <u>to transcribing</u> the spoken word,
            B
    <u>is difficult</u> to learn but <u>permits</u> great speed.
       C   D

19. Vitamins, <u>often</u> marketed using well-
                  A
    known cartoon characters, <u>available is</u> in
                                  B
    flavored chewable tablets that <u>appeal</u> to
                                       C
    the tastes of <u>children</u>.
                      D

20. The principal island of Mauritius, <u>located</u>
                                           A
    in the Southwest Indian Ocean, <u>has</u> a
                                       B
    central plateau and volcanic mountains

    that <u>rise</u> to a height of 820 <u>in</u> meters.
           C   D

21. New York City <u>has</u> <u>more</u> miles of subway
                      A   B
    track <u>than</u> any <u>another</u> city.
             C   D

22. <u>A</u> fetish is <u>an</u> inanimate natural or cultural
       A   B
    object <u>believed to</u> have magical power
              C
    from a will of <u>their</u> own.
                      D

23. The <u>true</u> genius of the Roman Empire <u>was</u>
           A   B
    not so much a talent for military conquest

    <u>and</u> the ability <u>to administer</u> the large
       C   D
    territories under its control.

24. <u>To make</u> fiberglass, molten material
       A
    is <u>forced</u> through a kind of sieve, thus
          B
    <u>forming</u> it into threads that can be <u>using</u> in
       C   D
    the manufacture of various products

    including draperies.

25. Mercury is the <u>metal only</u> existing <u>as</u> a
                      A   B
    liquid at ordinary temperatures and <u>is</u> used
                                            C
    in barometers, thermometers, and electric

    <u>switches</u>.
       D

26. Marble, a term <u>loosely</u> applied to <u>any</u>
                       A   B
    limestone that is suitable as a building or

ornamental <u>stone</u>, is found in various <u>color</u>
         C   D
depending on the types of impurities

present.

27. *Moby Dick* by Herman Melville, the story

of a whaling captain's <u>obsessive</u> search for
                      A

a white whale, is an exciting sea <u>story</u>, a
                            B

heavily <u>symbolic</u> inquiry into good and
          C

evil, and <u>of one</u> the greatest novels ever
         D
written.

28. Mastadons, a term <u>covering</u> several
                    A
prehistorical <u>mammal</u> of the extinct genus
            B
mammut, were forest <u>dwellers</u> that <u>lived</u> in
                  C   D
Africa during the Oligocene epoch.

29. <u>An</u> influential civil-rights lawyer and
A
<u>the first</u> African-American appointed to
B
the Supreme Court, Thurgood Marshall

was particularly <u>concerned to</u> civil rights
                  C

and <u>economic</u> justice.
      D

30. Loam, <u>composed of</u> sand, silt, clay, and
         A
organic matter, <u>has</u> a porous <u>texture</u> that
            B   C

permits <u>their</u> high moisture retention and
       D
air circulation.

31. Linguisitics is the <u>scientific</u> study of
               A
language, covering structure as well as the

<u>history</u> of the relation of languages to one
B
another and language's <u>cultural</u> place in
                  C
human <u>behaving</u>.
      D

32. Fertilizer, <u>which it is</u> added to the soil
           A
to replace <u>or</u> increase plant <u>nutrients</u>,
        B   C
<u>includes</u> animal and green manure, fish
C
and bone meal, guano, and compost.

33. <u>In</u> 1825 to 1918, when it was replaced by
A
the <u>larger</u> New York State Barge Canal,
     B
the Erie Canal provided <u>a</u> link <u>between</u> the
                  C   D
Atlantic Ocean and the Great Lakes.

34. The disease of measles <u>is characterized</u> by
                   A
fever, by <u>red</u> of the eyes, by white spots <u>in</u>
       B   C
the mouth, and by a facial rash that <u>spreads</u>
                        D
to the rest of the body.

7

35. Albert Einstein, <u>whose</u> special theory
                        A
    of relativity <u>dealt</u> with systems in uni-
                   B
    form motion with respect to one <u>another</u>,
                                      C
    <u>he received</u> the Nobel Prize in physics in
     D
    1921.

36. Intelligence-gathering organizations

    <u>provide</u> information that <u>is</u> essential <u>when</u>
      A   B   C
    government policy <u>makers</u> in the forma-
                       D
    tion of military strategies.

37. In modern electronic <u>appliances</u> with
                           A
    integrated circuits, it is usually less

    <u>costlier</u> to replace the entire unit <u>than</u>
      B   C
    to repair <u>a</u> single component.
               D

38. <u>Diamonds</u> of gemstone quality <u>vary</u> in
     A   B
    color, <u>bright</u>, cut, and <u>weight</u>.
            C   D

39. <u>As many as</u> 90 percent of the funds raised
     A
    by a typical <u>charitable</u> organization is
                  B
    <u>spent on</u> administrative expenses such <u>as</u>
     C   D
    salaries and office rental.

40. New York City, with its <u>harbor natural</u>,
                             A
    has always been a seaport even though

    <u>frequent</u> dredging is now needed to keep
     B
    the channels <u>deep</u> enough for today's
                  C
    giant container <u>ships</u>.
                     D

Evaluate Your Performance

Answer Key

1. A	11. B	21. D	31. D
2. B	12. C	22. D	32. A
3. B	13. A	23. C	33. A
4. A	14. C	24. D	34. B
5. B	15. B	25. A	35. D
6. B	16. C	26. D	36. C
7. B	17. A	27. D	37. B
8. C	18. B	28. B	38. C
9. D	19. B	29. C	39. A
10. A	20. D	30. D	40. A

HOUR 8

Review the Structure WarmUp Test

What You'll Do This Hour

- Review the Structure WarmUp Test

Your Goals for This Hour

- Your goals for today are:
- Review the Structure WarmUp Test

Review the Structure WarmUp Test

In Hour 7, you took the Structure WarmUp Test. We'll go over those problems and use them to pull together some of the important points discussed already.

1. **(A)** This item tests the order of basic elements:

SUBJECT	LINKING VERB	SUBJECT COMPLEMENT
Arles	is	where Van Gogh spent days

The "where" introduces a clause (modifying "Arles"), which has both a subject ("Van Gogh") and a verb ("spent").

(B) is incorrect because the word "it" has no logical connection to the other elements of the sentence. At first, "it" looks like a single word complement, e.g., "This is it." But then the clause "where Van Gogh spent" couldn't be the complement and would be out of a job in the sentence. As a result, a bunch of words would be hanging on at the end with nothing to connect them to the rest of the sentence.

(C) is incorrect because the "is" is superfluous, that is, it's stuck in there with no job to do.

(D) ends up with an extra "is that," a phrase that just doesn't connect to anything else in the sentence.

2. **(B)** The question that must be answered by the blank is: how are the researchers challenged? And (B) provides the answer. (A) is wrong, because you have a noun with no connection to anything else in the sentence. Similarly, putting another conjugated verb in there leaves you with just one more word, so (C) is wrong. (D) at least has the merit of coupling a potential subject with a verb, but this pair cannot function as the main subject and verb (that job is already taken) and there's nothing to make it a clause.

3. **(B)** The sentence has a complete structure:

SUBJECT	LINKING VERB	COMPLEMENT
Screwtape Letters	is	book

So the blank must do something to connect everything else to one of those elements. (B) does this by using "that" as a relative pronoun (referring to "book") to introduce an adjective clause ("that purports") which modifies "book."

COMPLEMENT	RELATIVE PRONOUN	VERB	RELATIVE CLAUSE COMPLEMENT
Book	that	purports	to be correspondence

.

So everything is tied together.

4. **(A)** This sentence needs a conjugated verb. The phrase "a potentially deadly gas" is an appositive that modifies or stands in for the subject of the sentence, carbon monoxide. So the basic structure of the sentence says "carbon monoxide" blank "no color." The blank must be a conjugated verb. (B) is incorrect because "which," a relative pronoun, would introduce an adjective clause. But that would leave the sentence with no main verb. (C) is wrong for a similar reason. (D) is incorrect because it commits the error of the superfluous subject. Carbon monoxide is the subject of the sentence; the "it" is unnecessary and therefore incorrect. Additionally, (D) would result in a double negative: "not have no color." Double negatives are not acceptable in standard written English.

5. **(B)** In this sentence, the subject is separated from the verb by a relative clause. So the basic order of elements is subject, "the use of the steel skeleton," modifier, introduced by "which," and verb, "was pioneered." The material inside of the commas is a nonessential relative clause. (C) and (D) are incorrect because "possibility" is a noun and "possibly" an adverb; neither of which can function as an adjective. In (A), "possible" is an adjective, but it modifies "construction" rather than "it."

6. **(B)** This sentence has a very simple structure: subject—verb—predicate adjective. "Complexities" is the subject, "are" is the verb, and "impossible" is the predicate adjective. (A) is incorrect because "though" is a conjunction that would be used to introduce a subordinate clause; but that would leave the sentence without a main subject. (C) is wrong for a similar reason. The phrase in (D) would reduce "complexities" to the status of an object of a proposition, leaving the sentence with no subject.

7. **(B)** This sentence needs a main verb. And only (B) provides it. As for (A), this seems to read "interest rates, the most," which looks like an adjective phrase to modify the "rates." But then the verb "are" has no logical connection to any other part of the sentence. The same is true of both (C) and (D). While it would not be inappropriate to include a modifier following "rates," it is still necessary to insure that there is a main verb.

8. **(C)** The defining characteristic of this sentence is a series of three parallel elements one of which must fill in the blank: blank, "flourished, and passed." Since these are three similar elements, they must have similar verb forms.

9. **(D)** This sentence is in all respects complete even without the blank. It has a subject "Howard Hughes," a verb, "was," and a predicate noun, "a pilot." To maintain the integrity of the sentence (so that you don't wind up with words that have no logical connection to something else in the sentence), the blank must create a phrase that modifies the subject. And that is why (D) is correct.

10. **(A)** A good way to analyze this sentence is to see that everything down to the blank constitutes an independent clause: "index" (subject) "gives"(verb) "value" (object). Since the integrity of the sentence does not depend upon what comes after the blank, it's necessary to include a structure that will connect everything following the blank with some component of the sentence that comes before. The most logical solution is a relative or adjective clause that modifies "value."

11. **(B)** This sentence becomes easier to understand if you strip out everything between the two commas: "the law school became" blank. The material between the two commas is an adverbial phrase that modifies "became"; the speaker includes it for its informational value, but it is not logically essential to the structure of the sentence. We are left with the task, then, of completing this sentence by explaining what the law school became. And that requires a noun or a phrase or clause functioning as a noun. (A) is incorrect because "what" may not introduce an adjective clause. Second, even with an appropriate relative pronoun the result would be a clause with the subject "schools" but no verb. And it is for this second reason that (C) is incorrect: "which the law schools." The result, is a failed attempt at adding an adjective clause because the result lacks a verb. Finally, (D) is incorrect because "that" seems to introduce a relative clause, but there is no verb to complete it.

12. **(C)** You can drop out everything between the two commas, and the sentence will maintain its integrity: it will have a subject and a verb. So the blank has to be completed in such a way that the material between the commas is logically connected to something in the sentence but doesn't compromise anything that's already in place. It's a job for a relative clause, and "which" is the appropriate relative pronoun to introduce a nonessential clause.

13. **(A)** A good way to analyze this sentence is to see that you could put a period after "empire" and have a complete thought and a grammatically correct sentence. Since the integrity of the sentence is already guaranteed, the blank must introduce an element that modifies some other element in the sentence. (A) does this by using a participle as an adjective to modify "empire."

14. **(C)** As written, the sentence has a subject, "incense-tree," but needs a main verb. Choice (C) provides one. (A) and (B) are incorrect because they want to introduce a relative clause, but in doing so they take the only logical candidate for a main verb and turn it into the verb of a relative clause. The resulting sentence is left without a main verb. Finally, (D) is incorrect because "being" is not a conjugated verb; the result is a fragment rather than a complete sentence.

15. **(B)** The sentence is lacking both a subject and verb. Neither (C) nor (D) includes a verb, so the result of using either of those choices is not a complete sentence. Both (A) and (B) contain the verb "are," a conjugated verb that is a perfectly good main

verb. The difficulty with (A) is that "they" would become the subject of the sentence; and that would seem to make "concerns" a predicate adjective, which it can't be because it's a noun.

16. **(C)** As written, "which" seems to refer to "nation," but that would make it the subject of a relative clause modifying "nation." The trouble with that reading is that the only other verb in the sentence is "warned" and it's associated with "he." In any event, it should be clear that "which" is intended to refer to "farewell address" since that is where the warning was issued.

17. **(A)** A good way to analyze this sentence is to see that everything that comes after the initial comma is a perfectly good sentence that doesn't need anything else. So the part that comes before will have to be connected with some other part of the sentence but not compromise the integrity of any of those parts. A good way to do this is simply to drop the "was." Now you have a participle used as an adjective that modifies the nearest noun, "transistor," and tells when the transistor was invented.

18. **(B)** As you learned in Hour 4, you can't mix the infinitive and gerund forms the way that (B) tries to do. The sentence can be corrected by simply using the infinitive.

19. **(B)** The subject of this sentence is "vitamins" and the verb is "is." "Available," then, is intended to be a predicate adjective that modifies "vitamins": Vitamins are available. The problem is that "available" is in the wrong place. The proper order for this sequence is: subject-verb-predicate adjective.

20. **(D)** The problem with (D) is that the phrase simply isn't idiomatic. With a denominate number, there is no need for an inverting preposition. Everything else in the sentence is in order. "Located" is a participle that modifies "Maritius" and tells where it's located; "has" is the verb for "island"; and "rise" is a plural verb that agrees with the two elements of the subject joined by "and."

21. **(D)** (D) is simply not idiomatic. The word should be "other." Everything else in the sentence is in order. "Has" is the main verb, and it is singular so that it agrees with "New York City." "More — than" is an English idiom used to make a comparison.

22. **(D)** The problem here is that "their" refers to "object," but "object" is singular and "their" is plural. So to correct the sentence, it would be necessary to change "their" to the singular "its." Notice that "a" and "an" are correctly used, as described in the review of Hour 5.

23. **(C)** The difficulty with this sentence is that it fails to use a proper idiom. The correct structure in English is "not so much this as that." The error could be corrected by substituting "as" for "and."

24. **(D)** It is a rule in English that a modal verb such as "may," "might," "could," or—as here—"can," must be completed by a conjugated or simple verb: "can be used."

25. **(A)** The error in this sentence is the order of words in the predicate adjective. Remember that the adjective should come before the noun: "only metal." Notice also that you have a series of parallel elements that is properly completed: "barometers," "thermometers," and "switches."

26. **(D)** The problem here is that a plural noun is required in (D), but "color" is singular. The word "various" could only refer to a plural noun, otherwise there would be no variation. Everything else in the sentence is in order. "Marble" is the subject, and the material within the commas is an appositive that restates what "marble" means. (A) is correctly written since you have an adverb modifying the verb "applied."

27. **(D)** Here is a good example of a sentence that has parallelism. You have a series of three elements: "story," "inquiry," and "novels." So (B) is correctly written, as is (C), since "symbolic" is an adjective modifying one of the nouns in that series. The problem is in (D): the "of" has no logical connection to anything in the sentence. Anytime that you find a word with no logical function that is just stuck into a sentence, it's probably the error that you're looking for.

28. **(B)** Here you have a singular count noun that should be plural: "several mammals." Everything else in the sentence is in order. "Covering" is a participle that modifies the subject "mastodons"; "dwellers" is a predicate noun for "mastodons"; and "lived" is the verb for the relative pronoun "that."

29. **(C)** The phrase "concerned to" would be idiomatic only if followed by a verb, e.g., "concerned to finish on time." To be followed by a noun, the phrase should be "concerned with." Everything else is in order. You have "an" modifying a word that begins with a vowel sound; you have an adjective "the first" modifying a noun "African-American;" and you have another adjective "economic" properly modifying the noun "justice."

30. **(D)** The problem with (D) is that "their" is a plural pronoun referring to "loam," a singular verb. So you need a singular pronoun: "its." Everything else is correct. "Composed" is a participle form used to modify "loam," and "composed of" is the proper idiom. "Has" is a singular verb and agrees with "loam." And "texture" is a noun that is the object of "has."

31. **(D)** Remember that a favorite trick of the TOEFL is to use a verb form where only a noun will do, and that is the problem with (D). You need a noun: "behavior." The other elements of the sentence are in order. "Scientific" is an adjective that modifies the noun "study"; "history" is a noun that helps to complete the thought "as well as"; and "cultural" is an adjective that can modify the noun "place."

32. **(A)** The problem here is that "which" seems ready to introduce a perfectly good relative clause: which is added . . . . But the "it" completely messes up everything. The "it" has to have a verb, but if "it" gets "added," then "which" as the subject of

the clause is left with no verb. In other words, you've got too many subjects and not enough verbs. While all of that is taking place within the commas, everything else in the main part of the sentence is okay.

33. **(A)** The "in" in (A) is just not idiomatic. In order to express a range of dates or a span of time, you'd have to use something like "From 1925 to 1918."

34. **(B)** Here's a vintage TOEFL problem: a series of elements that must be in parallel form but one of which is not. The series is supposed to be: "fever," "redness" "spots," and "rash." But that means that "red" is incorrect.

35. **(D)** There are some interesting points to be made here. First, notice that (A) uses a form of "who," and that is right since Einstein is a person. (B) is correct since "dealt" is a verb for the subject "theory." And (C) is the correct idiom. (Compare (C) with #21, above.) The problem is with the "he" in (D). It's an extra subject that has no role and simply disrupts the logic of the rest of the sentence.

36. **(C)** "When" is a conjunction that ordinarily is used to introduce an adverbial clause. The problem here is that there is no verb following "when," so it has to be wrong. Instead, "policy makers" has to be joined to the rest of the sentence in some other fashion, e.g., "for them."

37. **(B)** "Costlier" is the comparative form of the adjective "costly." The sentence should read "less costly."

38. **(C)** Again, you have a series of parallel elements that is disrupted by one of the elements: "color," "bright," "cut," and "weight." "Bright" should be "brightness." You can compare #34 above.

39. **(B)** Remember that noncount nouns cannot be modified by "many;" they have to be modified by "much." In this case, "funds" is a noncount noun that refers to an amorphous mass of dollars. You can count dollars, but you cannot count funds.

40. **(A)** The adjective "natural" should come before the noun it modifies: "natural harbor." In (B), "frequent" is an adjective with the correct form. (When "frequent" is used as an adverb, it has the *-ly* form: We eat there "frequently.") "Deep" modifies channels and has the correct adjective form, and "ships" is the object of the preposition "for" and its number (plural) is correct.

Part III

Reading Questions

HOUR 9

Test Your Reading Ability

What You'll Do This Hour

- Preview the Reading PreTest
- Take the Reading PreTest
- Evaluate Your Performance
- Q & A Session

Your Goals for This Hour

In this hour, you'll take the Reading PreTest. After you finish, you'll evaluate your performance.

Your goals for this hour are to:

- Get ready to take the Reading PreTest
- Take the Reading PreTest under timed conditions
- Score the PreTest and evaluate your performance
- Get answers to frequently asked questions

Preview the Reading PreTest

The Reading part of the TOEFL tests your reading comprehension ability. Here are the directions for this part.

> **DIRECTIONS:** In this part, you will read several passages. Each one is followed by questions based on the content of the passage. Choose the best answer to each question. Answer all questions based on what is *stated* or *implied* in that passage.

The Reading PreTest has 48 questions, and the time limit is 55 minutes. Set aside an hour or so during which you won't be disturbed, set a timer for 55 minutes (or use a watch or a clock), and do the PreTest.

Take the Reading PreTest

48 Questions • Time—55 minutes

> **DIRECTIONS:** In this part, you will read several passages. Each one is followed by questions based on the content of the passage. Choose the best answer to each question. Answer all questions based on what is *stated* or *implied* in that passage.

Questions 1–12

Geothermal energy offers enormous potential for direct, low-temperature applications. Unlike indirect applications, this new technology relies on the Earth's natu-
(5) ral thermal energy to heat or cool a house or multifamily dwelling directly without the need to convert steam or other high-temperature fluids into electricity, using expensive equipment.

(10) A geothermal system consists of a heat pump and exchanger plus a series of pipes, called a loop, installed below the surface of the ground or submerged in a pond or lake. Fluid circulating in the loop is
(15) warmed and carries heat to the home. The heat pump and exchanger use an electrically powered vapor-compression cycle— the same principle employed in a refrigerator—to concentrate the energy and to
(20) transfer it. The concentrated geothermal energy is released inside the home at a higher temperature, and fans then distribute the heat to various rooms through a system of air ducts. In summer, the pro-
(25) cess is reversed: excess heat is drawn from the home, expelled to the loop, and absorbed by the Earth.

Geothermal systems are more effective than conventional heat pumps that use the
(30) outdoor air as their heat source (on cold

days) or heat sink (on warm days) because geothermal systems draw heat from a source whose temperature is more constant than that of air. The temperature of (35) the ground or groundwater a few feet beneath the Earth's surface remains relatively stable—between 45°F and 70°F. In winter, it is much easier to capture heat from the soil at a moderate 50°F than from (40) the atmosphere when the air temperature is below zero. Conversely, in summer, the relatively cool ground absorbs a home's waste heat more readily than the warm outdoor air.

(45) The use of geothermal energy through heat-pump technology has almost no adverse environmental consequences and offers several advantages over conventional energy sources. Direct geothermal (50) applications are usually no more disruptive of the surrounding environment than a normal water well. Additionally, while such systems require electricity to concentrate and distribute the energy collected, (55) they actually reduce total energy consumption by one-fourth to two-thirds, depending on the technology used. For each 1,000 homes with geothermal heat pumps, an electric utility can avoid the installa-(60) tion of 2 to 5 megawatts of generating capacity. Unfortunately, only a modest part of the potential of this use for geothermal energy has been developed because the service industry is small and the price of (65) competing energy sources is low.

1. What does this passage discuss mainly?

   (A) The use of geothermal energy for home heating and cooling
   (B) The possibility of using geothermal energy to make electricity
   (C) The technical challenges posed by geothermal energy
   (D) The importance of conserving nonrenewable energy sources

2. According to paragraph 1, which of the following is *not* a difference between indirect geothermal technology and direct applications?

   (A) A need for expensive equipment
   (B) The use of high-temperature fluids
   (C) Converting energy to electricity
   (D) Reliance on geothermal energy

3. In the second paragraph, the passage compares the heat pump and exchanger to what?

   (A) The loop
   (B) A pond or lake
   (C) A refrigerator
   (D) A fan

4. According to paragraph 3, which of the following accomplish opposite results?

   (A) heat source and heat sink
   (B) heat pump and heat exchanger
   (C) ground and groundwater
   (D) outdoor air and soil

5. "Adverse" in line 47 is closest in meaning to

   (A) unsuccessful
   (B) harmful
   (C) proven
   (D) advantageous

6. "Stable" in line 37 is closest in meaning to
   (A) effective
   (B) constant
   (C) below zero
   (D) relatively cool

7. According to paragraph 3, the new technology is more effective than a conventional heat pump because
   (A) soil and groundwater temperatures fluctuate less than air temperatures.
   (B) heat is brought into a home during the winter and expelled during the summer.
   (C) ground temperature is close to groundwater temperature year-round.
   (D) cold air absorbs less heat than warm air.

8. "Waste" in line 43 is closest in meaning to
   (A) required
   (B) convenient
   (C) unwanted
   (D) unsanitary

9. The author regards the new technology as
   (A) promising but under-utilized.
   (B) dependable but costly.
   (C) inexpensive but unreliable.
   (D) unproven but efficient.

10. The passage implies that a rise in cost of conventional energy would have what effect?
    (A) An expanded reliance on direct geothermal technology
    (B) A decrease in cost for geothermal heating and cooling
    (C) A shift toward the use of conventional energy sources
    (D) A decrease in the number of homes using geothermal heating

11. Which of the following helps to illustrate why the new technology can be used for air conditioning as well as heating homes?
    (A) A pool of still water freezes faster than a running stream.
    (B) A drink of well water tastes cool on a hot summer day.
    (C) Refrigerated liquids stay colder than liquids at room temperature.
    (D) The temperature of surrounding air varies from winter to summer.

12. A logical continuation of the passage would be a discussion of
    (A) unique geological features of the Earth.
    (B) ways of expanding reliance on geothermal technology.
    (C) techniques for converting geothermal energy into electricity.
    (D) the environmental hazards to be faced in the next 20 years.

Questions 13–24

Perhaps the best-known of the ancient Greek religious festivals are the Panhellenic gatherings in honor of Zeus, at Olympia, where the Olympics origi-
(5) nated in 776 B.C. These and other festivals in honor of Zeus were called "crown festivals" because the winning athletes were crowned with wreaths, such as the olive wreaths of Olympia. Yet in ancient Greece
(10) there were at least 300 public, state-run religious festivals celebrated at more than

250 locations in honor of some 400 deities. Most of these were held in the cities, in contrast to the crown festivals which (15) were held in rural sanctuaries. In Athens, for example, four annual festivals honored Athena, the city's divine protectress, in addition to those that honored other gods. In all, some 120 days were devoted annu- (20) ally to festivals.

By far the largest event of the Athenian religious calendar, rivaling the crown gatherings in prestige, was the Great Panathenaic festival. The development of (25) the Panathenaic festival—the ritual embodiment of the cult of Athena—evolved from a purely local religious event into a civic and Panhellenic one. This transformation, and that of the image of Athena (30) from an aggressively martial goddess to a more humane figure of victory, parallels the great political change that occurred in Athens from 560 B.C. to 430 B.C., as it evolved from a tyranny to a democracy.

(35) Athenian reverence for Athena originated in a myth that recounts a quarrel between Poseidon and Athena over possession of Attica. In a contest arranged by Zeus, Athena was judged the winner and (40) made the patron goddess of Athens, to which she gave her name. The origin of the Panathenaia, however, is shrouded in mystery. Perhaps it was founded by Erichthonius, a prehistoric king of Athens. (45) According to legend, after having been reared by Athena on the Acropolis, he held games for his foster mother and competed

in the chariot race, which he reputedly invented. The first archaeological evidence (50) for the festival is a Panathenaic prize vase from 560 B.C., which depicts a horse race, so scholars infer that equestrian events were part of the festival.

Much more is known about the (55) Panathenaia after 566 B.C., when the festival was reorganized under the tyrant Peisistaros. At that time, the festival, in addition to its annual celebration, was heightened every fourth year into the Great (60) Panathenaia, which attracted top athletes from all over the region to compete for valuable prizes—such as 140 vases of olive oil for winning the chariot race— rather than for honorific wreaths.

(65) From the mid-sixth century B.C. until the end of antiquity, when the Christian emperors suppressed the pagan religions, the high point of Athenian religious life was the Great Panathenaia, held in July. (70) Every four years, some 1,300 painted amphorae were commissioned and filled with olive oil to be used as prizes. The accouterments of Athena—helmet, spear, and shield—figured prominently in the (75) iconic representations of the goddess on these vases and served to identify the stylized figure and to associate the festival with the goddess. So far as is known, none of the crown games commissioned any art (80) for their festivals. Yet, ironically, the images that are often associated with the modern Olympics are taken from the Panathenaic vases.

9

13. What does the passage primarily discuss?

   (A) The origins of the modern Olympic games
   (B) Minor religious festivals in ancient Greece
   (C) Athletic contests centered in ancient Athens
   (D) Use of military iconography on Greek pottery

14. Which of the following is *not* mentioned as a characteristic of the games at Olympia?

   (A) The games were held in honor of Zeus.
   (B) Winners were crowned with wreaths.
   (C) The games originated in 776 B.C.
   (D) The games were held in or near cities.

15. Which of the following best summarizes the parallel development referred to in the second paragraph?

(A)

Time	Athena	Festival	Government
Earlier	Symbol of Victory	Local, Religious	Tyranny
Later	Aggressive Warrior	Regional, Civic	Democracy

(B)

Time	Athena	Festival	Government
Earlier	Symbol of Victory	Regional, Civic	Democracy
Later	Aggressive Warrior	Local, Religious	Tyranny

(C)

Time	Athena	Festival	Government
Earlier	Aggressive Warrior	Local, Religious	Tyranny
Later	Symbol of Victory	Regional, Civic	Democracy

(D)

Time	Athena	Festival	Government
Earlier	Aggressive Warrior	Local, Religious	Democracy
Later	Symbol of Victory	Regional, Civic	Tyranny

16. The author implies that the suggestion that the Panathenaia originated under Erichthonius is

   (A) conclusively proved.
   (B) a theoretical possibility.
   (C) without any foundation.
   (D) a hoax perpetrated by Athenians.

17. "Equestrian events" mentioned in line 52 refers to activities involving

   (A) weapons
   (B) gods
   (C) horses
   (D) tyrants

18. Which of the following was *not* true of the Great Panathenaia?

   (A) It was held every four years.
   (B) Contestants competed solely for honor.
   (C) It began at the time of Peisistaros.
   (D) It was held in July.

19. What word has most nearly the same meaning as "amphorae" (line 71)?

   (A) vases
   (B) wreaths
   (C) representation
   (D) Panathenaia

20. "Iconic" (line 75) most nearly means

   (A) stylized depiction
   (B) religious statue
   (C) painted amphorae
   (D) assorted weapons

21. According to the passage, who is supposed to have created the chariot race?

   (A) Poseidon
   (B) Erichthonius
   (C) Peisistaros
   (D) Athena

22. According to the passage, the archaeological evidence for the Panathenaia dates from

   (A) 776 B.C.
   (B) 566 B.C.
   (C) 560 B.C.
   (D) 430 B.C.

23. The author of the passage regards the association of imagery of Athena with the modern Olympic games as

   (A) sacrilegious
   (B) misguided
   (C) well-founded
   (D) hasty

24. Where in the passage does the author mention objects traditionally associated with Athena?

   (A) Lines 5–9
   (B) Lines 49–53

   (C) Lines 57–64
   (D) Lines 72–78

Questions 25–36

Alcohol abuse and dependence are serious problems affecting 10 percent of adult Americans, and the toll is high: 3 out of 100 deaths in the United States can
(5) be linked directly to alcohol. In addition to traffic crashes, injuries in the home and on the job, and serious long-term medical consequences, alcohol abuse has been implicated in aggression and crime. The cost
(10) of alcohol abuse and alcohol dependence is estimated to be as high as $1 trillion annually.

Although patterns vary, it is possible to classify drinkers as social drinkers, al-
(15) cohol abusers, and alcohol-dependent persons. While alcohol consumption is never entirely a risk-free activity, these categories represent a range from relatively benign to extremely problematic.

(20) An evaluation of treatment for any alcohol-related disorder must be situated historically. For nearly 200 years, the explanation of alcoholism as a disease competed with explanations in which
(25) character or moral defects were believed to lead to problematic drinking behavior. It wasn't until the 1930s that serious consideration was given to the concept of alcoholism as a disease with psychological,
(30) biochemical, endocrinological, and neurological implications. Even as late as the 1960s, some researchers still defined alcoholism broadly to include any drinking having harmful consequences.

(35) Evidence accumulated, however, suggesting that alcohol abuse and alcohol

dependence are distinguishable. "Alcohol abuse" refers either to transitory or long-term problems in accomplishing basic liv-
(40) ing activities in which alcohol is impli-cated, and "alcohol dependence" describes a severe disability in which dependence brings about a reduction in the individual's ability to control the drinking behavior.
(45) This delineation was endorsed in 1987 by the Institute of Medicine, which defined alcohol abuse as "repetitive patterns of heavy drinking associated with impair-ment of functioning and/or health" and
(50) discussed alcoholism (dependency) as a separate phenomenon. Alcohol depen-dence is associated with additional symptoms such as craving, tolerance, and physical dependence that bring about
(55) changes in the importance of drinking in the individual's life, and impaired ability to exercise behavioral restraint.

   The distinction has important clinical implications. For some nondependent al-
(60) cohol abusers, drinking patterns may be modified by exhortations or by societal sanctions. For alcohol-dependent persons, exhortations and sanctions are insufficient, and the goal of modified drinking inap-
(65) propriate. The goal for these persons is abstinence, and a range of treatment op-tions is available, including pharmaco-logic interventions, psychotherapy, and counseling. But even alcohol-dependent
(70) persons do not constitute a homogeneous group. They are not identical in personal-ity, life experiences, family characteristics and social status. Knowledge of the dif-ferences among alcohol-dependent per-
(75) sons is important because research shows

that alcoholism treatment methods are dif-ferentially effective according to patient characteristics.

25. What does the passage mainly discuss?

   (A) The history of alcoholism as a treatable disease
   (B) The difference between alcohol abuse and alcohol dependence
   (C) The injurious consequences associated with alcohol consump-tion
   (D) The early view of alcohol abuse as a moral problem

26. According to paragraph 2, which of the following represents the progression from least-serious to most-serious?

   (A) social drinking, alcohol abuse, alcohol dependence
   (B) social drinking, alcohol depen-dence, alcohol abuse
   (C) alcohol abuse, social drinking, alcohol dependence
   (D) alcohol dependence, alcohol abuse, social drinking

27. It can be inferred that the author would consider the conclusions mentioned in line 31 as

   (A) unfounded rejections of the traditional model.
   (B) scientific advances, but only partially correct.
   (C) conclusively proven and valid for current models.
   (D) irrelevant to the subject of the discussion.

28. In paragraph 3, the author contrasts which of the following?

(A) disease and moral defects

(B) psychological and biochemical implications

(C) alcoholism and harmful consequences

(D) disorder and alcoholism

29. Which of the following is *not* mentioned as an implication of the early disease model of alcoholism?

(A) social implications

(B) psychological implications

(C) endocrinological implications

(D) neurological implications

30. Which of the following is *not* mentioned in paragraph 4 as characteristic of alcohol dependence but not alcohol abuse?

(A) long-term problems

(B) craving

(C) tolerance

(D) physical dependence

31. "Homogeneous" (line 70) means

(A) may be modified

(B) are identical

(C) is important

(D) research shows

32. Where in the passage does the author cite an authority in support of the argument?

(A) Paragraph 2

(B) Paragraph 3

(C) Paragraph 4

(D) Paragraph 5

33. Where in the passage does the author outline different courses of treatment?

(A) Paragraph 2

(B) Paragraph 3

(C) Paragraph 4

(D) Paragraph 5

34. The mention of suicide as a consequence of alcohol-related depression would be an appropriate addition to which of the following sentences?

(A) In addition to traffic crashes, injuries in the home and on the job, and serious long-term medical consequences, alcohol abuse has been implicated in aggression and crime.

(B) It wasn't until the 1930s that serious consideration was given to the concept of alcoholism as a disease with psychological, biochemical, endocrinological, and neurological implications.

(C) The goal for these persons is abstinence, and a range of treatment options is available, including pharmacologic interventions, psychotherapy, and counseling.

(D) They exhibit differences in personality, life experiences, family characteristics, and social status.

35. The passage is primarily concerned with

(A) drawing a distinction.

(B) refuting a theory.

(C) cataloguing sources.

(D) criticizing behavior.

36. The most logical continuation of the passage would be

(A) further information about alcoholism as a moral problem.

(B) an explanation of the physical effects of alcohol on the brain.

(C) a brief historical summary of the attitudes toward alcohol.

(D) more detailed discussion of treatments for alcohol dependence.

9

Questions 37–48

Legislatures are increasingly becoming highly professionalized bodies. There have been profound changes in the organization of legislative life, shifts in the
(5) location of power, and alterations to the instruments by which power is exercised.

James S. Young's account of Washington, D.C. from 1800 through 1828 describes a community of sojourners, people
(10) temporarily in a place with little or no expectation of remaining long. Congressmen lived in boarding houses, and the boundaries between the makeshift social life of residents and their political duties were
(15) indistinct. Young's Washington was a city of cliques formed around regional and sectional affinities. For the modern legislator, social life has receded to the periphery. Legislators live in apartments and
(20) have less to do with one another in groups outside of the formal interactions of the legislative body. Organized political units—conferences, caucuses, committees—have replaced the more personal
(25) clique arrangements of an earlier period. Additionally, membership is more likely to be a career in itself rather than a temporary status or a capstone to another career. Indeed, members describe them-
(30) selves in terms of their status. When asked to list their primary occupation, most describe themselves not as lawyers or business executives but as "legislators."

A second set of changes involves the
(35) internalization of control of the legislative body. In earlier periods, it was the Chief Executive who set the agenda for the body as whole. For example, the Chief Executive proposed the budget, and the
(40) legislature largely approved it. Or the Chief Executive exercised control through a veto power that was regarded as nearly absolute. Now, legislatures are more likely to propose an agenda and ignore that of
(45) the Chief Executive, and to make it clear that a veto can be overridden when the issue is of sufficient importance to the membership. External control also used to reside in the hands of local party leaders who
(50) controlled nominations. Now, control over nominations is more centralized and under the direction of legislative leaders.

Finally, there is the change in what counts as an instrument of power. Career
(55) legislators plan to be reelected, so influencing a member's chances for reelection becomes an important instrument of leadership. Leaders within the body itself now control the means to a successful campaign
(60) and distribute money and other assistance in exchange for loyalty. Additionally, "member items," budget allocations to specific districts over which members have considerable control, are an important tool
(65) of leadership. And there is growth of centers of policy activity where a legislator has created a special area of influence through expertise and the development of special relationships with influential groups.

37. What is the main point of the passage?

 (A) The Chief Executive is now less important than the legislature.

 (B) Legislative power is centered in the hands of a few.

 (C) Democracy is at risk because of recent political changes.

 (D) Legislatures are now highly professional organizations.

38. Which of the following best describes the relationship among the second, third, and fourth paragraphs?

   (A) Three independent arguments in support of a contention
   (B) One main argument followed by two minor arguments
   (C) A claim, a rebuttal, and an answer to the rebuttal
   (D) Three arguments presented in order of their importance

39. Which of the following terms used by the author helps to define "sojourner" (line 9)?

   (A) community
   (B) temporarily
   (C) boundaries
   (D) indistinct

40. A "clique" (line 16) is a

   (A) governmental agency.
   (B) legislative body.
   (C) political party.
   (D) social grouping.

41. Which of the following means most nearly the *opposite* of "periphery" (line 18)?

   (A) center
   (B) permanent
   (C) elected
   (D) later

42. Which of the following phrases could best be substituted for "capstone" (line 28)?

   (A) crowning achievement
   (B) acceptable alternative
   (C) political aspiration
   (D) second choice

43. Which of the following is *not* an example of external control (paragraph 3)?

   (A) Political influence of the Chief Executive
   (B) Veto power of the Chief Executive
   (C) Local party control over nominations
   (D) Centralized direction of nominations

44. The controls mentioned in paragraph 4 would be *least* effective if used on

   (A) a first-term career legislator.
   (B) a member facing stiff reelection opposition.
   (C) a junior member who hopes for a prestigious party appointment.
   (D) a member who has already announced retirement.

45. If the author wished to draw a distinction between direct and indirect instruments of power, which of the following would express that distinction?

(A)

Direct	Indirect
Distribution of campaign money	Control of member items
Relations with influential groups	Policy expertise

(B)

Direct	Indirect
Distribution of campaign money	Policy expertise
Control of member items	Relations with influential groups

9

(C)

Direct	Indirect
Policy expertise	Control of member items
Distribution of campaign money	Relations with influential groups

(D)

Direct	Indirect
Policy expertise	Distribution of campaign money
Relations with influential groups	Control of member items

46. Where does the author mention a survey?

(A) Paragraph 1
(B) Paragraph 2
(C) Paragraph 3
(D) Paragraph 4

47. Which of the following best describes the organization of the passage?

(A) The author states a thesis and then supports it with evidence.
(B) The author describes a popular position and then refutes it.
(C) The author explains the historical roots of a political problem.
(D) The author outlines the defects of a political institution.

48. Which of the following would be the most appropriate for the author to include in a fifth paragraph?

(A) Examples of the effects of professionalization on laws passed
(B) An analysis of the declining power of the Chief Executive
(C) More details on the social life of nineteenth-century Washington, D.C.
(D) The names of prominent members of the legislature

Evaluate Your Performance

1. A	13. C	25. B	37. D
2. D	14. D	26. A	38. A
3. C	15. C	27. B	39. B
4. A	16. B	28. A	40. D
5. B	17. C	29. A	41. A
6. B	18. B	30. A	42. A
7. A	19. A	31. B	43. D
8. C	20. A	32. C	44. D
9. A	21. B	33. D	45. B
10. A	22. C	34. A	46. B
11. B	23. B	35. A	47. A
12. B	24. D	36. D	48. A

Use this graph to see how you did.

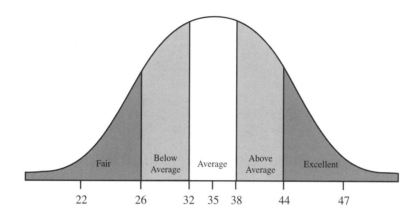

Fair	Below Average	Average	Above Average	Excellent

22   26   32   35   38   44   47

Q & A Session

Q: Does the TOEFL always use passages on such odd topics?

A: Yes. That's one of the design features of the TOEFL: unusual topics. And in the next hour, you'll learn strategies for reading the passages that will make it easy to handle even the strangest subjects.

Q: Is it typical to have questions that seem to ask about the same thing, for example, the "main topic?"

A: Again, the answer is "yes." The questions that you just answered are carefully designed TOEFL questions. In Hour 11, you'll learn more about how to identify the different types and what kinds of right and wrong answers are used by the TOEFL. That way, you'll be better prepared.

Hour 10

Teach Yourself Reading (I)

What You'll Do This Hour

- Get All the Inside Info on Reading
- Reading for Comprehension
- Workshop A
- Q & A Session

Your Goals for This Hour

Today, you'll begin teaching yourself how to answer TOEFL Reading questions. "Reading," as the name suggests, is a reading selection (passage) followed by questions based on the content of the selection. You'll learn how to use your reading ability to maximize your performance on this kind of question. Here are your goals for this hour:

- Get inside information on the Reading section
- Learn how to TOEFL-read passages
- Get answers to frequently asked questions

Get All the Inside Info on Reading

The description given in the directions for Reading makes everything sound simple:

DIRECTIONS: In this part, you will read several passages. Each one is followed by several questions about it. Choose the best answer to each question. Answer all questions on the basis of what is *stated* or *implied* in that passage.

That sounds like: read a selection and then answer some questions. But, in fact, Reading is not quite so simple.

First, the TOEFL chooses passages that you won't be familiar with. Then specially designed TOEFL questions are posed. TOEFL reading questions ask about things that you're not usually asked about on your tests at the university. All of this will be discussed in this chapter.

Inside the Selection

The "selection," which is also called the "passage," is the reading material upon which the questions are based. A selection can be about almost anything: a scientific theory, animal behavior, a historical event, and so on.

Two factors tend to make the Reading section of the TOEFL more difficult that you might expect:

1. Unpredictable topics
2. Special questions

Let's take a look at each of these factors and how they work. Knowing what the rules of the game are will give you an important edge.

Unpredictable Topics

The TOEFL uses a bewildering variety of topics for its Reading selections. Consider just a few that have appeared recently:

Winterthur: a private estate that is also a museum*

The origin of modern comic strips*

The matrilineal structure of the Anasazi people[*]

Bird bill as an evolutionary advantage of oystercatchers[*]

TOEFL, Test Preparation Kit (Educational Testing Service: 1998), pp. 180, 184, 212, 252

Fortunately, you're not expected to know anything about these topics—other than what you read on the TOEFL itself. Still, the fact that there are literally endless possibilities for the TOEFL to choose from automatically makes Reading more difficult than it might seem at first. The best advice on this count is "Don't panic." Yes, the topic may be obscure. You may not know anything about the topic before you read the selection, but everything you need to answer the questions is there for you.

NOTE

> Reading is not a test of anything you've learned in school. You're not expected to know anything about the topics, other than what you read on the TOEFL.

10

Inside the Questions

Most of the reading you do for school is "informational." You're supposed to read a chapter in the history book and get ready to answer questions such as "Why did the war start?" and "Who won?" and "Who benefited from it?" A few TOEFL Reading questions are like this, but most are not.

Most TOEFL Reading questions ask about elements of the selection that you don't usually think about. So to do well on the TOEFL, you need to think about these other elements. And the best way to do that is to get familiar with the kinds of questions you'll be asked.

The questions used by the TOEFL are about

- The main idea of the selection.
- The points specifically made by the author.
- The structure of the selection.
- The ideas implied in the selection.
- The meaning of an important word.

It's important to learn what each of the five types of questions is asking for and what a correct answer will probably look like.

NOTE   The five question types reflect the TOEFL's theory that Reading involves three skills: general understanding (thesis and development questions), specific understanding (specific-point questions and vocabulary-in-context), and drawing further conclusions.

Inside the Choices

One of the other striking differences between the exams you're used to taking and the TOEFL Reading is the answer choices. The wrong choices on the TOEFL are called "distractors." They're called distractors because they are supposed to distract your attention away from the right answer—that is, they're supposed to make the right answer harder to find. Look at the following example:

> The history of western medicine can be traced to Hippocrates, a Greek physician who lived on the island of Cos. Few particulars are known about the life of Hippocrates, but the establishment of the school of medicine on Cos is regarded as his most important achievement. The school emphasized reason and observation and regarded disease as having natural, not supernatural, causes. Reason and observation are important elements of modern medicine. In addition to a systematized body of empirical knowledge free of superstition, the school of Hippocrates evolved as a tradition of the highest standards of conduct. Today, the Hippocratic oath, which defines the duties and moral obligations of a physician, is taken by all medical students upon completion of their training.

What is the passage mainly about?

    (A) The life of Hippocrates

    (B) The text of the Hippocratic oath

    (C) Hippocrates as the father of modern medicine

    (D) Superstitions during the time of Hippocrates

The correct answer is **(C)**. The passage discusses the origins of modern medicine. Notice that all four choices refer to Hippocrates, the main figure in the passage. So it's not enough just to match one or two words from an answer choice to the text of the passage. Instead, you have to carefully read what each choice says. (C) is correct because it points out that the passage is about Hippocrates in the role of father of modern medicine.

So the Reading continues into the choices, which are as much a part of the Reading as the selections themselves.

You need to learn about the patterns that characterize right and wrong answers to each of the question types. But we'll save this important feature until Hour 11, and in this hour concentrate on the passages.

NOTE   The correct choice is surrounded by "distractors" that are meant to draw your attention away from the right answer.

Reading for Comprehension

The first thing you have to do is read the selection, but you can't read like you usually do. Instead, you have to read for the things that the TOEFL has put there for you to find. Here is the approach, broken down for you step-by-step:

ACTION PLAN   **Reading for Comprehension**

1. **Read the first sentence of each paragraph and the last sentence of the selection.** This is like getting an outline of the selection.

2. **Track the development.** Ask yourself about the organization of the selection; ask yourself why the author is doing each important thing in the selection.

3. **Read through details.** Don't try to memorize details. Try to understand what point is being made; but more important, make sure that you understand the function of the detail in the structure of the selection.

4. **Summarize the development.** After you've finished reading and before you go to the first question, pause to summarize in your mind the development of the selection and the author's main point.

Step 1 gets you over the initial hurdle of the strange topic. Here are the key sentences taken from a passage used by the TOEFL:*

THE PASSAGE	WHAT YOU LEARN
1st Paragraph Birds that feed in flocks commonly retire together in roosts.	The passage is about birds. More specifically it's about a unique aspect of their behavior: they feed in flocks and roost in flocks.
2nd Paragraph The second possible benefit of communal roosts is that they act as "information centers."	The phrase "second possible benefit" tells you that the author is giving a list of possible benefits. Look for other elements in the list as you read.

THE PASSAGE	**WHAT YOU LEARN**
3rd Paragraph Finally, there is safety in numbers at communal roosts.	The phrase "finally" tells you this is the last element in the list of "possible benefits": safety.
Last Sentence The birds on the edge are at greatest risk since predators find it easier to catch small birds perching at the margins of the roost.	The last sentence gives a possible disadvantage to roosting in flocks: the birds on the edge are most likely to be attacked by predators.

The key sentences give you a "road map" of the selection. They can tell you where you're going and where you've been. So pay careful attention to them.

TOEFL Kit, p. 142.

In addition to providing you with a roadmap, the key sentences often give you the correct answer to a thesis question. And thesis questions are very common.

> **TIP**
>
> The first sentence of a paragraph is often the topic sentence. So reading the first sentences of all the paragraphs is like getting an outline of the selection. You may have to scroll a little, but it will be worth the effort.

Step 2 of the Action Plan concentrates on the development of the selection, a key part of Reading. Like Step 1, Step 2 also does two things. First, you are tracking the development of the selection, and some questions ask directly about development of the selection. Second, a clear understanding of the structure is essential to being able to assess the significance of details.

> **TIP**
>
> Pay attention to transition words. Some transition words signal a continuation of a line of thought: *additionally, moreover, not only . . . but also, another, furthermore,* and *for example.* Other transition words signal a reversal in a line of thought: *however, on the other hand, but,* and *yet.* And still others signal a conclusion: *therefore, thus, in sum,* and *in short.*

Step 3 of the Action Plan makes sure that you don't waste a lot of time on details. Your main objective is to understand what role the details play in the development of the selection without needing to memorize anything. TOEFL Reading is an "open book" test. You can always go back to the selection if you need to look up something.

> **CAUTION**   Don't waste time learning information that won't raise your score. Many details won't be tested, so don't worry about them. Mark their location in your mind; come back and look them up if you need to.

Step 4 of the Action Plan helps you to digest what you've just read. Having a clear idea of the overall development of the selection is essential both to answering a thesis question and to understanding how the various parts of the argument fit together.

Now let's apply the Action Plan for reading to a selection. (This selection is longer than a typical TOEFL selection, but it provides a lot of material to discuss.)

10

Government bailouts of failing banks are harmful because they create incentives that aggravate the underlying economic problems that give rise to the crisis. Indeed,
(5) moral-hazard incentives are the villain in the recent, unprecedented wave of financial system collapses. Banks willingly and knowingly take on more risks—especially default risks—than they would if they were
(10) not protected by government safety nets. In extreme cases, banking collapses lead to the fiscal insolvency of governments that bail out banks and to exchange-rate collapse. In the absence of safety net distor-
(15) tions, economic shocks would encourage the opposite behavior: a reduction in bank risk exposure to reassure bank debt holders. But overly generous protection of banks insulates them from market disci-
(20) pline and makes them willing to increase risk in the wake of adverse shocks. Banks are not the only entities protected by government safety nets: large, politically influential firms often receive implicit pro-
(25) tection from the government on their debts, which encourages a similar tendency to bear risk.

The mechanism by which the bailout is usually funded, the general rev-
(30) enue fund, also results in economic dislocation because it requires large increases in taxation of average citizens to transfer resources to wealthy risk-takers who would otherwise lose money. Tax
(35) increases are always distortionary and accentuate the unequal wealth distribution. In addition, there is a longer term cost from the way bailouts affect the political process. Bailouts encourage
(40) crony capitalism in emerging market economies and thus stunt the growth of democracy and reform. Bailouts also undermine democracy and economic competition in industrialized countries be-
(45) cause they are often a means for the executive to provide subsidies to international lenders and foreign governments without legislative approval under the guise of emergency assistance.

(50)   It is possible to provide banks with emergency protection without bailouts through a responsible lender of last resort, provided that the plan ensures market discipline. This presupposes, however, an *eco-* *(55)* *nomic* and not a *political* definition of emergency liquidity assistance. Politicians and bureaucrats often declare a "liquidity crisis" and give "emergency" assistance when there is no real crisis, just because it *(60)* is politically expedient to give money to a powerful interest. Thus, the moral-hazard incentive reemerges at the political level, and special interests will surely fight to preserve the mechanism that affords them the *(65)* luxury of moral-hazard risk assumption. The challenge, then, is to design an alternative to bailouts that will survive the attack of special interests.

Step 1: Read the first sentence of each paragraph and the last sentence of the selection.

The first sentence tells you the author thinks that bailouts are harmful. The first sentence of the second paragraph (which includes an "also" signal) tells you that taxation to fund bailouts is a bad idea. The first sentence of the third paragraph says there is an alternative to the present policy. And the final sentence mentions again the need for an alternative to bailouts.

Step 2: Track the development.

Read the passage, paying careful attention to the logical development.

In the first paragraph, the author states that moral-hazard incentives are the cause of financial system collapses and goes on to explain that moral-hazard incentives aggravate the effects of economic shocks by encouraging banks to take even greater risks when they should be playing it safe. Collapses have other harmful effects, and other institutions are affected as well.

The second paragraph describes other harmful effects of bailouts. The "also" in the first sentence of the paragraph signals that the author is continuing with the list of harmful effects of bailouts. The "in addition" in the middle of the paragraph lets you know that the flow of the argument is continuing in the same direction. And the "also" in the last sentence of the paragraph signals yet another harmful affect of bailouts.

The third paragraph introduces a different or competing point of view: there is an alternative to bailouts. The author describes what the alternative might look like. Finally, the "then" in the last sentence lets you know that you are looking at a conclusion.

Step 3: Read through details.

The long list of harmful effects of bailouts is obviously important, but you don't have to memorize anything. The first paragraph discusses moral-hazard risk, which is defined implicitly. The second paragraph talks about tax implications and political consequences.

And the final paragraph addresses the practical difficulties of introducing a plan with market discipline.

Step 4: Summarize the development.

The author says that bailouts are harmful in a lot of different ways. There is an alternative to bailouts, but whether such a plan would ever be accepted is questionable.

Now it's time for you to practice reading the TOEFL way, by doing the following workshop.

Workshop A

The Drill portion of this workshop consists of two reading selections. Analyze them, using the Action Plan for Reading in the way we used it with the preceding passage. Then read the Review part to check your understanding.

10

Drill

Passage 1

Scholars have tended to confuse the "I am, I exist" of Descartes' *Meditations* and the "I think, therefore I am" which appears in Descartes' *Discourse on Method* writ-
(5) ten three years earlier. In the *Discourse,* "therefore" signals a logical deduction, but it is missing in the formulation of the *Meditations*. Additionally, the doubt that is so important in the *Meditations* but not in the
(10) *Discourse* is part of the philosophical problem Descartes hopes to solve: no one can demonstrate for all persons the certainty of the "*I* am, *I* exist." That's something each individual ego must establish for itself.
(15)   The distinction between the earlier and later formulations is also supported by the development of Descartes' thought from the *Discourse* to the *Meditations*. In both works, Descartes' skepticism about knowl-
(20) edge is central, but there is a difference of degree. In the *Discourse,* the skeptical at-

titude is a firm policy of refusing to believe anything that might be infected with falsity; but in the *Meditations,* skepticism
(25) reaches a crisis. Descartes adds the hypothesis of the *malin genie,* which, he fears, might have deceived him regarding even those things that are taken for granted, such as body, movement, and place. Skepticism
(30) cannot be maintained at this level, and doubt turns back on and destroys itself. The very fact of doubting creates the certainty Descartes was looking for: "'I am, I exist,' must be true every time I say it."
(35)   The "I am, I exist" that results from the intensified skepticism of the *Meditations* is not a reformulation of the "I think, therefore I am" of the *Discourse;* it is a claim about existence rather than logic. Respect
(40) for this crucial distinction would do a lot to clarify scholarly research into the significance of Descartes' philosophical thought.

Passage 2

How is history different from the natural sciences such as chemistry and physics? The historian distinguishes between the outside of an event and its inside. The (5) outside of the event is everything that can be described in terms of physical bodies: Caesar crossed the Rubicon with soldiers and later Caesar's blood covered the floor of the Roman Senate. The inside of the (10) event is intention: Caesar *defied* the constitutional authority of Rome and was killed by assassins who *believed* they were defending the constitution.

Historical study is distinguished from (15) natural science in two ways. The historian is concerned with objective conditions and will read letters, examine documents, interview witnesses, and visit sites; but the physical objects and surroundings are im-(20) portant only insofar as they provide access to the inner of the event. On the one hand, the historian employs investigative tools neither needed by nor available to the natural scientist because the historian inquires (25) after the "why" of the event. On the other hand, the task of the historian is somewhat simpler than that of the natural scientist because once that question has been answered, there is no further question to be (30) raised.

There is no reason for a historian to look behind the intention to find a supervening law because there are no laws of historical development. And this is a consequence of (35) the view that the inside of the event is what distinguishes a historical event from a natural one. A natural or purely physical event can only be regarded as a particular classified under a universal or general law, but (40) the inside of the event is a thought, unique, and as such, not subject to law-like explanation.

Review

Now you check your analysis against ours.

Passage 1

Step 1: Read the first sentence of each paragraph and the last sentence of the selection.

In the first sentence, the author states that scholars have tended to confuse two different points in Descartes' writings; in the first sentence of the second paragraph, the author continues with the distinction (note the "also supported"); in the first sentence of the third paragraph, the author reiterates the importance of the distinction; and in the last sentence of the passage, the author concludes that the distinction drawn in the selection would help researchers understand Descartes' philosophy.

Step 2: Track the development.

The first paragraph sets forth the thesis of the selection and gives a point in support of the distinction the author draws: the missing "therefore." Then the second paragraph develops a second reason (the "also" in the first sentence is important): Descartes' philosophical skepticism grew stronger and stronger. And the final paragraph sets forth the conclusion of the argument.

Step 3: Read through details.

There are some details in the passage that you may or may not need to understand.

Step 4: Summarize the development.

Pause for 15 to 20 seconds and summarize this development in your own mind: The author argues that some scholars have overlooked an important distinction in Descartes' writings, discusses that distinction, and then concludes that scholars would benefit from paying attention to the differences outlined.

Passage 2

Step 1: Read the first sentence of each paragraph and the last sentence of the selection.

In the opening sentence, the author poses a question: How are history and science different? In the first sentence of the second paragraph, the author announces that there are two important differences. In the first sentence of the third paragraph, the author explores some aspect of this discussion (the "supervening law" issue, though what that means is not yet clear). And finally, the passage concludes with the statement that the inside of an event (what that is will become clear as you read) is unique and not law-like.

Step 2: Track the development.

Your second pass is a complete read-through, and you'll be able to fill in the blanks that your preview left open. The first paragraph provides further explanation of the distinction between history and science. The second explores that distinction by developing "two ways" in which they differ. And the final paragraph draws a lesson from the distinction.

Step 3: Read through details.

There is some, but not a lot of detail in the passage. Just make sure you don't waste time. In the first paragraph, for example, there is no reason to start studying the information about Julius Caesar in the same way you would if this were going to be a test in history.

Step 4: Summarize the development.

Pause and summarize the development in your own mind.

And that's how to read specifically for the TOEFL exam. Tomorrow, you'll come back to the passage when we talk about the questions and answers for Reading.

Q & A Session

Q: **What if I don't know a whole lot about bailouts, or Descartes, or history versus science?**

A: Then you're normal. You're not expected to know anything at all about the Reading selections—except how to read them. Everything you need to answer the question is right there in the selection. And you can answer questions even when you don't understand everything that you've read.

Q: **Why is it so important to read things out of order?**

A: The preview steps help you identify the main theme of the selection. This is important for two reasons. First, if you know what the central thesis is, then you can understand how all the parts of the selection fit together. (If you don't know the main thesis, then the selection looks like a bunch of unrelated points and won't make much sense.) Second, by getting the main point from the preview, you already have the correct answer to any main idea or thesis questions that might be asked.

This Hour's Review

1. Reading is not just reading and answering questions. Everything about Reading—the passages, the questions, and the answers—has been specially designed for the TOEFL.

2. You have an Action Plan for reading the selection that is designed to give you everything you need to know to answer questions without getting sidetracked. In the next hour, you'll learn about the questions and answers that go with passages.

Hour 11

Teach Yourself Reading (II)

What You'll Do This Hour

- Identifying the Question Stems
- Patterns of the Right and Wrong Answer Choices
- Workshop B
- Q & A Session

Your Goals for This Hour

Now you know how to read the selection. In this lesson, you'll be concentrating on questions and answer choices in order to learn how to identify questions that belong to a certain category and how the wrong answers differ from the correct response. Here are your goals for today:

- Learn to recognize question patterns
- Learn to recognize right and wrong answer choices
- Get answers to frequently asked questions

Identifying the Question Stems

Every TOEFL question stem fits one of five categories, and the right and wrong answers are carefully written to fit the type of question. So the next step is for you to learn to recognize each of the five types of question.

> **NOTE**
>
> TOEFL questions are completely predictable. You don't even need to read the passage to know which of the categories a question belongs to.

ACTION PLAN

Identify each question as you come to it by its characteristic wording:

1. **Thesis.** Thesis questions typically use a phrase like "main idea," "main purpose," or "primary concern."

2. **Specific detail.** Specific-point questions typically use a phrase like "according to the passage," "according to the author," or "the author . . . ."

3. **Development.** A development question may include a phrase such as "in order to," or it may directly ask "why" the author introduces an idea.

4. **Implication.** Implication questions use words such as "inferred" or "suggests."

5. **Vocabulary-in-context.** Vocabulary-in-context questions mention a word in a particular line and ask for a definition.

Each of the five kinds of question asks about a different aspect of reading. If you can recognize each question type by its characteristic wording, then you'll be in a better position to know what kind of answer the TOEFL is looking for.

Thesis questions always ask about the main point or the central theme of the passage. They are usually phrased like this:

The author is primarily concerned with . . .

The passage is chiefly concerned with . . .

Which of the following best expresses the main idea of the passage?

Every selection is edited so that it has a central thesis.

> The phrases "main idea" and "primarily concerned" always signal a thesis question.

Specific-detail questions always ask about an idea that is stated somewhere in the selection. Here are some examples:

According to the passage, the Missalifu Ice Floe is unusual because . . .

According to the author, early inhabitants of the Lesser Antilles had what type of kinship relationships?

The author compares the ocean waves to which of the following?

For each question like this, the correct answer is an idea explicitly mentioned somewhere in the selection.

> Phrases like "according to the passage" and "the author" signal a specific-detail question.

11

Development questions ask about the structure of the selection and the author's reason for introducing an idea or making a particular point. Here are some examples:

Which of the following best explains why the author introduces the Freedom of Information Act in the second paragraph?

Why does the author mention Benedetto Croce in the first paragraph?

Which of the following best describes the overall structure of the selection?

The correct answer to a development question always explains *why* the author did something in the selection.

> The phrases "in order to" and "why does" signal development questions.

Implication questions ask about inferences that you can draw from the text of the selection. The following examples illustrate the typical wording of an implication question:

Which of the following conclusions can be inferred from the discussion of the solar mass of a supernova in paragraph 3?

The author suggests which of the following about the extinction of species in the atoll?

Words such as "inferred" and "suggests" signal implication questions.

> **TIP**
> The phrases "implies," "suggests," and "inferred" signal implication questions. Other key phrases are "most likely" and "attitude."

The fifth and final type of question is called "vocabulary-in-context." These questions are usually phrased as follows:

The author uses the term "clandestine" in line 23 to mean . . .

In line 36, "fractured" most nearly means . . .

> **TIP**
> A question that includes a word in quotation marks and a line number is probably a vocabulary-in-context question. If it specifically asks about "meaning," then it is definitely a vocabulary-in-context question.

The following table summarizes the discussion of the five question types.

QUESTION TYPE	KEY WORDS	CORRECT ANSWER
Thesis	main idea, mainly concerned with, primarily concerned with	Summarizes the main point or theme of the selection
Specific detail	according to the author, according to the passage	Answer is stated in the passage for you to find
Development	why does the author	Explains why the author introduces the idea or mentions the points
Implication	inferred, suggests	Answer not stated in the passage but it is inferable from what the author says
Vocabulary-in-context	Cites a word and gives a line reference	The meaning of the word in the context of the passage (not necessarily its first dictionary meaning)

Patterns of Right and Wrong Answer Choices

Just as the passages and questions are specially designed for the TOEFL, so too are the answer choices. Right answers are right because they fit the pattern for that particular question type; wrong answers are wrong because they fit the pattern for wrong choices for that question type. Here's how to handle them both:

ACTION PLAN **After you have identified the question type, identify the right answer.**

Thesis Questions

Right Answer: Describes the main theme of the selection

Wrong Answers: Describe only a subpart of the selection or refer to material not included in the passage

Specific-Detail Questions

Right Answer: Specifically mentioned in the text (although perhaps not in the same words)

Wrong Answers: Nowhere mentioned in the text, a distorted rendering of a point mentioned in the text, or a point mentioned that does not answer the question asked

Development Questions

Right Answer: Explains *why* the author introduces a specific point or *how* the entire selection is organized

Wrong Answers: Fail to explain *why* the author makes a certain point or fail to explain *how* the selection is organized

Implication Questions

Right Answer: A statement logically inferable from the text of the selection

Wrong Answers: Statements that do not follow from the text because they are not supported by what the author specifically says

Vocabulary-in-Context Questions

Right Answer: A synonym for the word that appears in the selection

Wrong Answers: Words that cannot substitute for the word in the text

Now let's apply the Action Plan for answers to the questions for the "bailout" passage that you read earlier. (You read the "bailout" passage in Hour 10. You may want to reread it now before you try answering the questions. Also, feel free to refer to the passage as often as you need to.)

11

Thesis Questions

1. What is the main point of the selection?

    (A) The use of general tax revenues to fund is inequitable.

    (B) Bank bailouts weaken democratic institutions and slow economic reform.

    (C) Government bailouts cause avoidable economic harms.

    (D) Governmental manipulation of financial markets encourages risk-taking.

The correct answer is **(C)**. (A) and (B) refer to subparts of the discussion: (A) to the discussion in the second paragraph on taxation, and (B) to the discussion in the third paragraph. So neither can be a correct answer to a thesis question. (D) goes beyond the scope of the selection. Notice, for example, that (D) doesn't mention bailouts. It, too, must be wrong. (A) and (B) are too narrow; (D) is too broad; (C) is just right.

2. The author is primarily concerned with

    (A) proving that government bailouts are inequitable.

    (B) highlighting the threat posed by bailouts.

    (C) arguing that an alternative plan can avoid the harms caused by bailouts.

    (D) demonstrating that moral-hazard incentives have caused financial failures.

The correct answer is **(C)**, for the reasons noted in the discussion of the preceding question. (A), (B), and (D) are all topics the author discusses, but they are subparts of the discussion. Because they refer to subparts and not to the main thesis, none of the three could be the correct choice.

3. What is the most appropriate title for the selection?

    (A) Inequitable Taxing Policies and Bailouts

    (B) Bank Bailouts as a Threat to Democracy and Economic Reform

    (C) Market Discipline as an Alternative to Harmful Bailouts

    (D) Moral-Hazard Incentives: The Dangers of Government Bailouts

The correct answer is **(C)**, for the reasons given above. The only difference between this question and questions 1 and 2 is its format: "What is the best title?" You should apply the Action Plan for thesis questions to this type of question, just as you would to the others. (A) and (B) are wrong because, like (A) and (B) of the two earlier questions, they refer to subparts of the passage (tax and reform). (D) also refers to only a part of the selection. To be sure, the moral-hazard incentives offered by bailouts are an important topic of the selection, but (D) makes no mention of that other important element: how to fix the problem.

Minor points that are mentioned in the selection may look good, but a minor point is not an answer to a main-point (thesis) question.

Specific-Detail Questions

4. According to the passage, tax increases used to fund bailouts

   (A) lead directly to the collapse of exchange rates.

   (B) shift power from the executive to the legislature.

   (C) encourage crony capitalism in emerging market economies.

   (D) aggravate existing inequities in wealth distribution.

The correct answer is (D). You'll find the reference that you need in the second sentence of the second paragraph. (E) doesn't exactly quote from the selection, but it is a pretty close restatement of the point that the author makes. The other choices refer to aspects of the passage, but even though they mention facts that appear in the selection, they are not answers to the question asked: What are the tax consequences of bailouts?

5. The passage mentions all of the following as a harmful effect of bailouts *except*:

   (A) making moral-hazard risks more attractive

   (B) arbitrarily redistributing wealth

   (C) weakening democratic institutions

   (D) increasing the number of banking institutions

The correct answer is (D). Notice that this question uses what is called a "thought reverser": *except*. This is a fairly common feature of this type of question. The "*except*" means that four of the five ideas are facts mentioned in the selection. The one that is not mentioned is the correct answer. You'll find the ideas mentioned by (A), (B), and (C) in the selection, but the idea of an increase in the number of banking institutions does not appear there.

A point mentioned in the text may look like a good answer to a specific-detail question but still be wrong. The correct answer must meet two criteria: It must be explicitly stated in the text *and* responsive to the question asked. Some wrong answers meet the first but not the second criterion.

Development

6. Which of the following best describes the logical development of the selection?

    (A) Describes a problem and then proposes a possible solution

    (B) Refutes one explanation and then advances a new theory

    (C) Defines a key concept and then discusses examples of the concept

    (D) Lists several possible causes of a phenomenon and then analyzes one

The correct answer is (A). This development question is similar to a thesis question, except that it asks you about the *form* of the development rather than the *content*. (A) is correct for the reasons given earlier in the discussion of thesis questions. (B) is wrong because, while the author criticizes a practice, the author does not refute a theory. (C) is wrong because the author does not define a key concept; in other words, the author uses "bailout" without offering a formal definition. (D) is incorrect because the author does not analyze just one cause or effect.

7. Why does the author mention politically influential firms at the end of paragraph one?

    (A) To contrast the behavior of banks with that of nonfinancial institutions

    (B) To draw a distinction between bailouts with acceptable consequences and those with unacceptable consequences

    (C) To demonstrate that the problem of moral-hazard risk is not restricted to banks

    (D) To reconcile the need for liquidity assistance with dangers of abuse

The correct answer is (C). The author explains that bailouts create moral-risk incentives for banks, and then adds that this affects other firms as well. (A) must be wrong since the author wants to suggest that the behavior of the nonbanking firms is like that of banks—at least when it comes to bailout incentives. (B) must be wrong for the same reason, since the author regards the consequences as unacceptable in both cases. (D) would be an interesting answer had the question asked about the author's proposal: the author recognizes that a trade-off will be necessary. But the question did not ask for that answer.

8. What is the logical function of the final paragraph?

    (A) The author quantifies the extent of the problem discussed earlier.

    (B) The author clarifies a key term that was used earlier in an ambiguous manner.

    (C) The author begins a discussion of a new problem more serious than the one described earlier.

    (D) The author outlines a possible alternative to the policies criticized earlier.

The correct answer is (D). This type of question occupies a kind of middle ground between questions that ask about the overall logical development of the selection (see question 6) and those that ask about the logical significance of a particular point (see question 7). But there's no mystery in how to approach it. (D) correctly states that the last paragraph contains the author's alternative solution. (A) is wrong because the author never offers quantification of the problem. (B) is wrong because the author does not clarify terminology, and you shouldn't confuse the point about the "economic" and "political" definitions in the final paragraph. The author there is not really defining terms but rather prescribing what ought to qualify as a definition: liquidity should be defined as an economic phenomenon and not be used as a term to justify government policy on an ad hoc basis. (C) is wrong because the alternative solution is not a new problem.

TIP

Treat a development question that asks about the overall structure of the passage as you would treat a thesis question. The correct answer will summarize the development without being too narrow or too broad.

Implications

9. It can be inferred that the economic definition of liquidity assistance mentioned in line 39

   (A) is narrower than the political definition.

   (B) is used primarily by government officials.

   (C) covers more cases than the political definition.

   (D) obscures the need for liquidity assistance.

The correct answer is **(A)**. In the final paragraph, the author calls for an economist's use of the term liquidity and disparages the use of the term to justify government bailouts that are merely politically expedient. You can infer that the economist would apply the term to fewer cases than the politician would. (B) is "in the right pew but the wrong church." (B) correctly implies that government officials use the term in a special way, but the danger is not that they use it "primarily" but that they use it in a bad fashion. (C) must be wrong for the reasons that (A) is correct. (D) is wrong for the same reason that (B) is correct: the term is used not to obscure need but to find need where there is none.

10. The author implies that the decision to provide subsidies to a foreign government should be

   (A) the prerogative of the legislature.

   (B) a function of the need for assistance.

   (C) determined by the executive.

   (D) contingent upon a commitment by the recipient to reduce moral-hazard risks.

The correct answer is (A). In the second paragraph, the author says that bailouts are often a subterfuge for the executive branch to funnel moneys to a foreign government or firm without the approval of the legislative; and this practice, according to the author, is antidemocratic. So you can infer that the author believes this type of policy should be subject to legislative approval. (B) is incorrect since the author questions whether there really is a need for assistance. (C) is an interesting observation, but it does not answer the question asked. (D) is wrong because no such string is presently attached, and that is a problem, according to the author.

11. It can be inferred that in the absence of a government-guaranteed safety net, nonfinancial firms would respond to an economic shock by

   (A) increasing risk to reassure debt holders.

   (B) reducing exposure to asset risk.

   (C) shifting economic resources to foreign markets.

   (D) transferring funds from one shareholder group to another.

The correct answer is (B), and the reference you need is in the comparison of nonfinancial firms to banks in the first paragraph. Since the author suggests that there is a parallel to be drawn between the two, you can infer that nonfinancial firms react to moral-hazard incentives in the same way that banks do: they'll take the guarantee and increase risk. (A) is wrong because increasing risk does not reassure debt holders. (C) and (D) simply go beyond anything suggested by the selection; in other words, where does the passage mention foreign markets or different shareholder groups?

 TIP

The correct answer to an implication that uses "inferred," "implies," or "suggests" is not stated in the text in so many words, but it is strongly supported by the text. So stay close to home; don't wander too far from what is specifically stated.

12. The author is most likely addressing a meeting of

   (A) government policy makers.

   (B) leaders of emerging market countries.

   (C) heads of politically influential firms.

   (D) directors of banks and other financial institutions.

The correct answer is (A). You don't have any way of knowing where this article appeared. In fact, it is excerpted from the testimony given by an economist before a Congressional committee in a hearing on bailouts. While you could never reach that precise conclusion (except as a wild guess), you can figure out that it is probably addressed to policy makers who have the authority to entertain arguments on the alternative plan suggested in the last paragraph. It would not be addressed to foreign leaders, nor to private firms, nor to tax experts. Those readers might have an interest in the topic, but the structure of the argument (identify the problem and propose a solution) indicates that none of those are the primary audience.

> **TIP**
>
> Implications that use the phrases "most likely" and "least likely" are the most abstract of all and therefore the most difficult. If you get stumped on one, you should probably just guess.

13. The author's attitude toward moral-hazard incentives is one of

    (A) tolerance.

    (B) condemnation.

    (C) unconcern.

    (D) endorsement.

The correct answer is **(B)**. The author is critical of moral-hazard incentives. Indeed, the very choice of phrasing to describe the phenomenon, *moral*-hazard, suggests that the author has very strong negative feelings about the phenomenon.

> **TIP**
>
> Often the answer choices to a judgment question can be arranged on a scale from 1 to 5, with 1 the most negative emotion and 5 the most positive. Then you can easily decide whether the author's judgment is positive or negative (eliminating two or three choices) and from there, how strong the judgment is (leaving you with the correct choice).

Vocabulary-in-Context

14. In line 19, "insulates" means

    (A) warms

    (B) protects

    (C) excludes

    (D) satisfies

The correct answer is **(B)**. The author is saying that the promise of a bailout makes financial institutions immune from the economic forces that threaten them.

15. In line 49, "guise" means

   (A) pretense

   (B) hope

   (C) confidence

   (D) promise

The correct answer is **(A)**. The author is explaining that bailouts are sometimes used when there is no real emergency. In that case, they're just an excuse to give something away.

 TIP | The correct answer to a vocabulary-in-context question is almost never the most common meaning of the word. Look for a secondary or other unusual meaning.

Workshop B

This workshop will give you the opportunity to apply what you have just learned about right and wrong answers to the workshop passages from Hour 10. You'll probably need to refer to the passage to refresh your memory.

Drill

Answer the following questions. Start by trying to determine which of the five categories the question belongs. Then think about what makes a right answer to that type of question and make your selection. Look carefully at the wrong answers as well, and see whether you can figure out *why* they're wrong. Then compare your thinking to the explanations in the Review part of this chapter.

Passage 1

1. What is the main idea of the passage?

   (A) Descartes' *Discourse on Method* was published three years earlier than the *Meditations*.

   (B) Most scholars have been unable to understand the finer points of Descartes' philosophy.

   (C) Descartes' "I think, I exist" is not identical to "I think, therefore I am."

   (D) The central theme of Descartes' philosophy is doubt rather than certainty.

2. The word "it" in line 6 refers to

   (A) *Meditations*
   (B) *Discourse on Method*
   (C) therefore
   (D) "I am, I exist"

3. The word "infected" in line 23 most nearly means

   (A) diseased
   (B) contaminated
   (C) granted
   (D) supported

4. The word "hypothesis" in line 25 most nearly means

   (A) theory
   (B) doubt
   (C) assumption
   (D) attitude

5. Which word in the passage has the meaning most similar to the word "skepticism?"

   (A) degree
   (B) crisis
   (C) policy
   (D) doubt

6. According to the author, Descartes feared that the *malin genie* might deceive him about *all but* which of the following?

   (A) solid objects
   (B) motion through space
   (C) physical location
   (D) existence of ego

7. It can be inferred that the *malin genie* does not appear in the *Discourse* because Descartes had

   (A) already solved the problem of existence.
   (B) not yet begun to doubt so deeply.

   (C) made a mistake reading other works.
   (D) been deceived as to its existence.

8. The author says that in the *Meditations* doubt finally results in

   (A) falsity.
   (B) philosophy.
   (C) existence.
   (D) certainty.

9. What would be an appropriate topic for the author to take up next?

   (A) Specific mistakes by other scholars that the distinction would correct
   (B) A brief biographical description as it pertains to Descartes' thought
   (C) A discussion of the influence of Descartes on subsequent philosophers
   (D) A comparison of Descartes' *malin genie* with those of other writers

10. Which of the following correctly summarizes Descartes' thought, according to the author?

    (A)

Date	Publication	Kind of Doubt	Conclusion
Earlier	*Meditations*	Mild	I am, I exist
Later	*Discourse*	Extreme	I think, therefore I am

    (B)

Date	Publication	Kind of Doubt	Conclusion
Earlier	*Meditations*	Extreme	I am, I exist
Later	*Discourse*	Mild	I think, therefore I am

11

(C)

Date	Publication	Kind of Doubt	Conclusion
Earlier	*Discourse*	Mild	I think, therefore I am
Later	*Meditations*	Extreme	I think, I exist

(D)

Date	Publication	Kind of Doubt	Conclusion
Earlier	*Discourse*	Mild	I am, I exist
Later	*Meditations*	Extreme	I think, therefore I am

Passage 2

1. The author is primarily concerned to
   - (A) explain why Caesar crossed the Rubicon.
   - (B) contrast history with the natural sciences.
   - (C) defend history as equal to the natural sciences.
   - (D) demonstrate that history lacks rigor.

2. In the first paragraph, the author does which of the following?
   - (A) Asks a question and provides an answer
   - (B) Mentions a theory and refutes it
   - (C) Generalizes on a handful of examples
   - (D) Attacks the credibility of another scholar

3. According to the author, the historian regards objective conditions as
   - (A) completely irrelevant to the historical inquiry.
   - (B) an aid to answering questions about intention.
   - (C) accessible only by using scientific means.
   - (D) the only circumstances worth studying.

4. The author implies that a supervening law would be used by a
   - (A) natural scientist.
   - (B) historian.
   - (C) powerful ruler.
   - (D) military leader.

5. What does the author say about the role of law-like explanations in history?
   - (A) There are no historical laws.
   - (B) Historical laws are very reliable.
   - (C) It is hard to discover historical laws.
   - (D) Historical laws sometimes don't work.

6. Which of the following would be regarded by the author as closest to history?
   - (A) geology
   - (B) biology
   - (C) psychology
   - (D) zoology

7. The word "intention" in line 32 most nearly means
   - (A) inquiry
   - (B) motivation
   - (C) description
   - (D) fact

8. The author mentions all of the following as objective conditions *except*:

   (A) correspondence
   (B) documents
   (C) eyewitness accounts
   (D) intentions of participants

9. Which of the following is a correct application of the author's theory of history to the events described in paragraph 1?

(A)

Outside of the Event	Inside of the Event
Caesar crossed the Rubicon.	Caesar defied the Constitution.
Caesar was assassinated.	Caesar's killers believed they were defending the Constitution.

(B)

Outside of the Event	Inside of the Event
Caesar was assassinated.	Caesar defied the Constitution.
Caesar crossed the Rubicon.	Caesar's killers believed they were defending the Constitution.

(C)

Outside of the Event	Inside of the Event
Caesar crossed the Rubicon	Caesar was assassinated.
Caesar's killers believed they were defending the Constitution.	Caesar defied the Constitution.

(D)

Outside of the Event	Inside of the Event
Caesar defied the Constitution.	Caesar crossed the Rubicon.
Caesar was assassinated.	Caesar's killers believed they were defending the Constitution.

10. What is the author's attitude toward history as a discipline?

   (A) It is flawed when compared to the natural sciences.
   (B) It is an independent discipline with its own procedures.
   (C) It is superior to physics, chemistry, and other sciences.
   (D) It cannot produce any research that has real value.

11

Review

Passage 1

1. **(C)** This is a thesis question. The phrase "main idea" is the characteristic tag. The thesis of the selection is set forth in the very first sentence, and it reappears in the last sentence. (C) provides the best restatement of the thesis. (A) is wrong because this idea is a minor detail in the selection. (B) is wrong because it too is a subsidiary idea. While it is true that the author thinks that other scholars have made a mistake, the more important question is what kind of mistake and how to correct it. Finally, (D) is also an idea that is important in the selection; but, again, it is not the central thesis. This item is typical of thesis questions. The correct answer restates the main point of the selection, whereas the wrong answers refer to ideas mentioned along the way that are part of the development but not the central thesis.

2. **(C)** This is a detail question. It's included to determine whether you understand one of the points that is specifically made by the author: the "therefore" of "I think, therefore I am" is missing from "I am, I exist." If you were having trouble here, you could substitute each answer choice for the "it" in the selection to find which answer seems to make the most sense.

3. **(B)** This is a vocabulary-in-context question. Remember that with such a question, the correct answer to a commonly used word like "infected" is probably not going to be its usual meaning. So (A) is probably not going to be correct. In fact, the correct answer is (B). Descartes was worried that falsity might creep into almost anything, thereby contaminating the purity of truth.

4. **(C)** This is a vocabulary-in-context item. Again, the correct answer is probably not going to be (A), because "theory" is the most common synonym of "hypothesis." Instead, the correct answer is (C). The *malin genie* is added as an assumption. In essence, Descartes was saying, "Let's also assume that there is this *malin genie* who goes around fooling us."

5. **(D)** This is a vocabulary-in-context question. And this item reminds you that a tip like "Avoid a common synonym" is not supposed to be a substitute for thinking. In this case, skepticism is synonymous with doubt.

6. **(D)** This is a specific detail question. The words "According to the author" almost always signal this type of question. And the answer to the question is always in the text of the selection. Here, however, we have a wrinkle: the words *all but* turn the question inside-out. Three of the four choices are mentioned in the text. The one that is not mentioned is the correct answer. You'll find (A), (B), and (C) mentioned in paragraph two.

7. **(B)** This is an implication question. The correct answer to an implication question is a statement that can be inferred from the text, but inferred doesn't mean that you have to have a logical proof for the correct answer. Instead, you can think in terms of what the author implies or suggests. In this case, the author suggests that the *malin genie,* which shows up in the *Meditations,* was part of the more extreme doubt of the later work. So you can infer that the *malin genie* doesn't get mentioned earlier because the doubt is not so serious.

8. **(D)** This is a specific-detail question. The last sentence of the second paragraph specifically says: doubting creates the certainty.

Passage 2

1. **(B)** This is a thesis question, and you find the answer in the first and last sentences of the passage. The author is contrasting history and natural science. (A) is a part of the passage, that is, the author uses the case of Caesar's crossing the Rubicon to explain the difference between history and natural science. But an example or an illustration is not the central thesis. There is also an element of (C) in the passage because the author does think that history is worthwhile. But, again, (C) is not the main idea discussed. While the author would surely agree that history is a valid form of study, the author's main point is that history and science have different goals and different procedures. (D) is surely wrong because the author believes that history is a valuable discipline.

9. **(A)** This is an implication question. There is no guarantee that the author would take up any of these topics, and that's why the question stem reads "appropriate." Remember that the thesis of the selection is that other scholars have misread Descartes. So once the author has outlined the source of their error and corrected it, it would be appropriate to go on and talk about how this insight could be applied to particular examples.

10. **(C)** This is a specific-detail question. The "according to the author" is your clue. Admittedly, there are several parts to the choices, but it's just a matter of looking at the passage to make sure that you have correctly read what the author specifically said.

11

2. **(A)** This is a structure question. The author begins the discussion by posing a question and providing an answer.

3. **(B)** This is a specific-detail question. The "according to the author" is a common tag for this type of question. So you know the correct answer is stated in the selection. In the second sentence of the second paragraph, the author states that the objective conditions are of interest to a historian because they help to get at the "why" of the event.

4. **(A)** This is an implication question. The author doesn't specifically say that supervening laws are scientific laws (such as, a law of physics), but that conclusion is implied by the text because it is the universal or general law that makes a natural event what it is.

5. **(A)** This is a specific-detail question, so the answer is stated somewhere in the text of the selection (although maybe not in exactly the same words used in the question). In the very last sentence, the author specifically says that the inside of the event, which is the essence of a historical event, is not subject to law-like explanation.

6. **(C)** This is an implication question. The author doesn't mention geology, biology, psychology, or zoology; but you can apply what you learned in the text to determine what the author would probably say about these disciplines. The natural sciences are those that look for predictive laws (like physics and chemistry), so geology, biology, and zoology would go into that category. History deals with a unique aspect of an event—the intentions. And psychology, too, deals with mental events.

7. **(B)** This is a vocabulary-in-context question. The intention is the reason for the action, and the word that comes closest (of the four you are given) is motivation.

8. **(D)** This is a specific-point question, and the reference you need is the second sentence of the second paragraph.

9. **(A)** This is an implication question. The first paragraph has the information you need.

10. **(B)** This is an implication question because you have to infer something from the passage. And an attitude question is a particular kind of implication question, because you need to make a judgment about the author's attitude from clues provided in the selection. In this case, the author distinguishes between history and science and explains how history, by the very nature of its inquiry, is different from natural science. The author doesn't apologize for history; the author doesn't claim history is superior—just that history is different from physics.

Q & A Session

Q: **Will I be asked to identify questions by type on the TOEFL?**

A: No. You won't be asked to show how much you know about the test itself. But knowing how the test is constructed gives you a big edge. For example, you're not reading a passage as you would a regular assignment. You're reading only for those things that the TOEFL will test. And you're not just answering questions; you're consciously asking "What kind of question is this, and what sort of choice should I be looking for?" That approach is a real score booster.

Q: **If I can find the right answer directly, do I have to worry about the wrong answers?**

A: Two points. First, yes, as you practice you should be concerned about wrong as well as right answers. That way, you learn to recognize the wrong choices for what they are—wrong! And you'll find it easier to avoid them in the future. Second, yes, because eliminating three wrong choices is as good as finding the right choice—by the process of elimination.

This Hour's Review

11

1. In this hour, you developed an Action Plan for identifying the different types of questions used by the TOEFL. That's important because you can focus your attention on the question asked.

2. You also developed an Action Plan for answer choices:

   Why the right answer is right

   Why the wrong ones are wrong

3. Now you have the complete action plan:

   How to read the selection

   How to identify the question type

   How to choose the right answer

HOUR 12

Review the Reading PreTest

What You'll Do This Hour

- The Reading Action Plan
- Review the Reading PreTest
- Q & A Session

Your Goals for This Hour

In this hour, you'll assemble the entire Action Plan from Hours 10 and 11. Additionally, you'll review the Reading PreTest that you took in Hour 9. You'll see how your Action Plan would have helped you score higher on the PreTest.

Your goals for this hour are:

- Assemble the Action Plan for Reading
- Review the Reading PreTest
- Get answers to frequently asked questions

The Reading Action Plan

In Hours 10 and 11, you developed a detailed Action Plan for TOEFL Reading. You learned how to read TOEFL selections, how to identify TOEFL Reading questions by type, and how to distinguish the right answer from the wrong ones. Here is the entire Action Plan:

 Read for Comprehension

1. **Read the first sentence of each paragraph and the last sentence of the selection.**
2. **Track the development.**
3. **Read through details.**
4. **Summarize the development.**

Identify each question as you come to it by its characteristic wording:

Thesis

Specific detail

Development

Implication

Vocabulary-in-context

Identify the right answer.

Thesis Questions

Right Answer: Describes the main theme of the selection

Wrong Answers: Describes only a subpart of the selection or refer to material not included in the passage

Specific-Detail Questions

Right Answer: Specifically mentioned in the text (although perhaps not in the same words)

Wrong Answers: Nowhere mentioned in the text, a distorted rendering of a point mentioned in the text, or a point mentioned that does not answer the question asked

Development Questions

Right Answer: Explains *why* the author introduces a specific point or *how* the entire selection is organized

Wrong Answers: Fail to explain *why* the author makes a certain point or fail to explain *how* the selection is organized

Implication Questions

Right Answer: A statement logically inferable from the text of the selection

Wrong Answers: Statements that do not follow from the text, either because they are not supported or because they go too far

Vocabulary-in-Context Questions

Right Answer: A synonym for the word that appears in the selection

Wrong Answers: Words that cannot substitute for the word in the text

Now let's return to the Reading PreTest that you took in Hour 9.

Review the Reading PreTest

Here are the passages and questions that make up the Reading PreTest that you took in Hour 9. Following each passage and each question is an analysis using the Action Plan.

12

You've already graded your work on the PreTest in Hour 9, using the answer key. So the purpose of revisiting the PreTest is not to see how you did. Rather, the objective is to look at these same questions from a higher perspective, using what you learned in Hours 10 and 11. You're not so much concerned with *what* is the correct answer as with *why* it is the correct answer and *why* the other answers are wrong. To get the most out of the review, you should look back at your own work on the PreTest so that you can pay careful attention to those items you missed.

Now let's take another look at the PreTest.

Questions 1–12

Geothermal energy offers enormous potential for direct, low-temperature applications. Unlike indirect applications, this new technology relies on the Earth's
(5) natural thermal energy to heat or cool a house or multifamily dwelling directly, without the need to convert steam or other high-temperature fluids into electricity, using expensive equipment.

(10) A geothermal system consists of a heat pump and exchanger plus a series of pipes, called a loop, installed below the surface of the ground or submerged in a pond or lake. Fluid circulating in the loop is
(15) warmed and carries heat to the home. The heat pump and exchanger use an electrically powered vapor-compression cycle— the same principle employed in a refrigerator—to concentrate the energy and to
(20) transfer it. The concentrated geothermal energy is released inside the home at a higher temperature, and fans then distribute the heat to various rooms through a system of air ducts. In summer, the pro-
(25) cess is reversed: excess heat is drawn from the home, expelled to the loop, and absorbed by the Earth.

Geothermal systems are more effective than conventional heat pumps that use the
(30) outdoor air as their heat source (on cold days) or heat sink (on warm days) because geothermal systems draw heat from a source whose temperature is more constant than that of air. The temperature of
(35) the ground or groundwater a few feet beneath the Earth's surface remains relatively stable—between 45° F and 70°F. In winter, it is much easier to capture heat from the soil at a moderate 50°F than from
(40) the atmosphere when the air temperature is below zero. Conversely, in summer, the relatively cool ground absorbs a home's waste heat more readily than the warm outdoor air does.

(45) The use of geothermal energy through heat pump technology has almost no adverse environmental consequences and offers several advantages over conventional energy sources. Direct geothermal
(50) applications are usually no more disruptive of the surrounding environment than a normal water well. Additionally, while such systems require electricity to concentrate and distribute the energy collected,
(55) they actually reduce total energy consumption by one-fourth to two-thirds, depending on the technology used. For each 1,000 homes with geothermal heat pumps, an electric utility can avoid the installa-
(60) tion of 2 to 5 megawatts of generating capacity. Unfortunately, only a modest part of the potential of this use for geothermal energy has been developed because the service industry is small and the price of
(65) competing energy sources is low.

Here's what your preview of the passage would have turned up:

Geothermal energy offers enormous potential.

A geothermal system consists of a bunch of components.

Geothermal systems are more effective than conventional.

Geothermal has no adverse environmental consequences, plus has other advantages.

Unfortunately, only a modest part of the potential has been developed.

The preview gives you a really good look at the development of the passage.

During your second pass, you run across a lot of detail, but now you know that you shouldn't get bogged down in it. For example, the technical discussion of the second and third paragraphs can be a little confusing, so bracket that information. Make a note of *where* the details are discussed; you can return to them if necessary.

Now let's go to the questions.

1. What does this passage discuss mainly?

   (A) The use of geothermal energy for home heating and cooling

   (B) The possibility of using geothermal energy to make electricity

   (C) The technical challenges posed by geothermal energy

   (D) The importance of conserving nonrenewable energy sources

(A) This is a thesis or main point question. Your preview of the passage, by itself, gave you enough information to choose answer (A). What's wrong with the other choices?

(B) goes beyond the passage, because the direct technology discussed in the passage does not require the conversion of geothermal energy to electricity. (That's why it is called a *direct* application.)

Choice (C) should remind you of the importance of reading each choice carefully. The author does discuss some technical aspects of using geothermal energy, but the passage does not address technical *challenges* (that is, difficulties or problems) as its central theme.

Finally, (D) is certainly a theme that can be found in the selection because the author does mention "environmental consequences." But remember that a minor point is not the main point, so (D) is wrong.

2. According to paragraph 1, which of the following is *not* a difference between indirect geothermal technology and direct applications?

   (A) A need for expensive equipment

   (B) The use of high-temperature fluids

   (C) Converting energy to electricity

   (D) Reliance on geothermal energy

(D) This is a specific-detail question. Remember that the answer to a specific-detail question is explicitly set forth in the text. (That's what the TOEFL means by *specific* detail.) And this question also has a thought-reverser—the *not*. So three of the four choices are specifically mentioned in the text; the one that is not mentioned is the correct answer. The task, then, is to look through the text to see what is mentioned and what's not mentioned.

12

You'll find (A), (B), and (C) mentioned in the first paragraph as differences between the two types of technology. (D), however, is not a *difference,* since both direct and indirect applications utilize geothermal energy.

3. In the second paragraph, the passage compares the heat pump and exchanger to what?

    (A) The loop

    (B) A pond or lake

    (C) A refrigerator

    (D) A fan

(C) This is another specific-detail question. In the second paragraph, the author says "the heat pump uses . . . the same principle employed in a refrigerator." There's nothing more to the question than that: find the reference, point and click, confirm your answer.

4. According to paragraph 3, which of the following accomplish opposite results?

    (A) heat source and heat sink

    (B) heat pump and heat exchanger

    (C) ground and groundwater

    (D) outdoor air and soil

(A) This is another specific-detail question, and the question stem guides you to the third paragraph. In the first sentence the author says that heat pumps use the outdoor air as a heat source (from which to draw energy) on cold days and a heat sink (into which to dump unwanted heat) on warm.

Why is (B) wrong? For one thing, the heat pump and exchanger work together. For another thing, they're mentioned in paragraph 2, but this question is based on paragraph 3. Remember that an idea mentioned in the text that does not answer the question asked is wrong—even though the idea is mentioned. And, as a rule, if the idea is mentioned somewhere else, it's not the correct answer.

As for (C) and (D), those pairs can accomplish the same result, although with differing degrees of efficiency.

5. "Adverse" in line 46 is closest in meaning to

    (A) unsuccessful

    (B) harmful

    (C) proven

    (D) advantageous

(B) This is a vocabulary-in-context question. The correct approach to such questions is to use the context in which the word appears to learn the meaning of the word. In the very next sentence, the author notes that direct geothermal applications are no more disruptive of the surrounding environment than a normal water well. So adverse must have a meaning like disruptive, and that would be harmful.

6. "Stable" in line 37 is closest in meaning to

    (A) effective

    (B) constant

    (C) below zero

    (D) relatively cool

(B) This is a vocabulary-in-context question. In the sentence immediately preceding the one with which we are concerned, the author refers to constant temperature. Therefore, a relatively stable temperature must mean constant.

7. According to paragraph 3, the new technology is more effective than a conventional heat pump because

   (A) soil and groundwater temperatures fluctuate less than air temperatures.

   (B) heat is brought into a home during the winter and expelled during the summer.

   (C) ground temperature is close to groundwater temperature year-round.

   (D) cold air absorbs less heat than warm air.

(A) This is a specific-detail question. The correct answer will be explicitly stated in the text at or near the location mentioned by the question's stem. You are referred to the third paragraph. There, the author specifically states that geothermal systems are more effective because they use a heat source whose temperature is more constant than that of air. Choice (A) makes this point, although not exactly in the same words.

What's wrong with (B)? First, as a matter of content, (B) simply defines a function of the heat pump. So (B) is not an explanation as to why the new technology is more effective than conventional technology. Second, as a matter of

test-taking strategy, the idea mentioned by (B) is found in paragraph 2 of the selection, not in paragraph 3. When a specific-detail question stem includes a reference, that's where you'll find the correct answer.

(C) is perhaps the second best answer, and it's a good reminder of the importance of reading all choices carefully. The phrase "is close" suggests the idea of stability that makes (A) the correct answer, but the choice when read in its entirety is wrong.

Finally, (D) is simply a misreading of the selection.

8. "Waste" in line 43 is closest in meaning to

   (A) required

   (B) convenient

   (C) unwanted

   (D) unsanitary

(C) This is a vocabulary-in-context question. As a general rule, an answer choice that is a common meaning of the word being tested is probably not correct. For this reason, you should avoid answer (D). To be sure, a common characteristic of waste is that waste is unsanitary. But that common connection should make you suspicious. The correct answer is (C). Remember that the heat-pump technology is designed to extract unwanted energy from the inside of the building and dump it outside. So, waste in this context means unwanted.

9. The author regards the new technology as

12

(A) promising but under-utilized.

(B) dependable but costly.

(C) inexpensive but unreliable.

(D) unproven but efficient.

(A) This is a special implication question: one that asks about the author's attitude toward something. We treat these as implication questions because the author's attitude or judgment is not specifically stated in the text. Therefore, as with other implication questions, you have to use clues within the text to arrive at your answer. The preview turned up some clues that are useful here. Remember that the author said this new technology is very promising though under-utilized. Clearly, this is answer (A).

Remember also that it is often possible to arrange answer choices to a question like this on a scale from negative to positive. If you find it convenient, you can use the scale of 1 to 4, with 1 as the most negative judgment and 4 the most positive. This scale cannot be applied with the same precision as a ruler, but it can help you organize your thinking about the answer choices. In this case, answer choice (C) is perhaps the most negative because it says that the technology is unreliable. The answer choice next to that appears to be (D), which states that the technology is unproven. Answer choice (B) begins to move into the positive range: the technology is dependable but costly. Finally, the most positive evaluation is provided by (A): promising but under-utilized. In fact, under-utilized is not an indictment of the technology itself, but of the public perception regarding the technology. So (A) would be the most positive value judgment, and (A) is consistent with the author's judgment in this case.

10. The passage implies that a rise in cost of conventional energy would have what effect?

(A) An expanded reliance on direct geothermal technology

(B) A decrease in cost for geothermal heating and cooling

(C) A shift toward the use of conventional energy sources

(D) A decrease in the number of homes using geothermal heating

(A) This is an implication question. The word "implies" clearly tags it as one. Information about the cost of conventional energy sources is provided in the final sentence of the passage. There the author explains that geothermal energy has been under-utilized in part because the price of competing sources is low. So what would happen if the price of competing sources rose? Geothermal energy would look more attractive, and there would be increased reliance upon it.

Remember that an implication question does not necessarily entail a logical deduction, although the correct answer to this question seems to be logically deducible from the passage.

Now let's look at the wrong answers. The other choices are attractive distractors because they use language that may capture your attention:

"decrease in cost," "shift toward," and "decrease in." But a decrease in cost is not the same thing as expanded reliance. And a shift toward conventional sources is not a shift toward new technology. Differences such as these can make the difference between a correct and an incorrect answer. So you have to read all choices, read all of each choice, and read everything carefully.

11. Which of the following helps to illustrate why the new technology can be used for air conditioning as well as heating homes?

 (A) A pool of still water freezes faster than a running stream.

 (B) A drink of well water tastes cool on a hot summer day.

 (C) Refrigerated liquids stay colder than liquids at room temperature.

 (D) The temperature of surrounding air varies from winter to summer.

(B) This as an implication question. It is one of those that requires you to take what you have learned from the passage and apply it to a new situation. The key to the working of a heat pump in general and geothermal energy in particular is the temperature differential between the space to be heated or cooled and the heat source. Only (B) suggests a situation in which there is a temperature differential.

12. A logical continuation of the passage would be a discussion of

 (A) unique geological features of the Earth.

 (B) ways of expanding reliance on geothermal technology.

 (C) techniques for converting geothermal energy into electricity.

 (D) the environmental hazards to be faced in the next 20 years.

(B) This is an implication question; the correct answer is not found in the text. This type of implication question poses some special challenges. It can be difficult because there is no way to demonstrate conclusively what the author might do next. So your job is to pick the most likely continuation. The last sentence ties the argument together: this great technology is under-utilized. Certainly, then, the author can go on to discuss ways of expanding reliance on the new technology.

(A) is wrong because, while geology figures prominently in the passage, this idea gives the author nothing to build upon. (C) is wrong because the author is discussing the direct geothermal applications; converting geothermal energy into electricity is an example of an indirect application. (D) is an idea in which the author would have some interest, but that does not mean it's an idea that would be logical for the author to take on immediately following the last paragraph of this selection.

12

Questions 13–24

Perhaps the best-known of the ancient Greek religious festivals are the Panhellenic gatherings in honor of Zeus, at Olympia, where the Olympics origi-
(5) nated in 776 B.C. These and other festivals in honor of Zeus were called "crown festivals" because the winning athletes were crowned with wreaths, such as the olive wreaths of Olympia. Yet in ancient Greece
(10) there were at least 300 public, state-run religious festivals celebrated at more than 250 locations in honor of some 400 deities. Most of these were held in the cities, in contrast to the crown festivals, which
(15) were held in rural sanctuaries. In Athens, for example, four annual festivals honored Athena, the city's divine protectress, in addition to those for other gods. In all, some 120 days were devoted annually to
(20) festivals.

By far the largest event of the Athenian religious calendar, rivaling the crown gatherings in prestige, was the Great Panathenaic festival. The development of
(25) the Panathenaic festival—the ritual embodiment of the cult of Athena—evolved from a purely local religious event into a civic and Panhellenic one. This transformation, and that of the image of Athena
(30) from an aggressively martial goddess to a more humane figure of victory, parallels the great political change that occurred in Athens from 560 B.C. to 430 B.C., as it evolved from a tyranny to a democracy.
(35) Athenian reverence for Athena originated in a myth that recounts a quarrel between Poseidon and Athena over possession of Attica. In a contest arranged by

Zeus, Athena was judged the winner and
(40) made the patron goddess of Athens, to which she gave her name. The origin of the Panathenaia, however, is shrouded in mystery. Perhaps it was founded by Erichthonius, a prehistoric king of Athens.
(45) According to legend, after having been reared by Athena on the Acropolis, he held games for his foster mother and competed in the chariot race, which he reputedly invented. The first archaeological evidence
(50) for the festival is a Panathenaic prize vase from 560 B.C., which depicts a horse race, so scholars infer that equestrian events were part of the festival.

Much more is known about the
(55) Panathenaia after 566 B.C., when the festival was reorganized under the tyrant Peisistaros. At that time, the festival, in addition to its annual celebration, was heightened every fourth year into the Great
(60) Panathenaia, which attracted top athletes from all over the region to compete for valuable prizes—such as 140 vases of olive oil for winning the chariot race—rather than for honorific wreaths.
(65) From the mid-sixth century B.C. until the end of antiquity, when the Christian emperors suppressed the pagan religions, the high point of Athenian religious life was the Great Panathenaia, held in July. Ev-
(70) ery four years, some 1,300 painted amphorae were commissioned and filled with olive oil to be used as prizes. The accouterments of Athena—helmet, spear, and shield—figured prominently in the
(75) iconic representations of the goddess on these vases and served to identify the stylized figure and to associate the festival with the goddess. So far as is known, none

of the crown games commissioned any art
(80) for their festivals. Yet, ironically, the images that are often associated with the
modern Olympics are taken from the
Panathenaic vases.

Here is what your preview should have
turned up:

> The best-known of the ancient Greek
> religious festivals were the gatherings
> at Olympia.

> By far the largest event of the
> Athenian religious calendar, rivaling
> the crown gatherings, was the great
> Panathenaic festival.

> Athenian reverence for Athena
> originated in a myth.

> Much more is known about the
> Panathenaic games after 566 B.C.

> From the mid-sixth century B.C. until
> the end of antiquity, the high point of
> Athenian religious life was the Great
> Panathenaia.

> Ironically, the images often associ-
> ated with modern Olympics are taken
> from Panathenaic vases.

Your second pass will turn up a lot more
detail in the first paragraph. Remember,
however, not to get bogged down. Make
a mental note of the location of the
details, and move on.

The second paragraph describes the
development of the Panathenaic festival.
Again, there is more detail. Note it in
your mind, and keep moving.

The third paragraph provides more
historical detail. It states specifically

that the origin of the Panathenaia is not
known but speculates that it might have
been founded by Erichthonius, a
prehistoric king of Athens. The fourth
paragraph continues this development
by noting that much more is known
historically about the Panathenaic games
after 566 B.C.

The final paragraph gives more information about the Great Panathenaia. It talks
about prizes and art. But much of this
detail may or may not show up in a
question. Learn where it's located and
keep moving.

13. What does the passage primarily
    discuss?

    (A) The origins of the modern
    Olympic games

    (B) Minor religious festivals in
    ancient Greece

    (C) Athletic contests centered in
    ancient Athens

    (D) Use of military iconography
    on Greek pottery

(C) This is a thesis or main idea
question. Remember the Goldilocks
principle (from the fairy tale about
Goldilocks and the three bears): not too
broad, not too narrow, but just right. In
this case, answer choice (C) is just right.
It refers to an athletic contest but
narrows the scope of that phrase to focus
on those of ancient Athens.

Choice (A) is too narrow because the
modern Olympic Games are mentioned in
paragraph 1 and again, in passing, in
paragraph 5. In fact, the author takes

great care to distinguish the games in honor of Zeus, which gave rise to the modern Olympics, from those held at Athens.

(B) is clearly wrong because most of the passage is concerned with the major religious festival at Athens.

Finally, (D) is too narrow. In the final paragraph, the author provides some detail about the decorations of the prizes commissioned for the games at Athens, and those details included military symbols, such as helmets, spears, and shields. But this discussion is confined to the last paragraph. Therefore, it cannot be the main idea of the passage.

14. Which of the following is *not* mentioned as a characteristic of the games at Olympia?

    (A) The games were held in honor of Zeus.

    (B) Winners were crowned with wreaths.

    (C) The games originated in 776 B.C.

    (D) The games were held in or near cities.

(D) This is a specific-detail question. Again, the question stem includes a thought-reverser: *not*. This means that three of the four answer choices will be specifically mentioned in the text; the one not specifically mentioned is the correct answer. Choice (A) is mentioned in the first paragraph: the games at Olympia were held in honor of Zeus. Choice (B) is mentioned: the winners

were crowned with wreaths. And the date of origin is given in that paragraph as 776 B.C. (D) is not mentioned as a characteristic of the games at Olympia. In fact, the first paragraph specifically says that crown festivals, which included those held at Olympia in honor of Zeus, were held in rural areas.

15. Which of the following best summarizes the parallel development referred to in the second paragraph?

(A)

Time	Athena	Festival	Government
Earlier	Symbol of Victory	Local, Religious	Tyranny
Later	Aggressive Warrior	Regional, Civic	Democracy

(B)

Time	Athena	Festival	Government
Earlier	Symbol of Victory	Regional, Civic	Democracy
Later	Aggressive Warrior	Local, Religious	Tyranny

(C)

Time	Athena	Festival	Government
Earlier	Aggressive Warrior	Local, Religious	Tyranny
Later	Symbol of Victory	Regional, Civic	Democracy

(D)

Time	Athena	Festival	Government
Earlier	Aggressive Warrior	Local, Religious	Democracy
Later	Symbol of Victory	Regional, Civic	Tyranny

(C) This is a specific-detail question, although you might not recognize it as such from the form of the question. The clue is "referred to." That phrase tells you that the correct answer is specifically given in the second paragraph.

In the second paragraph, the author discusses the evolution of the Great Panathenaic festival. According to the selection, it evolved from a purely local, religious event into a civic and Panhellenic one. Furthermore, this evolution paralleled the transformation of the image of Athena from an aggressively martial goddess to a more humane figure and symbol of victory. And that is paralleled as well by political changes that saw the evolution to democracy from tyranny.

16. The author implies that the suggestion that the Panathenaia originated under Erichthonius is

    (A) conclusively proved.

    (B) a theoretical possibility.

    (C) without any foundation.

    (D) a hoax perpetrated by Athenians.

(B) This is an implication question, and the word implied clearly signals it as such. The text does not specifically state what the author thinks of the theory that the Panathenaia originated under Erichthonius, but you can infer what that attitude probably is. In the third paragraph, the author refers first to legend; then the author cites archaeological evidence. The reference to archaeological evidence strongly suggests that the author believes that there is more than legend here. So the best description is "theoretical possibility." The other choices are much too strong. "Conclusively proved" places too much reliance on the passing reference to the scientific evidence; "without any foundation" and "a hoax" ignore the reference to the evidence.

17. "Equestrian events," mentioned in line 52 refers to activities involving

    (A) weapons

    (B) gods

    (C) horses

    (D) tyrants

(C) This is a vocabulary-in-context question. We are referred to the final sentence of the third paragraph. There the author mentions a horse race and notes that scholars infer that equestrian events were part of the festival. The juxtaposition of horse race and equestrian events is the clue that equestrian refers to horses.

12

18. Which of the following was *not* true of the Great Panathenaia?

    (A) It was held every four years.

    (B) Contestants competed solely for honor.

    (C) It began at the time of Peisistaros.

    (D) It was held in July.

(B) This is a specific-detail question. And, again, we have a question stem that includes a thought reverser: *not*. As you analyze the answer choices, any choice that is mentioned specifically in the selection is wrong; the one not specifically mentioned is the correct answer. In the last paragraph of the selection, we are given details about the Great Panathenaia: it was held every four years; it was held in July. That paragraph also tells us that the contestants did not compete solely for honors but for valuable prizes. Finally, it is in the third paragraph that you learn that the Great Panathenaia grew out of the Panathenaia when the festival was reorganized under the tyrant Peisistaros.

19. What word has most nearly the same meaning as "amphorae" (line 71)?

    (A) vases

    (B) wreaths

    (C) representation

    (D) Panathenaia

(A) This is a vocabulary-in-context question. You are referred to the second sentence of the last paragraph where the author mentions 1,300 painted amphorae. Later in that paragraph, the author refers to the decorations on those amphorae and calls them vases.

20. "Iconic" (line 75) most nearly means

    (A) stylized depiction

    (B) religious statue

    (C) painted amphorae

    (D) assorted weapons

(A) This is a vocabulary-in-context question. Keep in mind that an answer choice with a commonly associated meaning may be a distractor. In this case, (B) is a distractor because the word icon can refer to a religious statue. The meaning here is slightly different. The key word is stylized. The iconic representations were stylized figures.

21. According to the passage, who is supposed to have created the chariot race?

    (A) Poseidon

    (B) Erichthonius

    (C) Peisistaros

    (D) Athena

(B) This is a specific-detail question. The phrase "according to the passage" almost always signals specific detail, so the correct answer will be found specifically in the text. To learn about chariot races, you need to consult the third paragraph. There the author explains that legend had it that the chariot races were introduced by Erichthonius, a prehistoric king of Athens, who had been reared by Athena.

22. According to the passage, the archaeological evidence for the Panathenaia dates from

    (A) 776 B.C.

    (B) 566 B.C.

    (C) 560 B.C.

    (D) 430 B.C.

(C) This is a specific-detail question. Again, the phrase "according to the passage" is an unmistakable tag. You need information about the archaeological evidence for the Panathenaia, and that is found in the third paragraph. There the author states that the first archaeological evidence for the festival dates from 560 B.C.

23. The author of the passage regards the association of imagery of Athena with the modern Olympic Games as

    (A) sacrilegious

    (B) misguided

    (C) well-founded

    (D) hasty

(B) This is an implication question. The author never specifically renders a judgment on the presumed association between the modern Olympic Games and the imagery of Athena, but you can infer what that attitude probably is, based upon information given in the passage and the last sentence of the text. The author explains that the festivals held in honor of Zeus were crown festivals. The winners at the crown festivals were awarded wreaths, not valuable prizes. The games in honor of Athena were something altogether

different. That alone tells you that the author believes that the association is mistaken. Then, in the last paragraph, the author uses the word ironically. The association is ironic because the modern Olympic Games are supposed to be amateur games, but the Panathenaic games clearly awarded competitors valuable prizes.

24. Where in the passage does the author mention objects traditionally associated with Athena?

    (A) Lines 5–9

    (B) Lines 49–53

    (C) Lines 57–64

    (D) Lines 72–78

(D) This is a specific-detail question. You find the reference you need in the final paragraph.

Questions 25–36

    Alcohol abuse and dependence are serious problems affecting 10 percent of adult Americans, and the toll is high: 3 out of 100 deaths in the United States can
(5) be linked directly to alcohol. In addition to traffic crashes, injuries in the home and on the job, and serious long-term medical consequences, alcohol abuse has been implicated in aggression and crime. The
(10) cost of alcohol abuse and alcohol dependence is estimated to be as high as $1 trillion annually.

    Although patterns vary, it is possible to classify drinkers as social drinkers, alco-
(15) hol abusers, and alcohol-dependent persons. While alcohol consumption is never

12

entirely a risk-free activity, these categories represent a range from relatively benign to extremely problematic.

(20)   An evaluation of treatment for any alcohol-related disorder must be situated historically. For nearly 200 years, the explanation of alcoholism as a disease competed with explanations in which (25) character or moral defects were believed to lead to problematic drinking behavior. It wasn't until the 1930s that serious consideration was given to the concept of alcoholism as a disease with psychological, (30) biochemical, endocrinological, and neurological implications. Even as late as the 1960s, some researchers still defined alcoholism broadly to include any drinking having harmful consequences.

(35)   Evidence accumulated, however, suggesting that alcohol abuse and alcohol dependence are distinguishable. "Alcohol abuse" refers either to transitory or long-term problems in accomplishing basic (40) living activities in which alcohol is implicated, and "alcohol dependence" describes a severe disability in which dependence brings about a reduction in the individual's ability to control the drinking behavior. (45) This delineation was endorsed in 1987 by the Institute of Medicine, which defined alcohol abuse as "repetitive patterns of heavy drinking associated with impairment of functioning and/or health" and (50) discussed alcoholism (dependency) as a separate phenomenon. Alcohol dependence is associated with additional symptoms such as craving, tolerance, and physical dependence that bring about (55) changes in the importance of drinking in

(60) the individual's life, and impaired ability to exercise behavioral restraint.

The distinction has important clinical implications. For some nondependent alcohol abusers, drinking patterns may be (65) modified by exhortations or by societal sanctions. For alcohol-dependent persons, exhortations and sanctions are insufficient, and the goal of modified drinking inappropriate. The goal for these persons is (70) abstinence, and a range of treatment options is available, including pharmacologic interventions, psychotherapy, and counseling. But even alcohol-dependent persons do not constitute a homogeneous group. (75) They are not identical in personality, life experiences, family characteristics and social status. Knowledge of the differences among alcohol-dependent persons is important because research shows that alcoholism treatment methods are dif- (80) ferentially effective according to patient characteristics.

Let's began with the preview stage.

Alcohol abuse and dependence are serious problems.

Although patterns vary, it is possible to classify drinkers as social drinkers, alcohol abusers, and alcohol-dependent persons.

An evaluation of treatment for any alcohol-related disorder must be situated historically.

Evidence accumulated, however, suggesting that alcohol abuse and alcohol dependence are distinguishable.

The distinction has important clinical implications.

Knowledge of the differences among alcohol-dependent persons is important also.

Some previews yield more information that others, and this is a particularly good one. The first sentence establishes that both alcohol abuse and dependence are serious problems. In other words, you already know what the topic of the selection will be. Then the second paragraph distinguishes three sorts of drinkers: social drinkers, alcohol abusers, and alcohol-dependent persons. Apparently the passage will discuss the differences among these three groups. The third paragraph announces that this distinction has historical roots. Then paragraph 4 begins by saying evidence has accumulated suggesting that alcohol abuse and alcohol dependence are distinguishable. In other words, the second and third distinctions introduced in the second paragraph are not always one thing; only gradually did they diverge. In the next paragraph the author will tell us that this distinction has important clinical implications. That's a lot of information to be had just from a preview.

25. What does the passage mainly discuss?

(A) The history of alcoholism as a treatable disease

(B) The difference between alcohol abuse and alcohol dependence

(C) The injurious consequences associated with alcohol consumption

(D) The early view of alcohol abuse as a moral problem

(B) This is a thesis or main-idea question. The main focus of the passage is the difference between alcohol abuse and alcohol dependence. The author begins by giving you some historical background on this distinction and then discusses its clinical implications.

Choice (A) is too narrow. It is true that the author discusses the history of alcohol as a treatable disease, but that is only in order to situate the modern distinction historically.

Choice (C) is too narrow. The author acknowledges in passing that any drinking is risky behavior, but this is not the main point of the selection.

Choice (D) is also too narrow. Again, the author acknowledges that alcohol abuse was first viewed as a moral problem, but this view has since been rejected.

26. According to paragraph 2, which of the following represents the progression from least-serious to most-serious?

(A) social drinking, alcohol abuse, alcohol dependence

(B) social drinking, alcohol dependence, alcohol abuse

(C) alcohol abuse, social drinking, alcohol dependence

(D) alcohol dependence, alcohol abuse, social drinking

12

(A) This is a specific-detail question. The phrase "according to paragraph 2" clearly signals its status. The tripartite classification is given in the second paragraph: social drinkers, alcohol abusers, and alcohol-dependent persons.

27. It can be inferred that the author would consider the conclusions mentioned in line 31 as

    (A) unfounded rejections of the traditional model.

    (B) scientific advances, but only partially correct.

    (C) conclusively proven and valid for current models.

    (D) irrelevant to the subject of the discussion.

(B) This is an implication question. The overall development of the passage clearly indicates that the author regards this as a stage in the development of thinking about alcohol abuse—from viewing it as a moral problem to seeing it as a clinical problem with several grades of illness. Since the author endorses the view that it is important to recognize gradations of alcoholism, you can infer that the author believes that the view mentioned in paragraph 3, while more advanced than the earlier view that alcoholism is a moral problem, is still too crude. The best description of this is given by choice (B): an improvement, but more needs to be done.

(A) is directly contrary to the author's opinion because the author believes that

the newer model is entirely justified. (C) makes the opposite mistake. The author thinks that the model described in paragraph 3 did not go far enough. Finally, (D) is incorrect because the author thinks that the model mentioned in paragraph 3, while historically limited, represented an advance over earlier thinking.

28. In paragraph 3, the author contrasts which of the following?

    (A) disease and moral defects

    (B) psychological and biochemical implications

    (C) alcoholism and harmful consequences

    (D) disorder and alcoholism

(A) This is a specific-detail question. In that paragraph the author situates the new model historically. There the author contrasts the traditional view of alcoholism as a moral problem with the more modern view that alcoholism is a disease and should be treated as such.

29. Which of the following is *not* mentioned as an implication of the early disease model of alcoholism?

    (A) social implications

    (B) psychological implications

    (C) endocrinological implications

    (D) neurological implications

(A) This is a specific-detail question, and the word "mentioned" tells you that the answer will be found specifically in the text. You also have a thought reverser, *not*, which means that three of the choices (the wrong ones) will be mentioned in the text and one (the correct one) will not be mentioned. In the third paragraph, the author mentions psychological, endocrinological, and neurological implications. Missing from that list, however, is social implications.

30. Which of the following is *not* mentioned in paragraph 4 as characteristic of alcohol dependence but not of alcohol abuse?

    (A) long-term problems

    (B) craving

    (C) tolerance

    (D) physical dependence

(A) This is a specific-detail question. Again, the word "mentioned" flags it as a specific-detail question. In the last sentence of paragraph 4, the author lists the characteristics of alcohol dependence. In that list, you'll find craving, tolerance, and physical dependence. These are *additional* symptoms of dependence as opposed to alcohol abuse. (A) is the correct answer because "long-term problems" does not distinguish between the two grades of illness; both grades of illness have this in common.

31. "Homogeneous" (line 70) means

    (A) may be modified

    (B) are identical

    (C) is important

    (D) research shows

(B) This is a vocabulary-in-context question. The word "homogeneous" appears in the fourth paragraph. In the very next sentence, the author notes that persons are not identical in personality, life experience, family characteristics, or social status. Since they are different, you can infer that homogeneous refers to people who are alike. So the best answer here is "identical."

32. Where in the passage does the author cite an authority in support of the argument?

    (A) Paragraph 2

    (B) Paragraph 3

    (C) Paragraph 4

    (D) Paragraph 5

(C) This is a specific-detail question. The wording of the question stem tells you that somewhere in the passage the author cites an authority in an argument. Your task is to find that. The location you're looking for is paragraph 4, where the author cites the Institute of Medicine.

33. Where in the passage does the author outline different courses of treatment?

    (A) Paragraph 2

    (B) Paragraph 3

    (C) Paragraph 4

    (D) Paragraph 5

(D) This is a specific-detail question. The wording of the question tells you that somewhere in the passage the author outlines different courses of

12

treatment. Your task is to find where. In the first sentence of the fifth paragraph, the author says that the distinction between alcohol abuse and alcohol dependence has important clinical implications. This means important treatment implications. The author explains that nondependent alcohol abusers may be treated by a combination of methods, including exhortation and societal sanctions. The author goes on to explain that these are likely to be ineffective for alcohol-dependent persons.

34. The mention of suicide as a consequence of alcohol-related depression would be an appropriate addition to which of the following sentences?

   (A) In addition to traffic crashes, injuries in the home and on the job, and serious long-term medical consequences, alcohol abuse has been implicated in aggression and crime.

   (B) It wasn't until the 1930s that serious consideration was given to the concept of alcoholism as a disease with psychological, biochemical, endocrinological, and neurological implications.

   (C) The goal for these persons is abstinence, and a range of treatment options is available, including pharmacologic interventions, psychotherapy, and counseling.

   (D) They exhibit differences in personality, life experiences, family characteristics, and social status.

(A) This is a development question. The question is designed to determine whether you understand the structure of the argument. If you're able to position this additional sentence correctly, that's a pretty good indication that you understand how the author has developed the passage. In the first paragraph, the author refers to alcohol abuse and dependence as serious problems and lists some of their consequences: crashes, injuries, and long-term health consequences. It would be appropriate to add suicide to that list.

Answer choice (B) is incorrect. Although this sentence includes a list, the list consists of higher-order terms, such as psychological (a group term), rather than particular mental problems. (C) is incorrect because in that paragraph the author is talking about possible therapies. And finally, (D) is incorrect because in that part of the last paragraph the author is talking about tailoring treatment options to individual needs.

35. The passage is primarily concerned with

   (A) drawing a distinction.

   (B) refuting a theory.

   (C) cataloguing sources.

   (D) criticizing behavior.

(A) At first glance, you might think that this is a thesis or main-idea question. After all, it includes the characteristic wording "primarily concerned." But the answer choices indicate that the question is actually asking about the development of the passage. The confusion is not terribly important because regardless of what you call this question the task is to describe the main point or thesis in terms of the overall approach taken by the author.

The main focus of the passage is the distinction between alcohol dependence and alcohol abuse. This development is best described by (A).

Choice (B) might catch your eye. The author does address the theory that alcoholism is a moral problem rather than a medical one. The difficulty with this reading, however, is that the author does not attempt to demonstrate that this position is false; rather, the author takes for granted that it has already been proved false by history.

Choice (C) is incorrect because there's only a single source cited by the author, and that hardly constitutes a catalog. Choice (D) is incorrect because the author is not judgmental. While it is true that the author refers to groups that might be judgmental, to wit, those who regard alcoholism as a moral weakness, this is not the author's own point of view.

36. The most logical continuation of the passage would be

    (A) further information about alcoholism as a moral problem.

    (B) an explanation of the physical effects of alcohol on the brain.

    (C) a brief historical summary of the attitudes toward alcohol.

    (D) more detailed discussion of treatments for alcohol dependence.

(D) This is an implication question. It has that special form that asks you to select a topic that would be appropriate for the next paragraph. It's important to keep in mind that you'll never feel entirely comfortable with your choice of answers to a question like this.

The correct answer is (D). The author spends the last paragraph of the passage talking about treatment options for abuse and dependence. The author notes that therapies need to be adapted to individual needs since the group is not homogeneous. An appropriate continuation of the topic, then, would be further discussion of this notion.

Choice (A) is wrong. The idea that alcoholism is a moral problem is a historical notion that has been overruled. The author mentions it in order to provide background information for the reader, but then moves on to describe the modern view. So it would not help the reader to see more information about alcoholism as a moral problem.

(C) is wrong for a similar reason. The author mentions the neurological effects of alcoholism, but does not do so to prove that alcohol abuse has such effects; rather, the author mentions this to explain why alcoholism eventually

12

came to be regarded as a disease. The final paragraph is concerned with treatment options, not with diagnosis or harmful effects.

Answer choice (B) is wrong for the same reason that answer choice (A) is wrong.

Questions 37–48

Legislatures are increasingly becoming highly professionalized bodies. There have been profound changes in the organization of legislative life, shifts in the
(5) location of power, and alterations to the instruments by which power is exercised.

James S. Young's account of Washington, D.C. from 1800 through 1828 describes a community of sojourners, people
(10) temporarily in a place with little or no expectation of remaining long. Congressmen lived in boarding houses, and the boundaries between the makeshift social life of residents and their political duties were
(15) indistinct. Young's Washington was a city of cliques formed around regional and sectional affinities. For the modern legislator, social life has receded to the periphery. Legislators live in apartments and
(20) have less to do with one another in groups outside the formal interactions of the legislative body. Organized political units—conferences, caucuses, committees—have replaced the more personal clique arrange-
(25) ments of an earlier period. Additionally, membership is more likely to be a career in itself rather than a temporary status or a capstone to another career. Indeed, members describe themselves in terms of their
(30) status. When asked to list their primary occupation, most describe themselves not as lawyers or business executives but as "legislators."

A second set of changes involves the
(35) internalization of control of the legislative body. In earlier periods, it was the Chief Executive who set the agenda for the body as a whole. For example, the Chief Executive proposed the budget, and the leg-
(40) islature largely approved it. Or the Chief Executive exercised control through a veto power that was regarded as nearly absolute. Now, legislatures are more likely to propose an agenda and to ignore that of
(45) the Chief Executive, and to make it clear that a veto can be overridden when the issue is of sufficient importance to the membership. External control also used to reside in the hands of local party lead-
(50) ers who controlled nominations. Now, control over nominations is more centralized and under the direction of legislative leaders.

Finally, there is the change in what
(55) counts as an instrument of power. Career legislators plan to be reelected, so influencing a member's chances for reelection becomes an important instrument of leadership. Leaders within the body itself now
(60) control the means to a successful campaign and distribute money and other assistance in exchange for loyalty. Additionally, member items, budget allocations to specific districts over which members have considerable control, are an impor-
(65) tant tool of leadership. And there is growth of centers of policy activity where a legislator has created a special area of influence through expertise and the development of special relationships with
(70) influential groups.

37. What is the main point of the passage?

    (A) The Chief Executive is now less important than the legislature.

    (B) Legislative power is centered in the hands of a few.

    (C) Democracy is at risk from recent political changes.

    (D) Legislatures are now highly professional organizations.

(D) The main point of the entire passage is summarized for you in the very first sentence.

38. Which of the following best describes the relationship among the second, third, and fourth paragraphs?

    (A) Three independent arguments in support of a contention

    (B) One main argument followed by two minor arguments

    (C) A claim, a rebuttal, and an answer to the rebuttal

    (D) Three arguments presented in order of their importance

(A) After setting forth the main thesis of the passage, the author goes on to supply three independent arguments to support the contention that legislatures are now professionalized: one, permanent membership; two, internal control; three, new instruments of power.

39. Which of the following terms used by the author helps to define "sojourner" (line 9)?

    (A) community

    (B) temporarily

    (C) boundaries

    (D) indistinct

(B) The structure of the sentence referred to indicates that what follows the comma is supposed to be further explanation of what has come before. So the phrase "temporarily in place" is supposed to explain "sojourner."

40. A "clique" (line 16) is a

    (A) governmental agency.

    (B) legislative body.

    (C) political party.

    (D) social grouping.

(D) The context should make it clear that a clique is a small group of people.

41. Which of the following means most nearly the *opposite* of "periphery" (line 18)?

    (A) center

    (B) permanent

    (C) elected

    (D) later

(A) Traditionally, a legislator's personal life was intimately bound up with that of other legislators from the same region or locale. But in the modern legislature, the personal lives of its members are separate from their professional lives. So the personal life no longer has a central importance insofar as membership is concerned.

12

42. Which of the following phrases could best be substituted for "capstone" (line 28)?

    (A) crowning achievement

    (B) acceptable alternative

    (C) political aspiration

    (D) second choice

(A) A capstone is the top or final row of stones on a wall or similar construction. Thus, it is like the crown, in that it is on top of everything else.

43. Which of the following is *not* an example of external control (paragraph 3)?

    (A) Political influence of the Chief Executive

    (B) Veto power of the Chief Executive

    (C) Local party control over nominations

    (D) Centralized direction of nominations

(D) In paragraph 3 the author describes the "internalization" of control and mentions the executive's loss of power over the agenda and the veto, and the migration of control over the nominating process from the local to the central level. So centralized control is not an example of outside, but rather of inside, control.

44. The controls mentioned in paragraph 4 would be *least* effective if used on

    (A) a first-term career legislator.

    (B) a member facing stiff reelection opposition.

    (C) a junior member who hopes for a prestigious party appointment.

    (D) a member who has already announced retirement.

(D) The tools mentioned are effective because they affect a member's chances for reelection. A member who has already announced retirement is not interested in reelection.

45. If the author wished to draw a distinction between direct and indirect instruments of power, which of the following would express that distinction?

(A)

Direct	Indirect
Distribution of campaign money	Control of member items
Relations with influential groups	Policy expertise

(B)

Direct	Indirect
Distribution of campaign money	Policy expertise
Control of member items	Relations with influential groups

(C)

Direct	Indirect
Policy expertise	Control of member items
Distribution of campaign money	Relations with influential groups

(D)

Direct	Indirect
Policy expertise	Distribution of campaign money
Relations with influential groups	Control of member items

(B) The author does not draw such a distinction, but the four tools mentioned can naturally be categorized as those which are used directly to manipulate members (by threats and rewards) and those that derive from an informal power, such as prestige.

46. Where does the author mention a survey?

    (A) Paragraph 1

    (B) Paragraph 2

    (C) Paragraph 3

    (D) Paragraph 4

(B) In paragraph 2, the author mentions how members describe themselves when they are asked.

47. Which of the following best describes the organization of the passage?

    (A) The author states a thesis and then supports it with evidence.

    (B) The author describes a popular position and then refutes it.

    (C) The author explains the historical roots of a political problem.

    (D) The author outlines the defects of a political institution.

(A) The author states a thesis in the first paragraph and then offers three independent arguments or three separate pieces of analysis in support of the thesis. There is no indication that one is more important than the other.

48. Which of the following would be the most appropriate for the author to include in a fifth paragraph?

    (A) Examples of the effects of professionalization on laws passed

    (B) An analysis of the declining power of the Chief Executive

    (C) More details on the social life of nineteenth-century Washington, D.C.

    (D) The names of prominent members of the legislature

(A) The author makes a fairly persuasive case for the proposition that legislatures have turned into professional organizations and function very much like other business or organizations. A natural continuation of this line of thought would be to explore the issue of whether this type of legislature passes laws that are different in content from those passed in earlier eras.

12

Q & A Session

Q: I'm afraid that I'll waste a lot of time trying to figure what category a question belongs in. Should I really try to do that on the test?

A: Let's start to put things in perspective. The short answer to your question is "No, you shouldn't spend much time worrying about categories on your TOEFL." But that's because categorizing will be automatic for you.

You have to remember that when you took the Reading PreTest, you probably weren't even aware that there are categories. You were just busy answering questions, as though all the questions were alike. Now, you understand that there are different kinds of questions and that they have different kinds of answers.

In fact, it's probably already becoming automatic for you. Instead of thinking, "Let's see, this says "main idea" so it must be a thesis question, therefore . . . ," you see the phrase "main idea" and immediately start looking for the thesis without even pausing to think.

Until you reach that level of familiarity, however, you should keep asking yourself consciously, "What kind of question is this?"

Q: What about the preview? It seems to take some time.

A: Yes it does, but no matter how familiar you are with TOEFL Reading you should still do a preview. Why? Because each passage is different.

HOUR 13

Reading Workshop

What You'll Do This Hour

- Workshop A
- Workshop B
- Workshop C
- Q & A Session

Your Goals for This Hour

In this hour, you'll practice everything that you've learned so far about Reading in timed mode.

Your goals for this hour are

- Do Reading Workshop A
- Do Reading Workshop B
- Do Reading Workshop C
- Get answers to frequently asked questions

This hour's lesson includes three Workshops. Each workshop is a self-contained exercise—a reading passage with 10 questions followed by answer explanations. The time limit for the Drill portion of each workshop is 10 minutes, but you can take as much time as you need to review your work.

Because each Workshop is self-contained, you'll get the benefit of doing practice in timed mode without the need for spending an entire hour on an exercise. Plus, the 10-minute burst of activity won't be unduly tiring because you can catch your breath as you review.

Make sure you have a watch or a clock. And you may proceed.

Workshop A

10 Questions • Time—10 minutes

> **DIRECTIONS:** The passage below is followed by 10 questions based on the content of the passage. Answer each question based upon what is *stated* or *implied* in the passage. Mark you answer choices in your book.

This workshop consists of a Drill portion with a 10-minute time limit and a Review portion with no time limit. Mark your answers in your book.

Drill

Early criminal law, which grew out of the blood feud, was almost totally lacking in the modern ethical notion of wrongdoing. Wherever a barbaric society was orga-
(5) nized along the lines of blood kinship, revenge was aimed not at atonement for the bodily harm inflicted but for the humiliation suffered by the family unit. So, too, the primary goal of the early law was to
(10) provide an alternative to the feud by substituting a system of monetary compensation, and there emerged a definite tariff or *wer* with amounts reflecting the affront to clan dignity. Thus, the Welsh King Howell
(15) the Good decreed that a scar on the face was worth 80 pence, while the permanent loss of a thumb (an injury that would disable the hand) brought only 76 pence.

In a parallel development, the institu-
(20) tion of the *deodand* for cases involving a fatality required the surrender of the agent of death, whether that was a sword, a cart, a millwheel, or even an ox. It was not even required that the object have been under
(25) the direct control of the owner at the time, as in a case involving a sword hanging on a wall that fell, killing a visitor. The fact that early law attributed responsibility to insensible objects is further indication that
(30) the notion of ethical wrongdoing was a much later innovation.

1. What is the main topic of the selection?

   (A) The significance of *wer* and *deodand*
   (B) The history of the death penalty
   (C) The origins of the blood feud
   (D) Modern notions of criminal liability

2. The author cites the decree of King Howell the Good in order to

   (A) clarify the distinction between the *wer* and the *deodand.*
   (B) prevent misunderstanding about forfeiture in cases resulting in fatalities.
   (C) show that violence was common during the era of the blood feud.
   (D) prove that the *wer* compensated the clan for loss of honor.

3. The author's argument would be most strengthened by an early case in which

   (A) the *wer* for a visible bruise was double that for a similar bruise concealed by clothing.
   (B) the owner of an object had to forfeit it after using it to inflict injury.
   (C) the *deodand* did not apply because the instrument of death had been misused.
   (D) the payment was the same for two persons of unequal rank.

4. According to the selection, the primary purpose of the *wer* was to

   (A) deter people from injuring one another.
   (B) provided alternative dispute resolution.
   (C) punish wrongdoers for breaking the law.
   (D) prevent clan members from suing one another.

5. In line 19, the word "parallel" most nearly means

   (A) violent
   (B) unending
   (C) similar
   (D) legal

6. In line 29, the word "insensible" most nearly means

   (A) inanimate
   (B) dangerous
   (C) unconscious
   (D) useful

7. The author mentions the sword in line 22 because

   (A) people in violent societies frequently use arms.
   (B) it was not being used by anyone at the time of the death.
   (C) a sword is dangerous no matter who uses it.
   (D) a sword wound is usually worse than a farming injury.

8. In line 13, the word "affront" most nearly means

   (A) advancement
   (B) fatality
   (C) insult
   (D) atonement

13

9. In line 12, the word "definite" most nearly means

(A) changeable
(B) expensive
(C) optional
(D) fixed

10. The word "clan" in line 14 refers to what phrase used earlier in that paragraph?

(A) family unit
(B) blood feud
(C) ethical notion
(D) barbaric society

Review

Answer Key

1. A	4. B	7. B	10. A
2. D	5. C	8. C	
3. A	6. A	9. D	

1. **(A)** This is a thesis question. The main focus of the selection is the *wer* and the *deodand*. The author explains what they were, how they worked, and what about them made early criminal law different from later criminal law. (B) is wrong because the death penalty is never mentioned. (C) is incorrect because the blood feud is the author's starting point: out of the blood feud grew . . . . So a discussion of the origins of the blood feud would be a good topic for a different selection, but it's not the main topic here. And (D) would be a good topic for another selection to follow up on this one, but it is not the main idea of this selection.

2. **(D)** This is a structure question: *why* does the author do this? The author mentions the example of the scar and the loss of the thumb to show that a clan got more money for a scar than for a mangled hand—even though the loss of a digit would mean a loss of productivity. So the aim was not compensation for financial loss but for something else—namely, for the insult.

3. **(A)** This is an implication question. The author doesn't address any of the hypothetical cases given in the answer choices, but you can figure out which would be further proof for the author's contention. The goal of the *wer*, according to the author, was to compensate for a loss of honor or dignity, not for pain or suffering or physical injury. (A) gives another example of that distinction. The visible bruise is worth more than the same injury in a place that is not visible.

4. **(B)** This is a specific-detail question. (The "according to" is your clue.) In the first paragraph, the author explains that the primary goal of the early law was to avoid the violence of the blood feud, and it did this by setting up a system of compensation. In fact, the author actually uses the word "alternative" in the first paragraph.

5. **(C)** This is a vocabulary-in-context question. The second paragraph describes the *deodand,* which required the forfeiture of the object that caused death. The author uses the *wer* and the *deodand* to demonstrate that early criminal law was primarily concerned with compensation and not punishment. So the two institutions were similar.

6. **(A)** This is a vocabulary-in-context question. In this case, the "insensible" is referring to the sword that would be subject to forfeiture, and a sword is an inanimate object. It is, of course, also dangerous, but that is not the point. A tea kettle that fell off a shelf and caused a fatal head wound would have been subject to forfeiture as well. The word "unconscious" applies to a temporary lack of awareness; and, of course, a sword is an object that has no awareness.

7. **(B)** This is a development or structure question. You can recognize such questions because they ask *why* the author does something in the selection. And, importantly, the correct answer has to explain *why* the author did it. So *why* does the author mention the sword? In that paragraph, the author explains that the *deodand* is a system whereby the object that causes someone's death has to be given over to the clan of the person who was killed, regardless of what caused the death—a cart, an ox, or whatever. Then the author adds that this was required even when the object was something just hanging on the wall. So the most important element of the example is that the sword was just hanging there and fell for no apparent reason.

8. **(C)** This is a vocabulary-in-context item, and there are several clues to help you out. The word occurs in the phrase "affront to clan dignity," so you can conclude that the affront is some kind of harm to dignity. And that would have to be disrespect or insult. Also, early in the paragraph the author has used the term humiliation, which is like insult.

9. **(D)** This is a vocabulary-in-context item. The whole purpose of the *wer* was to create an alternative to the blood feud. To do that, it had to provide an authoritative alternative, one that would be accepted as fair. In this context, the word "definite" means fixed or established.

10. **(A)** This is a specific-detail question. It asks what the author said in paragraph 1. In that paragraph, "clan" must mean the same thing as "family."

13

Workshop B

10 Questions • Time—10 minutes

Electromechanical batteries, or EMBs, can power an electric car as well as electrochemical batteries. An EMB is a modular device that contains a flywheel integrated with a generator motor. The (5) EMB is "charged" by spinning its rotor to maximum speed with the motor in "motor mode." It is "discharged" by slowing the rotor to draw out the kinetically stored energy in "generator mode." (10)

Compared to stationary EMB applications such as wind turbines, vehicular applications pose two special problems. First, gyroscopic forces create problems (15) when a vehicle turns. The effects can be minimized by orienting the axis of rotation vertically, and by operating the EMB modules in pairs—one spinning clockwise and the other counterclockwise—so that (20) the net gyroscopic effect on the car is nearly zero.

The other problem associated with EMBs for vehicles is failure containment. The amount of kinetic energy stored is deter- (25) mined by the mass of the flywheel and its speed of rotation: the heavier the wheel and the faster it spins, the greater the energy stored. So it might seem that metal flywheels would be the automatic choice for EMBs. (30) The problem is that any spinning rotor has an upper speed limit determined by the

tensile strength of the material from which it is made, and when that limit is exceeded, the result is catastrophic failure. In other (35) words, the flywheel tears apart.

As it turns out, a low-density wheel can be spun up to a higher speed where it stores the same amount of kinetic energy as a heavier wheel spinning more slowly. Light- (40) weight graphite fiber, for example, is 10 times more effective per unit mass for kinetic energy storage than steel. And tests show that a well-designed rotor made of graphite fibers that fails turns into an amor- (45) phous mass of broken fibers. This failure is far more benign than that of metal flywheels, which typically break into shrapnel-like pieces that are difficult to contain.

1. The author's primary concern is to

   (A) discuss solutions to problems with the use of EMBs to power cars.

   (B) report on new technology that makes EMB-powered cars competitive with gasoline-powered vehicles.

   (C) prove that EMBs can operate more efficiently than conventional batteries.

   (D) design field tests to determine whether mobile EMBs can be used effectively.

2. The author mentions wind turbines in line 12 because they

(A) produce electricity.
(B) store energy.
(C) use wind power.
(D) do not move.

3. In line 16, the word "orienting" most nearly means

(A) reducing
(B) spinning
(C) aligning
(D) discharging

4. It can be inferred that a low-density flywheel with stored kinetic energy equal to that of a high-density flywheel is

(A) discharging energy as it spins.
(B) spinning in the opposite direction.
(C) rotating at a higher speed.
(D) made of graphite fibers.

5. In line 44, the word "amorphous" most nearly means

(A) shapeless
(B) weightless
(C) motionless
(D) worthless

6. It can be inferred that when a flywheel is slowing down it is

(A) gaining weight.
(B) spinning clockwise.
(C) moving horizontally.
(D) losing energy.

7. In line 46, the phrase "more benign" means

(A) less dangerous
(B) more reliable
(C) more stable
(D) less expensive

8. The author regards the new EMB technology as

(A) overrated.
(B) unattainable.
(C) promising.
(D) impractical.

9. The author states that the gyroscopic effect of EMB modules operating in pairs can be minimized if they are

(A) constructed of high-density metal.
(B) rotated in opposite directions.
(C) operating in their "motor" mode.
(D) spinning at high speeds.

10. Which of the following best describes the logical development of the selection?

(A) It mentions some technological challenges and describes some possible solutions.
(B) It identifies some technological problems and dismisses attempts to solve them.
(C) It outlines technological demands of an engineering application and minimizes their significance.
(D) It presents a history of a technological question but offers no answers.

13

Review

Answer Key

1. A	4. C	7. A	10. A
2. B	5. A	8. C	
3. C	6. D	9. B	

1. **(A)** This is a thesis or main-idea question. (A) correctly describes the passages, but it's worth remembering also that sometimes eliminating wrong choices can be just as effective as finding the right one. In this case, you can eliminate (C) and (D) because the passage is not "proof" or a "blueprint." And you can eliminate (B) because the author is not making such a comparison. Eliminating (B), (C), and (D) for those reasons gives you the same score as picking (A) directly.

2. **(B)** This is a development question that asks for an explanation of why the author does something. (In this case, the "because" does the job sometimes done by "why.") In the second paragraph, the author is discussing the first special problem associated with using EMBs in vehicles: gyroscopic effects. The author contrasts this application with the use of EMBs in stationary instruments. So "stationary" must be the key word, and that means "not moving." You can also figure this out by using the context: the turning vehicle poses problems. Well, a windmill doesn't move from its spot.

3. **(C)** This is a vocabulary-in-context question. In the second paragraph, the author is explaining how to set up the EMBs to

avoid the gyroscopic problems. So "orienting" means "aligning."

4. **(C)** This is an implication question. The author says that stored energy is a function of two factors: the mass of the wheel and the speed at which it spins. If a lighter-weight wheel has the same stored energy as a heavier one, then the lighter wheel has to be spinning faster.

5. **(A)** This is a vocabulary-in-context question. In the final paragraph, the author contrasts the failure of a metal wheel with the failure of a graphite fiber wheel. The metal wheel breaks into pieces of shrapnel with sharp edges; the fiber wheel doesn't. From the context, you can figure out that "amorphous" must mean lacking sharp edges, so "shapeless" is the best answer.

6. **(D)** This is an implication question. A flywheel stores energy by spinning, and the faster it spins, the more energy it stores. So if it is slowing down, it is losing energy.

7. **(A)** This is a vocabulary-in-context question. The breakdown of the fiber wheel does not result in the containment problem presented by the shrapnel created by a metal flywheel. So it must be less dangerous.

8. **(C)** This is an implication question—in particular, one that asks about the author's attitude. The author recognizes that there are problems with the new technology but thinks that solutions can be found. So (C) is the best description.

9. **(B)** This is a specific-detail question. In the second paragraph, the author offers this as one way of minimizing the gyroscopic effects of EMBs in cars.

10. **(A)** This is a development question that asks about the overall structure of the passage. The author introduces the idea of EMBs in the first paragraph and briefly describes how they work. Then, in the second paragraph, the author notes that, used in cars, EMBs pose special problems. One is the gyroscope problem that can be solved by mounting the flywheels vertically and spinning them in opposite directions. The other is the containment problem, which can be solved by using a graphite wheel. So (A) is the best description of the development of the selection.

Workshop C

10 Questions • Time—10 minutes

DIRECTIONS: The passage below is followed by 10 questions based on the content of the passage. Answer each question based upon what is *stated* or *implied* in the passage. Mark you answer choices in your book.

In 1848, gold was discovered in California, and newspapers quickly spread the word. President James K. Polk confirmed the discovery in his 1848 State of the Union
(5) message to Congress; the president's words and the knowledge that taking the precious metal was completely unregulated in California were enough to trigger the greatest national mass migration in U.S. history, and
(10) a global gold fever. People used their life savings, mortgaged their homes, sold everything they had to travel to California in hopes of becoming wealthy. At the time gold was discovered, there were approxi-
(15) mately 11,000 non-Native Americans living in California. Between the discovery and 1852, some 300,000 people, mostly young and male, traveled to California from all quarters.

(20)   Regardless of where the hopefuls came from, the months-long trip was perilous. A journey across the continent meant rough conditions and possibly attack by Indians or by other emigrants. Those com-
(25) ing by sea from Europe and the eastern United States had to travel around stormy Cape Horn. The sea journey could be shortened by going overland through the jungles of the Isthmus of Panama, but it
(30) was a region rife with cholera and other diseases. From San Francisco, getting to the mining areas was difficult. There was

13

little housing, disease was rampant, and prices for food were astronomically high.

(35)   There were tales of people finding thousands of dollars of gold in only a few weeks, but most miners just encountered hard times. To survive, some left mining or worked for wages in other men's opera-
(40) tions. The problem for many was that they couldn't afford to return home, and any news of other people striking it rich would renew hope. Many people lost, but a few lucky ones won. By 1860, approximately
(45) $600 million in gold had been mined— more than $10 billion in today's dollars.

1. In line 6, the word "precious" most nearly means

   (A) legal
   (B) scarce
   (C) beautiful
   (D) valuable

2. Why does the author mention that 300,000 people moved to California?

   (A) To demonstrate that many people became wealthy
   (B) To underscore the size of the migration
   (C) To show that they came from all over the world
   (D) To explain why so many miners failed to find gold

3. It can be inferred that some people mortgaged their homes in order to

   (A) get money to travel to California.
   (B) ensure a place to return to.
   (C) provide insurance against failure.
   (D) purchase gold from California.

4. It can be inferred that travelers who crossed the Isthmus of Panama

   (A) avoided the trip around Cape Horn.
   (B) generally came from the eastern U.S.
   (C) arrived in California after the gold rush.
   (D) paid less than others for their trip.

5. In line 30, the word "rife" most nearly means

   (A) devoid
   (B) filled
   (C) immune
   (D) suspected

6. The author mentions all of the following as difficulties facing travelers when they arrived in San Francisco except:

   (A) high food prices
   (B) a housing shortage
   (C) widespread disease
   (D) lack of work

7. In line 21, the word "perilous" most nearly means

   (A) dangerous
   (B) lengthy
   (C) uneventful
   (D) expensive

8. In line 41, "couldn't afford" most nearly means

   (A) weren't able to sell their gold
   (B) couldn't find transportation
   (C) didn't want
   (D) had no money

9. According to the selection, why did so many people move to California?

   (A) They hoped to become rich by mining gold.
   (B) The president encouraged them to go.
   (C) They wanted to open stores to sell goods to miners.
   (D) They had no homes of their own.

10. What is the main focus of the selection?

    (A) The California migration triggered by the discovery of gold
    (B) The conditions in San Francisco during the California gold rush
    (C) The various modes of transportation available during the mid-1800s
    (D) The demographic characteristics of the people who came to California

Review

Answer Key

1. D	4. A	7. A	10. A
2. B	5. B	8. D	
3. A	6. D	9. A	

1. **(D)** This is a vocabulary-in-context question. What was the major attraction of the gold? You could become rich. So "precious" must refer to the fact that gold is valuable.

2. **(B)** This is a development or structure question. *Why* does the author give you the 300,000 number? In order to compare it to the 11,000 and show in a dramatic fashion just how big the migration was.

3. **(A)** This is an implication question. A mortgage is a transaction whereby the owner of property borrows money and pledges the property to the lender as a guarantee of the loan. You don't need to know all this. You can figure out that it must have to do with getting money because the phrase "mortgaged their homes" appears in the sentence with "used their life savings" and "sold everything."

4. **(A)** This is an implication question. In the second paragraph, the author explains that the sea voyage took a route around Cape Horn. Travelers could shorten the trip by going overland through Panama. So you can infer that the overland route avoided the longer trip around Cape Horn.

5. **(B)** This is a vocabulary-in-context question. The author says that even the overland route was dangerous because of cholera and other diseases. They must have been abundant in the region.

6. **(D)** This is a specific-detail question. The author mentions (A), (B), and (C) in the last sentence of the second paragraph. But there is no mention of a "lack of work." (Indeed, the author implies that most people could find work, just not gold.)

13

7. **(A)** This is a vocabulary-in-context question. "Rough conditions," "attack," and "disease" all make it sound very dangerous.

8. **(D)** This is a vocabulary-in-context question. The author is explaining that many people failed, and you might expect that they would return home. But, the author says, they couldn't because they could not afford to do so. Given that many had sold everything to get to California in the first place, you can figure out that "afford" must mean able to pay for.

9. **(A)** This is a specific-detail question. The passage explains that the migration occurred because people thought they could become rich.

10. **(A)** This is a thesis or main-idea question. The focus of the question is the massive migration to California in response to the discovery of gold. The other ideas are mentioned in the selection, but they are details—not the main point.

Q & A Session

Q: **I felt more time pressure on one of the passages than on the others. Is that normal?**

A: Yes, and it can be attributable to a number of factors. Perhaps there was one passage you felt especially uncomfortable with because of the topic. Or perhaps you got off to a bad start on one and a particularly good start on another. Whatever the possible explanation, don't worry about it. Remember that the Reading on your TOEFL will include several passages to be done within an overall time limit (not like these workshops with a time limit for every passage). So, over the long haul, things should average out.

Q: **There are some questions that I miss, but I can't figure out why because the explanation makes perfect sense. What can I do?**

A: Be more careful. If you miss a question that later makes perfect sense to you when you review it, that means that it was not beyond your English ability. You missed it for another reason, usually lack of attention or excess speed.

HOUR 14

Reading WarmUp Test

What You'll Do This Hour

- Take the Reading WarmUp Test
- Evaluate Your Performance
- Q & A Session

Your Goals for This Hour

In this hour, you'll take the Reading WarmUp. After you finish, you'll evaluate your performance.

Your goals for this hour are

- Take the Reading WarmUp
- Score the WarmUp and evaluate your performance
- Get answers to frequently asked questions

Take the Reading WarmUp Test

48 Questions • Time—55 minutes

DIRECTIONS: In this part, you will read several passages. Each one is followed by questions based on the content of the passage. Choose the best answer to each question. Answer all questions based on what is *stated* or *implied* in that passage.

Questions 1–13

The buzzwords "information age" are widely used but often with only casual effort to unpack their meaning. For many, the term means little more than the fact
(5) that computers and associated technologies are implicated. Yet it is clear that we are in the throes of the third great transformation of human communication.

Before any form of communication
(10) was possible, there must have been human thought. We all have an experience of an inner life in which we look into our minds or reflect upon on our thoughts, but our inner thoughts are not, in and of them-
(15) selves, accessible to others. To be sure, a scream, a sigh, or a grunt may signal pain, satisfaction, or disapproval; but raw experience is not thought. Instead, what was needed was a system of symbols to ex-
(20) press thoughts in ways that were susceptible of understanding by others, that is, a code. Speech sounds represent cognitions; and as language has developed, increasing richness and subtlety of expression
(25) have become possible. With speech, the knowledge of individuals could not only be communicated, it could be accumulated, and so society began to acquire a common wisdom—stored usually in the
(30) brains of elders. By memorizing the accumulated knowledge and passing it on to successive generations by word of mouth, the product of human minds achieved a durability beyond the life of a
(35) single human.

The second transformation occurred with the development of a code that made use of graphic symbols to record speech. The earliest known use of graphics is the
(40) cave drawings of the Upper Paleolithic period, 30,000 to 10,000 B.C., but these drawings were not yet a primitive form of writing—only a way to represent important events in the same way as primitive
(45) music and dance. The first true use of graphic symbols to codify speech did not occur until around 3500 B.C., or about 500,000 years after humans evolved an oral tradition. The invention of the print-
(50) ing press, which made books, newspapers, magazines, and other printed matter available to everyone who could read, belongs to this second transformation.

We are now in the throes of a third
(55) transformation in communications, although when it began exactly is difficult to say. One might choose that evening of 1844 when Samuel Morse telegraphed the

message "What has God wrought!" Or
(60) possibly the invention by Charles Babbage
of the "Analytic Engine," a mechanical
device that prefigured the modern electronic computer. Or the ENIAC computer
developed during World War II—the first
(65) digital electronic computer. In any case,
it is estimated that it took about 150,000
years for human knowledge to first double,
then 1,500 years for it to double again, and
that it now doubles every 15 years or less.

1. What is the passage mainly about?

    (A) The beginning of the information
         age
    (B) Transformations in communication
    (C) The evolution of human speech
    (D) The transmission of knowledge

2. The passage is organized primarily as

    (A) an anthology.
    (B) a bibliography.
    (C) a chronology.
    (D) a typology.

3. According to the passage, pain, satisfac-
    tion, and disapproval are

    (A) basic thoughts.
    (B) word concepts.
    (C) raw experience.
    (D) psychological states.

4. Which of the following best describes the
    connection between a word and a thought?

    (A) The word represents the thought.
    (B) The word creates the thought.
    (C) The thought and word emerge
         together.
    (D) The thought echoes the word.

5. "Code" (line 22) most nearly means

    (A) system of symbols
    (B) accumulated knowledge
    (C) speech sounds
    (D) thought

6. "Common" (line 29) most nearly means

    (A) ordinary
    (B) shared
    (C) ancient
    (D) insignificant

7. In can be inferred that cave drawings oc-
    cupy a middle ground between

    (A) thought and word.
    (B) speech and writing.
    (C) writing and printing.
    (D) wisdom and computers.

8. According to the passage, graphic sym-
    bols were first used approximately how
    many years ago?

    (A) 150
    (B) 5,500
    (C) 10,000
    (D) 500,000

9. Which of the following is implied by the
    fourth paragraph?

    (A) Morse's telegraph and Babbage's
         Analytical Engine were forerunners
         of ENIAC.
    (B) Babbage's Analytical Engine was a
         more advanced version of Morse's
         telegraph.
    (C) ENIAC, like Babbage's Analytical
         Engine, was a mechanical comput-
         ing device.
    (D) Morse and Babbage developed
         ENIAC as a joint project.

14

10. The phrase "information age" (line 1) refers to

    (A) the world of prespeech.
    (B) the emergence of speech.
    (C) the invention of graphic symbols.
    (D) the third transformation.

11. If the author wished to discuss Egyptian hieroglyphics, the information should go into

    (A) Paragraph 1.
    (B) Paragraph 2.
    (C) Paragraph 3.
    (D) Paragraph 4.

12. What topic might the author logically take up next?

    (A) How humans evolved the physical capacity for speech
    (B) Why thought must exist before speech is possible
    (C) Where the earliest graphics symbols appeared on Earth
    (D) What the third transformation means for knowledge

13. The primary purpose of the passage is to

    (A) explain the significance of a phrase.
    (B) refute an accepted theory.
    (C) predict the course of the future.
    (D) propose a solution to a problem.

Questions 14–26

At the beginning of the nineteenth century, workers were differentiated by skill, income, and relative opportunities for advancement. The unskilled fared poorly.
(5) Laborers, weavers, and mill workers, who constituted perhaps 40 percent of the urban working class, received about a dollar per day. Skilled workers—variously known as craftsman, artisans, or mechan-
(10) ics—received nearly double that. The tools they owned and their proficiency in using them gave skilled workers marketable assets. Working independently or with others as journeymen in small shops directed
(15) by master craftsmen, who supervised the production of goods for a custom market, they could realistically anticipate becoming masters someday.

The technological and economical
(20) changes of the nineteenth century had a marked impact on American workers. Improvements in turnpikes or toll roads gave way to "canal fever" accompanied by the appearance of steamboats and, in the
(25) 1830s and 1840s, railroads. The resulting sharp reduction in transportation costs enabled sellers to compete successfully in distant markets, opening up great profit-making opportunities to efficient
(30) large-scale manufacturers. Limited custom-order and local trade gave way to a massive national market, inevitably affecting the conditions of the workers who produced for this market.

(35) Merchants increasingly assumed control not only over the sale of goods but also over their production. Their possession of substantial capital and easy access to credit enabled them to contract for mas-
(40) sive orders all over the country. The size of their operations enabled them to cut prices below those fixed by masters and journeymen.

On the surface, little seemed to have
(45) changed. In the typical shop the master was still the chief, and the craftsmen he

presided over still owned their tools. Their style of work in many cases differed little from what it had been in the eighteenth cen-
(50) tury. But now the merchant capitalist supplied the raw materials and owned and marketed the finished product made in the shop. The masters became small contractors employed by the merchant capitalist and, in
(55) turn, employing one to a dozen journeymen. Since the profits of masters came solely out of wages and work, they sought to lessen dependence on skill and to increase speed of output. To increase profits,
(60) masters demanded greater productivity from skilled workers and resorted to cheaper labor—prisoners, women, children, and the unskilled. Under the increasing economic pressure, the apprentice system
(65) eventually broke down.

14. What is the passage primarily concerned with?

(A) Compensation paid to laborers
(B) Changes in working conditions
(C) Development of transportation
(D) Categorizing workers by jobs

15. Which of the following was *not* a skilled worker?

(A) Mechanic
(B) Artisan
(C) Craftsman
(D) Weaver

16. Which of the following did not separate the skilled worker from the unskilled worker?

(A) Geographical location of the workplace
(B) Ownership of the tools of the trade

(C) Ability to use tools to make goods
(D) Prospect of advancement within the trade

17. "Proficiency" (line 11) most nearly means

(A) effort
(B) skill
(C) direction
(D) independence

18. The possibility of filling orders for a national market was due to

(A) changed conditions for all workers.
(B) new machinery for producing goods.
(C) advances in modes of transportation.
(D) decreased demand for local goods.

19. Which of the following did *not* contribute to the rise of the merchants?

(A) Easy access to credit
(B) Cheaper transportation
(C) Shortage of skilled labor
(D) Control over substantial capital

20. "Their" (line 37) refers to

(A) unskilled workers
(B) merchants
(C) masters
(D) journeymen

21. Masters who were under contract to merchants replaced skilled workers in order to

(A) reduce the cost of labor.
(B) lower the cost of materials.
(C) raise the price of finished goods.
(D) obtain local orders.

14

22. According to the passage, the most important change in the structure of the workplace was

   (A) the hierarchy of workers.
   (B) style of working.
   (C) ownership of tools.
   (D) financial arrangement.

23. What can be inferred about a typical shop at the beginning of the nineteenth century?

   (A) Masters owned all the tools.
   (B) Masters supplied raw material and sold finished goods.
   (C) Unskilled workers competed against skilled workers.
   (D) Finished goods had to be shipped long distances.

24. The "apprentice system" (line 64) refers to the

   (A) organization of workers according to skill and experience.
   (B) practice of paying skilled workers more than unskilled ones.
   (C) classification of industry by goods produced.
   (D) division of markets into local, custom, and national.

25. The passage is primarily concerned to

   (A) analyze an economic development.
   (B) argue for social reform.
   (C) encourage the use of skilled labor.
   (D) describe manufacturing processes.

26. The following sentence can be added to the passage.

   While the dollar of 1800 was worth at least seven or eight times as much as that of today, the wages of unskilled labor were too low to maintain a decent living.

Where is the most logical place to put it?

   (A) After "day" and before "Skilled" in line 8
   (B) After "workers" and before "Improvements" in line 21
   (C) After "changed" and before "In" in line 45
   (D) After "output" and before "To" in line 59

Questions 27–37

Fractur is a uniquely American folk art rooted in the Pennsylvania Dutch (Pennsylvania German) culture. In German, fraktur refers to a particular typeface used (5) by printers. Derived from the Latin fractura, a "breaking apart," fraktur suggests that the letters are broken apart and reassembled into designs. Fraktur as a genre of folk art refers to a text (usually (10) religious) that is decorated with symbolic designs.

Fraktur was primarily a private art dealing with the role of the individual in Pennsylvania Dutch society and its various rites (15) of passage: birth and baptism; puberty and schooling; courtship and marriage; and death and funeral rites. Special fraktur documents were associated with each: the Taufschein or Birth-Baptismal Certificate, (20) the Vorschrift for the student, the Trauschein for marriage, and the Denkmal or Memorial. Of these, the Taufschein and the Vorshrift are the most numerous. Wedding and death certificates are rare because (25) of the availability of alternative forms of memorialization: the wedding plate with its humorous inscription and the engraved tombstone.

In Pennsylvania during the early (30) settlement era, fraktur art flowered, at least in part, to fill an artistic vacuum that existed in the everyday world of the Pennsylvania Dutch farmer. While fraktur were produced by folk artists, these were (35) not studio artists producing public art for a wealthy clientele, but individuals who, in addition to their major occupation, produced private art for individuals. The great majority were either ministers in the (40) Lutheran or Reformed Church or schoolmasters in parochial schools. Because of the close association with religious life, fraktur was permitted as an art form in a culture that frowned upon public display (45) in general. As art, fraktur both delights the eye and refreshes the spirit with its bright colors, ingenious combination of text and pictures, and symbols drawn from folk culture. For example, mermaids (50) were often put on baptismal certificates to represent water spirits that, in Germanic mythology, were believed to deliver newborns to midwives who then took them to their waiting mothers. Still, (55) though art, fraktur was rarely displayed even in the home. Instead, it was usually kept in Bibles or other large books, pasted onto the inside lids of blanket chests, or rolled up in bureau drawers.

(60)   Fraktur is uniquely Pennsylvania Dutch, but manuscript art did develop in other American sectarian groups. The New England Puritans decorated family registers, the Shakers produced "spirit (65) drawings," and the Russian-German Mennonites created *Zierschriften* or ornamental writings.

27. What is the passage primarily about?

   (A) German influences on American art
   (B) Fraktur art of the Pennsylvania Dutch
   (C) Symbolism in German mythology
   (D) American manuscript folk art

28. By "private art" the author means that fraktur

   (A) were created by individual artists.
   (B) commemorated the lives of individuals.
   (C) exhibit Germanic influences.
   (D) were a form of manuscript art.

29. The wedding plate and the engraved tombstone correspond to the

   (A) *Taufschein* and *Vorschrift.*
   (B) *Taufschein* and *Trauschein.*
   (C) *Vorschrift* and *Denkmal.*
   (D) *Trauschein* and *Denkmal.*

30. "Flowered" (line 30) most nearly means

   (A) exhibited bright colors
   (B) served a useful function
   (C) grew and spread vigorously
   (D) challenged conventional wisdom

31. It can be inferred that the "artistic vacuum" (line 31) existed in part because

   (A) public displays of art were discouraged.
   (B) few people had real artistic talent.
   (C) fraktur art was primarily private art.
   (D) artistic resources were in short supply.

14

32. A mermaid symbol would be most likely to appear on a
    (A) *Denkmal*
    (B) *Trauschein*
    (C) *Taufschein*
    (D) *Vorschrift*

33. Which of the following is *not* a common characteristic of fraktur art?
    (A) Humorous inscriptions
    (B) Bright colors
    (C) Text and pictures
    (D) Folk symbols

34. The last sentence of the third paragraph serves further to demonstrate that fraktur
    (A) derived primarily from German roots.
    (B) was largely a private art form.
    (C) combined both text and pictures.
    (D) is uniquely American.

35. It can be inferred that the Puritans, the Shakers, and the Mennonites
    (A) were sectarian groups.
    (B) produced fraktur art.
    (C) emigrated from Germany.
    (D) were Lutheran or Reformed.

36. The following sentence can be placed in the passage.

    In fact, in Europe and also in Pennsylvania, the earlier word for such pieces of art was *Frakturschriften* or "Fraktur Writings."

    What is the most appropriate location?
    (A) The last sentence of the first paragraph
    (B) The last sentence of the second paragraph
    (C) The first sentence of the third paragraph
    (D) The last sentence of the third paragraph

37. Which of the following topics would be a logical continuation for the passage?
    (A) A discussion of the wedding plate and engraved tombstone
    (B) A biographical sketch of a typical Pennsylvania Dutch family
    (C) An analysis of the similarities between fraktur art and other manuscript art
    (D) A listing of well-known Pennsylvania Dutch fraktur folk artists

Questions 38–48

Lightning is basically an electrical discharge of immense proportions. Some 80 percent of lightning occurs within clouds; about 20 percent is cloud-to-ground light-
(5) ning; and an extremely small percentage is cloud-to-sky lightning.

Cloud-to-ground lightning begins when complex meteorological processes cause a tremendous electrostatic charge to build
(10) up within a cloud. Typically, the bottom of the cloud is negatively charged. When the charge reaches 50 to 100 million volts, air is no longer an effective insulator, and lightning occurs within the cloud itself.
(15) Ten to 30 minutes after the onset of intracloud lightning, negative charges called stepped leaders emerge from the bottom of the cloud, moving toward the Earth in 50-meter intervals at speeds of 100
(20) to 200 kilometers per second and creating an ionized channel. As the leaders near the

Earth, their strong electric field causes streamers of positively charged ions to develop at the tips of pointed objects con-
(25) nected directly or indirectly to the ground. These positively charged streamers flow upward.

When the distance, known as the striking distance, between a stepped leader and
(30) one of the streamers reaches 30 to 100 meters, the intervening air breaks down completely and the leader is joined to the Earth via the streamer. Now a pulse of current known as a return stroke, ranging
(35) from thousands to hundreds of thousands of amperes, moves at one-tenth to one-third the speed of light from the Earth through the object from which the streamer emanated and up the ionized
(40) channel to the charge center within the cloud. An ionized channel remains in the air and additional negative charges called dart leaders will quickly move down this path, resulting in further return strokes. It
(45) is this multiplicity that causes the flash to flicker. The entire event typically lasts about one second.

The return stroke's extremely high temperature creates the visible lightning and
(50) produces thunder by instantly turning moisture into steam. Most direct damage results from the heavy return stroke current because it produces high temperatures in the channel or from arcing at the point
(55) of ground contact. If the lightning current is carried by an enclosed conductor (for example, within a jacketed cable, through a concrete wall, or beneath a painted sur-face), entrapped moisture is turned into
(60) high-pressure steam that can cause a cable,

wall, or painted object to explode. Arcing frequently ignites combustibles.

Lightning causes hundreds of millions of dollars in property losses annually and
(65) the majority of forest fires. Lightning is also the leading weather-related killer in the U.S., causing from 100 to 200 deaths each year.

38. The passage is primarily
   (A) an explanation of the physics of lightning.
   (B) a description of weather conditions.
   (C) an analysis of when and where lightning will strike.
   (D) a discussion of a theory of electrical conductivity.

39. The passage talks mainly about what kind of lightning?
   (A) Cloud-to-ground
   (B) Cloud-to-cloud
   (C) Cloud-to-sky
   (D) Sky-to-cloud

40. Which of the following is *not* true of stepped leaders?
   (A) They are positively charged.
   (B) They emerge from the bottom of a cloud.
   (C) They move in 50-meter intervals.
   (D) They progress at 100 to 200 kilometers per second.

41. "Intracloud" means
   (A) between clouds.
   (B) within a cloud.
   (C) from cloud to sky.
   (D) from ground to cloud.

14

42. The striking distance is the distance between

(A) the ground and the cloud.
(B) a stepped leader and a dart leader.
(C) a dart leader and a return stroke.
(D) a steamer and a stepped leader.

43. The flickering appearance of a lightning
strike is created by

(A) the stepped movement of leaders.
(B) multiple return strokes.
(C) water being vaporized.
(D) arcing at ground contact.

44. Which of the following is *not* true of dart
leaders?

(A) They are negatively charged.
(B) They precede the initial return
stroke.
(C) They move down the ionized
channel.
(D) They trigger secondary return
strokes.

45. According to the passage, lightning damage is most often caused by

(A) stepped leaders.
(B) streamers.
(C) dart leaders.
(D) return strokes.

46. The following sentence can be added to
the passage.

These objects may include pine needles,
blades of grass, towers, raised golf clubs,
and human heads.

Where is the most appropriate point for
its inclusion?

(A) After "cloud" and before "Typically" (line 10)
(B) After "ground" and before "These"
(line 25)
(C) After "streamer" and before "Now"
(line 33)
(D) As the last sentence of paragraph 3

47. The passage answers which of the following questions?

(A) How does lightning cause the
associated thunder?
(B) How much energy is discharged by
a lightning strike?
(C) How frequently will lightning strike
a given object?
(D) How long does it take a cloud to
build up an electrostatic charge?

48. What topic might the author logically address in a continuation of the passage?

(A) Precautions to minimize lightning
damage
(B) Other weather phenomena that
cause injury
(C) Basic principles governing electricity
(D) Identifying different types of clouds

Evaluate Your Performance

Answer Key

1. B	13. A	25. A	37. C
2. C	14. B	26. A	38. A
3. C	15. D	27. B	39. A
4. A	16. A	28. B	40. A
5. A	17. B	29. D	41. B
6. B	18. C	30. C	42. D
7. B	19. C	31. A	43. B
8. B	20. C	32. C	44. B
9. A	21. A	33. A	45. D
10. D	22. D	34. B	46. B
11. C	23. B	35. A	47. A
12. D	24. A	36. A	48. A

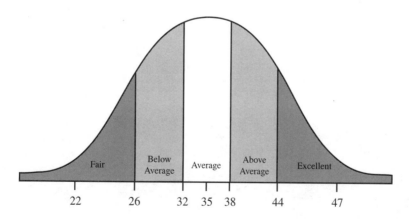

14

Q & A Session

Q: **Even now, I seem to have some trouble finishing under the time limit. Is there anything more I can do?**

A: Just make sure that you finish all the questions in the Reading part. While you don't want to miss questions due to carelessness, on balance your score will be better if you answer every item—even if you guess. If you're barely finishing, that's okay. But if you're running out of time, speed up.

HOUR 15

Review the Reading WarmUp Test

What You'll Do This Hour

- Review the Reading WarmUp Test
- Q & A Session

Your Goals for This Hour

In this hour, you'll review the Reading WarmUp by going over explanations for each of the items in the WarmUp that you took last hour.

Your goals for this hour are:

- Review the Reading WarmUp
- Get answers to frequently asked questions

Review the Reading WarmUp Test

Here are the explanations for the Reading WarmUp that you took last hour.

1. **(B)** The author begins by saying that people don't really understand the broader significance of the term "information." The passage then goes on to describe three successive transformations in human communications: speech, writing, electronic communications.

2. **(C)** The passage is organized historically or chronologically in the beginning there was thought without speech; then speech emerged and gave rise to communication and knowledge; then writing was invented; and now we have computers and electronic communications.

3. **(C)** In paragraph 2, the author states that screams, signs, and grunts are signals of raw experience—not thought.

4. **(A)** In paragraph 2, the author states that speech is a system of symbols that expresses private throughts.

5. **(A)** In that sentence, the author uses the phrase "that is" to signal that another way of describing the system of symbols is "code."

6. **(B)** The common wisdom is the wisdom of individuals that is stored in a single person's brain. So in this context, common means derived from all or shared.

7. **(B)** The second paragraph describes the emergence of thought, and the third paragraph describes the invention of writing. Cave drawings came after speech but before writing and were not, according to the author, full-fledged writing.

8. **(B)** The passage states that true graphic symbols or writing first appeared around 3,500 B.C.—or about 5,500 years ago.

9. **(A)** One way of getting the answer to this question is the word "prefigured." It tells you that the Morse telegraph and the Babbage "Analytic Machine" were earlier variations on the theme Or you might pick up on the fact that the telegraph is electronic, the Babbage machine a computing device, and the ENIAC an electronic computing device.

10. **(D)** Although the phrase "information age" appears in line 1, it is not discussed until the last paragraph. Remember that the author begins by saying that most people don't understand the real significance of the term. Paragraphs 2, 3, and 4 give the history needed to appreciate what the term really means.

11. **(C)** Hieroglyphics are a form of writing, so any information about that step in the development of communications belongs in the paragraph on writing.

12. **(D)** The development of the passage is chronological: speech, writing, then electronic communications. And in the second and third paragraphs, the author comments on the significance of each step in terms of human knowledge (stored common

wisdom and wider dissemination of knowledge). So it would be appropriate for the author to address that topic, a move that would also tie the passage up by further explaining the significance of the phrase "information age"—which was the starting point.

13. **(A)** The author notes that most people do not understand the real significance of the phrase "electronic communication" and goes on to unpack its significance.

14. **(B)** The passage first describes conditions at the beginning of the nineteenth century. It then goes on to talk about changes to the way that manufacturing shops were set up. The final paragraph explains the breakdown of the old system. So the passage is primarily concerned with the changes that occured to the labor market.

15. **(D)** Mechanic, artisan, and craftsman are mentioned in paragraph 1 as skilled workers. Weavers, however, are mentioned as an example of unskilled factory labor.

16. **(A)** Paragraph 1 describes the important features of the manufacturing system: skilled workers owned their own tools, they knew how to use them, and they could expect to move up the ladder. Location is not mentioned.

17. **(B)** The first paragraph distinguishes skilled and unskilled workers and describes the important characteristics of skilled workers. One of those characteristics was the ability to use the tools of the trade. So proficiency must mean skill.

18. **(C)** In the second paragraph, the author explains that the revolution in transporation lowered transportation costs and opened up national markets.

19. **(C)** In the third paragraph, the author explains that a new class—the merchant class—took control over the means of production. They were able to do so because they controlled capital, had access to credit, and could use the new transportation to fill orders in distant markets. The passage does not say, however, that a *cause* of this was a decline in labor skills. (Perhaps the collapse of the apprenticeship system lead to a decline in skills, but that is another matter.)

20. **(C)** In the final paragraph, the author is describing the result of the restructuring: the master became a small contractor. So "their" in this line refers to "masters."

21. **(A)** As the third paragraph explains, a masters compensation came from the price paid by the merchant less the cost of production. Since the merchant controlled the cost of the raw material, a master had control only over the cost of labor. So in order to increase profit, a master would try to lower the cost of labor.

22. **(D)** The opening sentence of the last paragraph notes that "on the surface" things seemed pretty much the same: the master was still in charge, the workers owned tools, and so on. What caused all of this to change? A profound change in the financial structure of the relationship between master and merchant.

23. **(B)** In the traditional shop, workers owned their tools and produced goods under the direction of the master for a specialty market. Under the new system, while workers still owned their tools and worked for a master, they produced goods for more general market. But in both cases, the master controlled the production and, it can be inferred, the raw materials.

24. **(A)** The "apprentice system" refers to the traditional organization that is the subject of the passage.

25. **(A)** The passage is primarily concerned with explaining how and why the traditional apprenticeship system changed.

26. **(A)** The sentence could be added to help the reader better understand the situation of laborers, but it needs to go in the place where the author is discussing wages.

27. **(B)** The passage is mainly about fraktur, a uniquely Pennsyvania Dutch form of folk art.

28. **(B)** In the second paragraph, the author explains that the purpose of fraktur was to commemorate important moments in an individual's life. This is to be seen in contrast to art intended primarily for public viewing.

29. **(D)** According to the second paragraph, the *Trauschein* was a fraktur to commemorate a marriage and the *Denkmal* a fraktur of rememberance.

30. **(C)** In this context, flowered means flourished or grew vigorously. A good clue is the juxtaposition of the word with "vacuum." In other words, there was little else in the way of art, but frakturs filled in the space.

31. **(A)** The phrase "frowned upon" means to disapprove or to discourage. So public displays were discouraged. Consequently, fraktur art was used to satisfy the artistic impulse.

32. **(C)** The *Taufschein* was the certificate for birth, and it was birth that would be symbolized by the mermaid or other water spirit.

33. **(A)** The humorous inscription is mentioned in paragraph two as a characteristic of a wedding plate—not a manuscript fraktur. The other characteristics are specifically mentioned by the author.

34. **(B)** Look closely at the list of locations where the fraktur might have been kept: in an important book, in a chest with bed linens, or in a bureau drawer. All are very private places and not open to public view.

35. **(A)** The author says that other sectarian groups also developed manuscript art and then lists the three mentioned here.

36. **(A)** If the sentence is to be inserted into the passage, it must go with the discussion of the origin of the word fraktur, and that is in the first paragraph.

37. **(C)** In the final paragraph, the author notes that other sectarian groups also produced manuscript art but adds that these were not frakturs. A natural extension of the passage then would be a comparison of fraktur art with other forms of manuscript folk art.

38. **(A)** The passage is primarily a description of the physical process that occurs when lightning strikes.

39. **(A)** Although the passage identifies three different types of lightning (cloud-to-cloud, cloud-to-ground, and cloud-to-sky), it focuses on cloud-to-ground, mentioning cloud-to-cloud only as a step in the sequence of events leading up to a lightning strike.

40. **(A)** Everything you need to answer this question is in the second paragraph. The author says that stepped leaders are negatively charged.

41. **(B)** Intra- is a prefix meaning within, so intracloud must mean within the same cloud. You could also deduce this by the juxtaposition of sentences three and four in the second paragraph.

42. **(D)** Striking distance is defined in the first sentence of the third paragraph.

43. **(B)** The last two sentences of the third paragraph answer this question: multiple

return strokes occur, and they give the appearance of flickering.

44. **(B)** The third paragraph is where you will find the discussion of dart leaders. There the author says they come after the initial return strong.

45. **(D)** This idea is explicitly stated in the fourth paragraph.

46. **(B)** "These objects" must refer to the pointed objects that direct the streamers, so the sentence should immediately follow that one.

47. **(A)** Paragraph 4 explains that it is the sudden vaporization of water into steam that causes the thunder clap. The other questions are not answered by the text.

48. **(A)** The final paragraph of the passage talks about the damage that is done by lightning. Having explained the mechanics of the lightning process and having noted that lightning causes damage, a good next step would be to tell the reader how to minimize the danger posed by lightning.

15

Q & A Session

Q: Will the computerized TOEFL be very much different from what I've been doing?

A: Obviously, there will be some important differences, but most of them won't make a difference. For example, on the computerized version, you won't lose time coding spaces on an answer sheet because you just "point and click." On the other hand, you do lose time on Reading when you have to scroll up or down to read the passage. You don't have that problem with a paper booklet. Don't let these things worry you; they all balance out.

Q: What about those "gimmick" questions?

A: The computer format gives the TOEFL writers some room to play around with different question formats. For example, they can give you a picture of a painting if the passage is about art. Or they can ask you to place a sentence in the passage by pointing and clicking instead of naming where it ought to go. (As we did with question 26 in the WarmUp, for example.) But again, they are careful to design things so that the gimmicks won't affect your score.

Part IV

Listening Questions

HOUR 16

Test Your Listening Skills

What You'll Do This Hour

- Preview the Listening Comprehension PreTest
- Take the Listening Comprehension PreTest
- Evaluate Your Performance
- Q & A Session

Your Goals for This Hour

Today, you'll take the Listening Comprehension PreTest, evaluate your performance, and make a judgment about where you stand. You'll also review the scripts of the Listening Comprehension and check the correct answers to the items used in the PreTest as a first step in your in-depth study of Listening Comprehension questions.

Your goals for this hour are

- Get ready to take the Listening Comprehension PreTest
- Take the Listening Comprehension PreTest under testing conditions
- Score the PreTest and evaluate your performance
- Review the correct answers

 NOTE   You can find all the scripts printed in Appendix A.

Preview the Listening Comprehension PreTest

The TOEFL uses the two different kinds of Listening Comprehension questions you learned about in Hour 1. You'll find these same kinds of questions in this hour's Listening Comprehension PreTest.

Short Conversations

Short conversations are brief verbal exchanges between two people. After the exchange, you'll hear a question that asks about the conversation. (The conversations and questions are *not* repeated.) Choose the best answer to the question. Here's an example:

[You'll hear]

Man: I wanted to show you something, but now I've forgotten what it was.

Woman: You said it was a photograph from your vacation and that it's in your pocket.

    Narrator: What will the man probably do?

         (A) Take the photograph from his pocket and show it to the woman.

         (B) Remember to take more photographs on his next vacation.

         (C) Have a copy made of the photograph and send it to the woman later.

         (D) Show the woman everything he has in his pocket.

    Correct answer: **(A)**

Longer Conversations and Talks

Longer conversations and talks are based upon extended verbal exchanges and followed by several questions. Here is an example:

Man: Let's go to the new restaurant that just opened on Main Street. It got a good review in last weekend's newspaper.

Woman: That's a good idea. I hear that it serves some very nice seafood dishes.

Man: My friend Mark ate there yesterday and had steamed lobster. The waiter took it right from a tank in the dining room and into the kitchen.

Woman: I don't know if I could eat a lobster that I saw swimming around in a tank. I'll probably have to order something like broiled fish.

Narrator: What do the man and the woman plan to do?

      (A) Visit an aquarium.

      (B) Have dinner with Mark.

      (C) Write a restaurant review.

      (D) Eat at a new restaurant.

Correct answer: **(D)**

Narrator: The woman says that she will not have lobster because

      (A) she doesn't like the taste.

      (B) the lobster might not be fresh.

      (C) she'll see it while it is alive.

      (D) her friend doesn't like lobster.

Correct answer: **(C)**

Talks are like excerpts from a lecture.

Take the Listening Comprehension PreTest

DIRECTIONS: The Listening component of the TOEFL consists of two different kinds of listening exercises: Short conversations (Part A) and talks (Part B).

Part A: Short Conversations

In a short conversation, you will listen to brief conversations between two people. Then you will hear a third person ask a question about what is said or implied by the speakers in the conversations.

The topics of short conversations concern student life. They might be about living arrangements, scheduling recreational activities, completing homework assignments, and similar topics. The speakers have many different reasons for speaking with each other, such as seeking advice, asking for information, or arranging schedules.

Some questions may ask you to select a paraphrase of what a speaker has said. Other questions may ask you to draw a further inference from the conversation.

Part B: Talks and Longer Conversations

Talks and longer conversations are about a variety of common topics that university students might encounter. For example, two students may be discussing a final examination, getting information from the library, or buying a train ticket. Or a talk might be a professor lecturing or leading a classroom discussion.

Following each talk or longer conversation are questions about the content of the exchange.

You will hear each conversation or talk *only once,* and the text is *not* displayed on the monitor screen.

For each question, choose the best answer, and indicate your response.

NOTE These questions reference Script 2 in Appendix A. Visit www.cambridgereview.com for audio transcripts.

Part A: Short Conversations

In this part, you will hear short conversations between two people. After each conversation, you will hear a question about the conversation. The conversations and questions *will not* be repeated. After you hear a question, read the answers and choose the best one.

Example

You'll hear:

Man: I missed the weather on the radio this morning.

Woman: The forecast wasn't certain, but I decided to carry an umbrella with me anyway.

Narrator: What does the woman imply?

    ✗(A) The forecast said it might rain.

    (B) No forecast was broadcast that morning.

(C) Weather is reported in the evening.

(D) The umbrella belongs to the man.

Sample Answer: **(A)**

You learn from the Dialogue that the man did not hear the morning weather forecast. The woman, however, did; and, based upon that information, she decided to carry an umbrella. You can infer, therefore, that the forecast mentioned the possibility of rain.

16

1.

(A) Turn down the volume of the television.

(B) Change the channel on the television.

(C) Begin looking for a new apartment.

(D) Watch more television in the future.

2.

(A) Tuition for school

(B) A sale on clothing

(C) A telephone bill

(D) Vacation plans

3.

(A) She doesn't like shopping.

(B) She doesn't have a light bulb.

(C) She doesn't know how to change a bulb.

(D) She prefers to eat in the dark.

4.

(A) He's not feeling well.

(B) He doesn't want to go.

(C) He has other plans.

(D) He's been to many clubs.

5.

(A) She earns a lot of money.

(B) Four hundred dollars is inexpensive.

(C) She can't afford to spend that much.

(D) She can borrow the money from friends.

6.

(A) The company's business is doing very well.

(B) She has mixed feelings about her new job.

(C) Most people would be very pleased with a new job.

(D) She is looking for a better job and will move soon.

7.

(A) The woman is an experienced hiker.

(B) The woman did not wear shoes while hiking.

(C) The woman will not go hiking again.

(D) The woman's shoes caused blisters.

8.

(A) The man had a difficult day.

(B) The man doesn't know how to cook.

(C) The man doesn't like what she cooked.

(D) The man is not hungry.

9.

(A) She will be able to tutor the man in elementary statistics.

(B) Professor Johnson does not plan to teach a seminar this semester.

(C) A course in elementary statistics should be required of every student.

(D) The man would probably find statistics useful in the seminar.

10.
- (A) Buy new drapes for the living room.
- (B) Paint the ceiling before hanging the drapes.
- (C) Hire a professional painter to do the ceiling.
- (D) Ask the woman to help him paint the ceiling.

11.
- (A) She changed her mind about offering a course in Medieval English.
- (B) She will offer a course in Medieval English next semester.
- (C) Her course in Medieval English has already been filled.
- (D) Medieval English is not her teaching speciality.

12.
- (A) No flights are leaving New York for Washington, D.C. that day.
- (B) The fare for the shuttle flight is very expensive.
- (C) Only passengers who arrive early will get seats on the flight.
- (D) It is not necessary to make a reservation for the shuttle flight.

13.
- (A) John should have planned the work on his paper more carefully.
- (B) Footnotes are not a required feature of the Sociology term paper.
- (C) John is afraid that the professor will not like the topic he's chosen.
- (D) Professor Williams made a late change in the due date of the papers.

14.
- (A) Read the article that the woman is copying.
- (B) Help the woman make a copy of the article.
- (C) Use one of the copy machines in the basement.
- (D) Leave without making the copies he needs.

Part B

In this part, you will hear longer exchanges. After each exchange you will be given two or three questions. Read the answer choices and choose the best one.

15. The conversation is mainly about
- (A) the wedding plans of Bob's cousin.
- (B) the assignments for Monday's classes.
- (C) Bob's travel plans for the weekend.
- (D) Mary's knowledge of the Boston area.

16. Which of the following does Mary consider to be advantages of the bus over the train?
- I. The Cost of a Ticket
- II. The Availability of Refreshments
- III. Frequency of Schedule
- IV. Quality of the Ride

(A) I and II
(B) I and III
(C) II and III
(D) III and IV

17. What will the man probably do next?

(A) Obtain schedule information.
(B) Purchase a train ticket.
(C) Cancel plans to go to Boston.
(D) Invite Mary to go to Boston.

18. The student's assignment is to

(A) learn about legislative hearings conducted by Congressional committees.
(B) report on the procedures followed by the U.S. Government Printing Office.
(C) prepare a paper on steps by which proposed legislation becomes law.
(D) compare laws on health care with laws on education or foreign affairs.

19. According to the librarian, a library that holds many but not all government publications is a

(A) partial depository.
(B) printing office.
(C) Congressional library.
(D) computerized library.

20. Put the following research steps in the order recommended by the librarian:

 I. Choose a piece of legislation.
 II. Select a topic.
 III. Return to the librarian.
 IV. Generate a printout.

(A) I, II, III, IV
(B) I, II, IV, III

(C) II, I, III, IV
(D) II, I, IV, III

21. The professor asks the student to return next week in order to

(A) learn more about the student's roommate from Afghanistan.
(B) give a quiz that will count toward a final grade in the course.
(C) discuss what topics should be taught in the course.
(D) determine whether the student knows enough to take the course.

22. According to the professor, which of the following topics will be studied in the course?

 I. The war between Afghanistan and the Soviet Union.
 II. The importance of Afghanistan as world energy provider.
 III. The conditions in which the Taliban came to power.
 IV. The fall of the Kabul government.

(A) I and II
(B) I and III
(C) II and IV
(D) III and IV

23. It can be inferred that

(A) this is the first meeting between the professor and the student.
(B) the professor knows the student's roommate from Afghanistan.
(C) the student has taken a course with the professor before.
(D) the student is not currently enrolled in the university.

24. According to the lecture, changing land use from farms to housing can cause an increase in

   (A) localized storm activity.
   (B) water runoff.
   (C) timber harvesting.
   (D) a river's drainage basin.

25. The lecture implies that the chance of a five-year flood in any given year is about

   (A) 1%
   (B) 5%
   (C) 20%
   (D) 25%

26. Match the season of the year with the likely cause of flooding:

   (A) Season   Cause
       Spring   Frontal Storms
       Summer   Cyclones
       Winter   Thunderstorms
   (B) Season   Cause
       Spring   Cyclones
       Summer   Frontal Storms
       Winter   Thunderstorms
   (C) Season   Cause
       Spring   Thunderstorms
       Summer   Frontal Storms
       Winter   Cyclones
   (D) Season   Cause
       Spring   Thunderstorms
       Summer   Cyclones
       Winter   Frontal Storms

27. The professor implies that floods are

   (A) completely predictable.
   (B) almost completely predictable.
   (C) somewhat predictable.
   (D) completely unpredictable.

28. What is the main point of the lecture?

   (A) The United States has many gangs.
   (B) Many youths are gang members.
   (C) Gang membership leads to crime.
   (D) At-risk youths don't commit crimes.

29. Statistics on which criminal activities show that gang membership leads to violent crimes?

   I. Drive-by Shootings
   II. Gun Ownership
   III. Automobile Theft
   IV. Drug-Selling

   (A) I and II
   (B) I and III
   (C) II and III
   (D) II and IV

30. According to the professor, the United States has approximately how many gangs?

   (A) 6,000
   (B) 16,000
   (C) 500,000
   (D) 600,000

31. According to the professor, what might prevent at-risk youths from joining gangs?

   (A) Making violent behavior illegal.
   (B) Creating for them a sense of belonging.
   (C) Explaining that gang membership is dangerous.
   (D) Putting gang members in jail.

32. The lecture is primarily about

   (A) Evolution of species
   (B) Circadian rhythms
   (C) Human biological clocks
   (D) Chemicals in bacteria

33. According to the researchers, concentrations of chemicals associated with kaiABC

    (A) increased during the day and decreased at night.

    (B) decreased during the day and increased at night.

    (C) increased during the day and during the night.

    (D) remained the same during the day and the night.

34. It can be inferred that circadian rhythms in bacteria are controlled by

    (A) kaiABC cells

    (B) proteins

    (C) Seiko watches

    (D) light bulbs

35. The lecture is primarily about

    (A) the workings of world financial markets.

    (B) the need to attract foreign investment.

    (C) recent events on the New York Stock Exchange.

    (D) a rise and fall of the stock market 100 years ago.

36. The Northern Pacific Corner was remarkable because

    (A) large syndicates were unable to maintain stock prices.

    (B) members of the financial public invested in the company.

    (C) stock prices rose very rapidly in a short time.

    (D) relatively few shares of stock were sold.

37. According to the lecture, the unprecedented availability of capital was due to what factors?

    I. Rising prices in the stock market

    II. Pledges by syndicates of credit

    III. Excellent harvest in the United States

    IV. Favorable exports of manufactured goods

16

    (A) I and II

    (B) I and III

    (C) II and III

    (D) III and IV

38. The main purpose of the discussion is to

    (A) outline the history of the study of folklore.

    (B) identify some important folk artists.

    (C) refine the definition of fine art.

    (D) define what constitutes folklore.

39. The professor concludes by saying that

    (A) folklore cannot be the object of scholarship.

    (B) the study of folklore is a type of scholarship.

    (C) scholarship should focus exclusively on fine art.

    (D) folklore and fine art cannot be distinguished.

40. The term *folklore* was coined by

    (A) George Balanchine

    (B) T.S. Eliot

    (C) Martha Graham

    (D) William J. Thomas

Evaluate Your Performance

Use the answer key to check your work. Then total the number of questions you answered correctly and evaluate your performance, using the graph below.

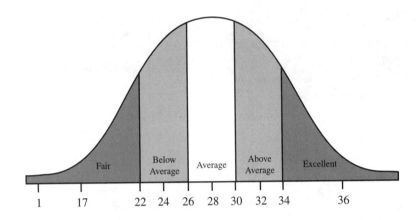

Answer Key

1. A	11. A	21. D	31. B
2. C	12. D	22. D	32. B
3. B	13. A	23. A	33. A
4. B	14. C	24. B	34. A
5. C	15. C	25. B	35. D
6. B	16. B	26. C	36. C
7. D	17. A	27. C	37. D
8. A	18. A	28. C	38. D
9. D	19. A	29. A	39. B
10. B	20. C	30. B	40. D

Q & A Session

Q: What are the main differences between Parts A and B of the Listening Comprehension?

A: There are two important differences. One, Part A uses shorter conversations, and Part B uses conversations and talks or lectures. Two, in Part A, you'll get one question per conversation; in Part B, you'll get two, three, or four questions per conversation or talk. You need to use different approaches for Part A and Part B, and you'll develop Action Plans for both types in Hours 17,18, and 19.

Q: How does the computer experience differ from the PreTest I just took?

A: Aside from the obvious difference that you just took a paper-and-pencil–based test and not a computer-based test, there is one important difference: the timing. The computer keeps track of the passing time. And you have to answer and confirm your answer before it permits you to move on to the next item.

16

HOUR 17

Teach Yourself Listening (I)

What You'll Do This Hour

- Get All the Inside Info on Short Conversations
- Learn Methods for Answering Questions
- Workshop
- Q & A Session

Your Goals for This Hour

Short conversations are brief exchanges between two people followed by a question posed by a narrator. Your goals for this hour are

- Get all the inside info on short conversations
- Learn methods for answering questions
- Get answers to frequently asked questions

Get All the Inside Info on Short Conversations

Short conversations have a very simple structure, and they are very consistent from item to item. With few exceptions, they all share these characteristics:

1. One person speaks; the other person speaks; then a third person or narrator asks a question.

2. The voices of the speakers are clearly distinguishable. Most often, if the first speaker is a man, then the second is a woman; and if the first speaker is a woman, then the second is a man. Occasionally, you may have two different women or two different men speaking one after the other. So you will not have any difficulty telling when one speaker finishes and the other begins.

3. The narrator is yet a third voice, and the voice of the narrator is clearly distinguishable from those of the speakers. Also, whereas the intonation and inflection of the speakers' voices is designed to enliven the exchange and make it realistic, the narrator's voice is flat, neutral, even clinical. You won't confuse the narrator (the one with the question) and the other two speakers.

4. If you are taking the TOEFL on computer, a visual will probably appear on the screen showing the two speakers; but, in reality, it's not much help. You might expect it to contain some clues, such as a snowy background or a cafeteria setting if either of those is relevant, but it won't. The visual is really just there so that the screen won't be blank. It won't help you answer questions.

These points may not at first seem to be very significant; but, in fact, they tell you exactly what you can do to improve your performance on this part.

> **NOTE**
> If you are taking the TOEFL on computer, you'll be given headphones to listen to the conversations. If you are taking the paper-and-pencil version, the class will hear a tape played by the proctor.

Learn Methods for Answering Questions

Because short conversations have such a simple structure, one or two strategies are all that you need. Here is your Action Plan for short conversations.

ACTION PLAN
1. **Ignore the visual on the monitor.**
2. **Listen to what the first speaker says.**
3. **Concentrate on what the second speaker says.**
4. **Ignore what the narrator says.**

Here's how the Action Plan works.

1. Ignore the visual on the monitor.

As was mentioned earlier, the picture on the monitor doesn't offer any clues to the content of the conversation. The visual display may actually be distracting because the speakers may not seem to match up with the voices that you're hearing. (In fact, the photographs were taken on location, but the audio portion seems to have been done in a studio.) So you can close your eyes, or stare into space, or look at the screen if you want to, but don't try to learn anything there.

17

TIP

The speakers are ordinary people talking about things they do almost every day, so eliminate choices that are out of the ordinary:

CHOOSE	DON'T CHOOSE
He will borrow his friend's car tomorrow to go to the beach.	He will buy a car tomorrow to go to the beach.
They both like to fish.	They'll go deep-sea fishing together over the weekend.
She'll find the book in the library.	Her new book has just been published.
He'll look for his wallet in the house.	He'll report a stolen wallet to the police.
She's going to spend her vacation in Florida where it's warm.	She's moving to Florida where it's warm.

2. Listen to what the first speaker says.

You should listen to what the first speaker says, but it's not really very important. The following short conversation will show you why not:

Man: I heard that you were going to have a picnic in the park yesterday. How did it go?

Woman: It poured! We postponed it until next weekend.

    Narrator: What does the woman imply?

        (A) She does not like going to the park.

        (B) The park was filled with people.

        (C) There wasn't enough food at the picnic.

        (D) The picnic had to be rescheduled.

And the correct answer is (D): "it poured" means it rained, and that is why the picnic was postponed or rescheduled.

Now, to learn whether the first speaker's comment is very important, imagine that the conversation was garbled so that you could *not* hear the second speaker:

Man: I heard that you were going to have a picnic in the park yesterday. How did it go?

Woman: Xx xxxxxx! Xx xxxxxxxxx xx xxxxx xxxx xxxxxxx.

    Narrator: What does the woman imply?

        (A) She does not like going to the park.

        (B) The park was filled with people.

        (C) There wasn't enough food at the picnic.

        (D) The picnic had to be rescheduled.

The x's indicate that you can't hear the second speaker. Can you answer the question asked just based on what the first speaker said? The answer is "no." The woman could have said:

    Woman: I didn't like it because that park is not very clean.

And then (A) would have been the right answer. Or she might have said:

    Woman: I didn't enjoy it because the park was much too crowded.

And then (B) would have been the right answer. Or she might have said:

    Woman: It wasn't a very good picnic because there were too many people for the amount of food.

And then (C) would have been the right answer.

Of course, there will only be one correct answer, but what this demonstrates is that the first speaker's comment is not particularly important. It provides you with a reference or a starting point (the picnic), but it doesn't really help you answer the question. You don't want to ignore the first speaker entirely, but don't waste a lot of energy on the first remark.

3. Concentrate on what the second speaker says.

Although the first speaker's comment is useful only as a general reference, the second speaker's comment is absolutely critical. Now let's imagine that you couldn't hear the first speaker but you could hear the second speaker:

Man: X xxxxx xxxx xxx xxxx xxxxx xx xxxx x xxxxxx xx xxx xxxx xxxxxxxxx. Xxx xxx xx xx?

Woman: It poured! We postponed it until next weekend.

Narrator: What does the woman imply?

  (A) She does not like going to the park.

  (B) The park was filled with people.

  (C) There wasn't enough food at the picnic.

  (D) The picnic had to be rescheduled.

And even though you don't know what the man said, you know that the only possible choice is (D) because it's the only one that makes any sense in light of what the woman said.

17

 TIP

Use your common sense. The situations are realistic, so ask yourself, "What would I think or do in this situation?" Your answer is probably the correct answer. For example:

THE SITUATION	THE MOST LIKELY TOEFL ANSWER
You have a dentist appointment and a class at the same time.	Ask the professor for permission to miss class.
Your long-distance telephone bill seems too high.	Check the list of phone calls that were made.
You can't figure out how to set the time on the VCR.	Find the instruction manual.
You hate soggy, water-logged pasta.	Don't overcook the spaghetti.
You spilled water on the kitchen floor.	Mop it up.
You spilled coffee on someone's clothing.	Apologize and offer to have it cleaned for them.

4. Don't worry about what the narrator says.

In the short conversations, the narrator may seem to ask a variety of questions such as:

What does the woman mean?

What does the man imply?

What will the woman do?

What can be inferred from the conversation?

But really all of these questions can be collapsed into one: Which of the following answer choices makes sense in light of the conversation?

> Think of all questions as asking: "Which of the following answer choices makes sense, given the conversation you just heard?"

While you'll hear what the narrator says, it's not likely to be particularly useful. Instead, treat every question by the narrator as asking just one thing: Which of the choices makes sense, given what the speakers have said?

> The question appears on the screen as the narrator speaks.

So the key to short conversations is what the second speaker says. When you trim away all the excess verbiage, here's what you're left with:

First speaker: ———

Second speaker: If I were you I'd skip it, because you've got a class first thing in the morning.

    Narrator: ———

        (A) Go to sleep.

        (B) Videotape the program.

        (C) Watch another channel.

        (D) Set the alarm clock.

And the correct answer is (A).

And here's another example:

Man: ———

Woman: I guess it's time to get out the vacuum cleaner.

    Narrator: ———

        (A) The man's apartment needs cleaning.

        (B) The man's sister should visit at another time.

        (C) The man's sister will be glad to see him.

        (D) The man's sister should stay somewhere else.

The correct answer is **(A)**.

And here is one final example:

Woman: ———

Man: We'll just have to have a good time without you.

Narrator: ———

        (A) The man doesn't want to go to the party.

        (B) The woman will finish her assignment before the party.

        (C) The woman won't be going to the party.

        (D) The party will not begin until late.

The correct answer is **(C)**.

> Eliminate as many "silly" answers as you can before you guess. The fact that two people are talking about an introductory course in physics doesn't make one of them an astrophysicist; the fact that students are permitted to use calculators on a test doesn't mean that the professor is going to give everyone a new calculator.

TIP

Avoid answer choices with strong *negative* emotions. The speakers are basically nice people.

CHOOSE	AVOID
She will talk to her roommate about the stereo.	She will yell at her roommate to tell her to turn down the stereo.
He will congratulate Cecilia on winning the award, even though he wanted to win.	He's going to tell Cecilia that she didn't deserve the award.
He notices that she has a new hair style.	He tells her that her new hair style is ugly.
She appreciates the gift.	She doesn't like that artist.

Workshop

This workshop consists of a drill and a review. It will let you practice the Action Plan for short conversations.

For the drill, you should refer to Script 3 in Appendix A. You'll read *only* what the second speaker says. You won't read the first speaker, and you won't read the narrator asking a question. Instead, choose the answer that makes the most sense given what the one speaker has said. Indicate your response by circling the letter of the answer choice in your book. There is no time limit for the drill.

After you have finished the drill portion of the Workshop, then you should compare your choices to the answer key provided.

NOTE

These questions refer to Script 3 in Appendix A. Visit www.cambridgereview.com for audio transcripts.

Drill

Read Script 3 and answer the following questions.

Question 1

(A) Watch the movie at midnight.
(B) Go to bed.
(C) Watch another program.
(D) Set the alarm clock.

Question 2

(A) The copies will be very expensive.
(B) He hasn't finished writing the report.
(C) The copy center used to open earlier.
(D) He won't be able to get copies before class.

Question 3

(A) New running shoes are now on sale.
(B) She will wear old shoes for the five-kilometer run.
(C) She needs a new pair of running shoes.
(D) She's not sure what size shoes she wears.

Question 4

(A) He is an accomplished musician.
(B) He doesn't really like classical music.
(C) He works as an usher at the concert hall.
(D) He is a serious student of music.

Question 5

(A) She has already promised the newspaper to someone else.
(B) She wants the newspaper back when the man is finished.
(C) She no longer has the newspaper.
(D) She doesn't want to lend the newspaper to anyone.

Question 6

(A) He is a vegetarian and doesn't eat meat.
(B) He made a mistake with the woman's order.
(C) He forgot to place the woman's order.
(D) He'll eat the hamburger instead of the vegetarian special.

Question 7

(A) She's been very busy writing a paper.
(B) She's decided that she no longer likes coffee.
(C) She enrolled in another economics course.
(D) She has been out of town on vacation.

Question 8

(A) He has changed his mind about going to the restaurant.
(B) He will be ready to leave before 1 o'clock.
(C) He will go directly to the restaurant.
(D) He doesn't like the restaurant they've chosen.

17

Question 9

(A) He did not know his whistling was disturbing the woman.
(B) He can't understand why the woman is unable to concentrate.
(C) He thinks that the woman can teach herself to whistle.
(D) He wants the woman to repeat what she said.

Question 10

(A) Everyone enjoyed Dr. Roberts's retirement dinner.
(B) Dr. Roberts has always liked being with people.
(C) Many people have always liked Dr. Roberts.
(D) Very few people attended the retirement dinner.

Question 11

(A) He was not really interested in addressing the Issues Group.
(B) He would like to accept but has a prior engagement.
(C) He made another commitment several weeks ago.
(D) He hopes that the woman will not ask him again.

Question 12

(A) The man is usually an early riser.
(B) Clouds are blocking the sunlight.
(C) She is not feeling particularly well.
(D) The man doesn't like getting up early.

Question 13

(A) She doesn't need an air conditioner.
(B) The man has not been uncomfortable.
(C) The man doesn't have a window fan.
(D) The man's air conditioner can't be fixed.

Question 14

(A) He is not very lucky.
(B) He doesn't play the lottery.
(C) He wins as often as anyone.
(D) He hopes that he will win soon.

Question 15

(A) The book does not belong to the library.
(B) He's not yet finished with the book.
(C) The woman is not going to the library.
(D) The book is already overdue.

Question 16

(A) Most of the drivers don't know where they're going.
(B) They should have expected traffic to be heavy.
(C) It's not important whether they're on time.
(D) They'll probably be on time for the game.

Question 17

(A) He doesn't care about dog shows.
(B) He never watches television.
(C) He wishes he had a pet.
(D) He hopes the woman saw the dog show.

Question 18

(A) The weather is not likely to affect classes.
(B) The radio station is not broadcasting at night.
(C) An announcement won't be made until the morning.
(D) The radio functions as an alarm clock.

Question 19

(A) He doesn't know where Miriam is.
(B) Miriam and Jan have the same address.
(C) He's been trying to contact Jan.
(D) Miriam knows Jan's new address.

Question 20

(A) The last bus has already left.
(B) She's afraid the bus will leave without her.
(C) She doesn't understand the man.
(D) She can't help the man.

Question 21

(A) He doesn't enjoy camping.
(B) He'll go camping instead of doing chores.
(C) He's been waiting for time to do some work.
(D) He wants the woman to help him with his work.

Question 22

(A) The man should have used a better tape recorder.
(B) The man needs to have the microphone repaired.

(C) The microphone was too far from the speakers.
(D) Recording a meeting is difficult.

Question 23

(A) He didn't buy a sweater.
(B) He thought the sweater was overpriced.
(C) He bought the sweater on sale.
(D) He decided that he didn't like the sweater.

Question 24

(A) Sue has recently moved.
(B) The woman has no idea where Sue is.
(C) The man needs to check his sources in the library.
(D) Sue spends a lot of time in the library.

Question 25

(A) She agrees that the reading assignment is too demanding.
(B) She feels that the professor is not being unreasonable.
(C) She doesn't plan to attend class tomorrow.
(D) She thinks that the man is being too critical.

Review

1. B	8. C	15. B	22. C
2. D	9. A	16. D	23. A
3. C	10. C	17. A	24. D
4. B	11. B	18. C	25. A
5. A	12. A	19. D	
6. B	13. A	20. D	
7. A	14. A	21. C	

Q & A Session

Q: **How can I be sure that my response to a situation would also be the TOEFL response?**

A: You can't be *sure,* but it's a good bet. The situations of the speakers are the same kinds of situations you'd normally find yourself in: you need to borrow someone's notes, you want to get something to eat, you're trying to find a ride to another city, you hope your paper will get a good grade, and so on. Whatever you would do in those situations is probably what the TOEFL speakers are going to do.

Q: **What do you mean by "The speakers are basically nice people"?**

A: The test-writers are given a set of "sensitivity guidelines." They are told not to write questions that would offend anyone. Some people might be offended by reactions such as yelling at someone else, ridiculing their dress, or attacking their honesty. So the test-writers just don't do that.

Q: **What should I do if I can't figure out the answer?**

A: Guess, and move on to the next question. Once you've determined that you just don't know the answer, there's no point in wasting time. Choose, confirm, and move on.

This Hour's Review

1. Short conversations have a very simple structure: the first speaker says something; the second speaker says something; the narrator asks the question. The visual display on the monitor is not useful.

2. The key element in the short conversation is what the second speaker says. While you probably don't want to ignore anything completely, you should concentrate on the second speaker's comment.

3. Common sense can take you a long way. Think about what you would do in the situation, and look for an answer choice that is similar. Avoid answer choices that suggest strong negative emotions.

HOUR 18

Teach Yourself Listening (II)

What You'll Do This Hour

- The Function of Idioms
- Common English Idioms
- Conversations with Idioms
- Workshop
- Q & A Session

Your Goals for This Hour

In the last hour, you learned that the second speaker's statement is the most important element of a TOEFL conversation. And you saw that you should concentrate on that element. In this hour, you'll learn about the importance of idioms as the source of correct answers. Here are your goals for this hour:

- Learn why the TOEFL tests idioms
- Review a list of important English idioms
- Develop an Action Plan for idiom questions
- Get answers to frequently asked questions

The Function of Idioms

Like other languages, English has phrases and sentences that cannot be translated literally plus phrases and sentences that, while susceptible to a literal translation, have additional, non-literal meanings. These are phrases and sentences such as:

- This lecture is not very interesting; in fact, I'm *bored to death.*
- I know Mike's not here. I told him about the meeting; but with him, it's *in one ear and out the other.*
- I don't have any antique watches of the sort you've described right now, but I'll *keep my eye out* for one.
- Cindy's involved in an important deal right now, so her vacation plans are *up in the air.*

The first speaker is not dead; Mike doesn't have a hole that runs through his head from one ear to the other; the shopkeeper is not going to remove his eye from the socket; and you won't find Cindy's vacation plans by looking up in the sky. But to someone who speaks English, these expressions make sense.

Such phrases, which are also called idioms, present special problems. Since you usually cannot learn the meanings by translating them literally, you have to have heard them before or infer their meanings from context. Either way, they can be a pretty good measure of someone's command of the language, and that's why they are used by the TOEFL.

So you'll find some conversations that test whether you know the meaning of a commonly used English idiom. It would be a good idea for you to go back to your own books and notes to look for such expressions that you may have learned but forgotten about. Additionally, we prepared a list of commonly used English idioms of the sort that are used by the TOEFL

Common English Idioms

Here is the list of common English idioms. You should review it to make sure you know those that you've studied before and to learn the meanings of those that you have not seen before. Then later in this hour, you'll get a chance to hear some conversations using the idioms in the list and answer TOEFL type questions.

NOTE

You can find an extended list of English idioms in Appendix B.

A bird in the hand is worth two in the bush. Something you already have is more valuable than something you might possibly get. *A bird in the hand is worth two in the bush; I'll take a B in history even though I might have gotten an A in English with more work.*

A fool and his money are soon parted. A foolish person with money soon loses it. *Ian got paid on Friday, but now he's broke; it's like they say, "A fool and his money are soon parted."*

A friend in need is a friend indeed. A true friend will help someone in need. *Elaine got out of bed at 4:00 in morning to come pick me up when my car broke down; a friend in need is a friend indeed.*

A little bird told me. The information comes from source the identity of which the speaker is not willing to reveal. *I can't tell you how I know about the grades; let's just say a little bird told me.*

A little knowledge is a dangerous thing. Partial knowledge can be incorrect resulting in embarrassment or even harm. *Carl said he knew how to fix the engine, but he only made things worse; a little knowledge is a dangerous thing.*

Able to take only so much. Capable of enduring only limited amount of discomfort or inconvenience. *I'm quitting my job tomorrow; I can only take so much.*

Absent without leave, also **A.W.O.L.** A military phrase meaning absent without permission, applied in other contexts as well. *He was absent without leave from our third period lab class.*

Ace in the hole. A hidden asset, something held in reserve against an emergency. *I have an ace in the hole: my brother knows the dean.*

Acquired taste. A liking for food, drink, or anything else that has to be acquired. *The music of composer Philip Glass is an acquired taste.*

Act one's age. Behave maturely. *If John would only act his age, he wouldn't embarrass himself like that.*

Actions speak louder than words. What someone does is a truer measure of what they believe that what they say. *Mike said he wanted to go to law school, but he never applied; and you know that actions speak louder than words.*

Add insult to injury. To make an already bad situation worse. *Then the professor added insult to injury by telling us we're also responsible for David Copperfield.*

18

After all is said and done. In the final analysis. *There were parts of the course I didn't like, but after all is said and done, it was a good learning experience.*

Ahead of the game. Early, ahead of schedule. *Beverly took an introductory statistics course at the community college, so she's ahead of the game.*

Alive and well, also **alive and kicking.** Healthy, doing well. *I ran into Dean in the library the other day, and he's alive and kicking.*

All for the best. On balance, good. *I was sorry to hear you did not get the assistant-ship, but maybe it's all for the best since you won't have the teaching responsibilities either.*

All Greek to me. Unintelligible. *Don't ask me about statistics; it's all Greek to me.*

All hours. Very late into the night. *I'm tired; I was up to all hours preparing for the economics final.*

All over but the shouting. Everything is over but some administrative functions. *Now that we're finished with finals, it's all over but the shouting.*

All set. Everything in readiness. *We're all set; I made the reservations, ordered the cake, and arranged for the decorations.*

All systems are go. Everything is ready. *All systems are go; the bus will pick us up at 9:00 in the morning.*

All that glitters is not gold. Something may appear to be attractive and valuable but isn't really. *Carl got over his disappointment at not getting the assistantship when he learned how many hours were required; it just goes to show you that all that glitters is not gold.*

All thumbs. Clumsy or inept. *Don't even ask me to change a light bulb; I'm all thumbs.*

All wet. Mistaken, wrong headed. *Kim is all wet; he wasn't there and doesn't know exactly what happened.*

All work and no play makes Jack a dull boy. Play and recreation are essential. *As they say, all work and no play makes Jack a dull boy, so I'll be at the party tonight instead of studying.*

All's well that ends well. An event that has a happy ending is good even if things went wrong along the way. *We had a flat tire on the way to the church, but the wedding was beautiful; and all's well that ends well.*

An ounce of prevention is worth a pound of cure. It's better and easier to prevent something bad from happening than to correct it after it's occurred. *Just remember an ounce of prevention is worth a pound of cure; I would fix that leak before it gets any worse.*

Any port in a storm. When a situation is dire, any solution is preferable to no solution at all. *It's any port in the storm; I don't really want to room with Jack but that's my only alternative.*

Apples and oranges. Referring to concepts that are not at all alike. *Economics or psychology; that's like comparing apples and oranges.*

Around the clock. Continuously or continually. *Tina has been studying around the clock; she hasn't even stopped to eat.*

As a rule. Usually, almost always. *As a rule, Jack is in the library at this time, but I haven't seen him.*

As a last resort. Only if everything else fails. *I'll take physics as a last resort, but I really want to take French.*

As busy as a beaver. Very busy. *With three finals coming up this week, I've been busy as a beaver.*

As clear as crystal. Easily understood, very clear. *Now the idea of the dialectic is as clear as crystal to me, but Mary had to explain it for three hours.*

As clear as mud. (Irony) Not clear at all, incomprehensible. *The professor's explanation of the Krebs cycle was as clear as mud; I don't think I'll ever understand.*

As cool as a cucumber. Calm and collected under pressure. *Kathy is as cool as a cucumber; the professor gave us a pop quiz, and she didn't even looked surprised.*

As different as night and day. Completely different. *Prof. Smith and professor Jones are as different as night and day; Prof. Smith is always in his office and glad to talk, but professor Jones's door is always closed.*

As dry as dust. Very dull, very boring, uninteresting. *I don't think that anyone enjoys Dr. Johnson's course in ancient legal concepts, it's dry as dust.*

As easy as pie. Very easy. *It's no wonder that there's a waiting list to get into Fine Arts 101; it's as easy as pie, and everyone gets an A.*

As easy as falling off a log. See as easy as pie.

As free as a bird. Completely free, carefree. *I finished my last exam, and now I'm as free as a bird.*

As good as done. Almost finished. *Our term papers are not due until next week, but mine is already as good as done.*

As plain as day. Plain, simple, easy to understand. *Bob explained the structure of the symphony to me, and now it's plain as day.*

As regular as clockwork. Dependable, regular. *I should have known that Peter would return the book on time; he's regular as clockwork.*

18

As the crow flies. Measured directly from point-to-point. *Jan's house is only three miles as the crow flies, but we have to go around the stadium, so the trip is actually longer.*

Asleep at the switch. Not paying attention. *I forgot that the assignment was due today; I guess I was asleep at the switch.*

At any rate. Anyway. *At any rate, the course was worth it, because Dr. Adams is such an interesting lecturer.*

At once. Immediately. *I'll start working at once; you'll have an outline in the morning.*

At one's wit's end. Having exhausted one's mental resources. *I'm at my wit's end; I don't see how I can possibly have this paper finished by tomorrow.*

At that rate. At a certain speed, or by doing something as it's been done before. *Andy has written only three pages in the last month; at that rate, he won't be finished until Christmas.*

At the last minute. At the latest possible hour, at the last possible chance. *Dick came through at the last minute; he dropped the assignment on the professor's desk at exactly 4:59.*

At worst. Under the most unfavorable circumstances conceivable. *I got an A on the mid-term, B for lab, so at worst I'll get a B in the course.*

Conversations with Idioms

Here is your Action Plan for answering questions when the conversation uses an idiom:

1. **Concentrate on the second speaker's statement. Use your knowledge of English idioms to pick the correct answer.**

2. **Eliminate all answer choices that use the literal meaning of the idiom.**

3. **Use the context to figure out the meaning of the idiom.**

Here's how it works.

First, your approach to conversations that use idioms should also focus on what the second speaker says. And if you know the meaning of the expression, that should be sufficient to get the answer. Here is an example:

Man: Are you finished with that report yet?

Woman: No, I'm going to take my time and make sure that it's done right.

Narrator: What does the woman imply?

(A) She will hurry up and finish the report.

(B) The report will not be ready immediately.

(C) She plans to take the report somewhere.

(D) She doesn't intend to do the report.

The correct answer is **(B)**. "Take one's time" means to proceed at a deliberate place, so (A) must be wrong. (C) and (D) are just confused readings of the what the woman says. She doesn't indicate that she or the report is going anywhere, and she certainly doesn't say that she won't do it. What she means is that she will proceed carefully and make sure that the report is done correctly.

 TIP

> If the second speaker uses an idiom, the correct answer probably states the meaning of the idiom.

Second, a literal translation of the idiom or some variation on that idea is probably going to be incorrect. Why? The whole point of using an idiom in the question is to learn whether or not you understand how it is commonly used by English speakers—not how it might be literally translated using a diction. Here is an example:

Woman: Were you able to follow the professor's lecture?

Man: Not me. I was completely lost.

Narrator: What does the man imply?

    (A) He was not able to understand the lecture.

    (B) He didn't know where the classroom was located.

    (C) The woman was unable to find the lecture hall.

    (D) The professor did not speak very clearly.

The correct answer is **(A)**. The idiom "was lost" in this context has nothing to do with finding one's way around physical space, so you can eliminate both (B) and (C). Instead, "lost" means "lost" in a figurative way.

 CAUTION

> An answer choice that uses the literal translation of an idiom is probably wrong.

18

Third, you can use the context to figure out the meaning of the idiom. Here is an example:

Woman: I've got to get back to the library. I still haven't finished the reading assignment for tomorrow's class.

Man: Me neither. So I guess it's back to the salt mines for both of us.

Narrator: What does the man imply?

    (A) Both he and the woman could use some salt.

    (B) The library is not a very pleasant place to work.

    (C) Both he and the woman have a lot of hard work to do.

    (D) Neither he nor the woman are fast readers.

The correct answer is **(C)**, and you should be able to figure out the answer from the context even if you aren't familiar with the idiom. The woman says that she still has a lot of work to do. The man says that he too has work to do. Working in a mine is probably hard work, so you can infer that the idiom means to work hard.

NOTE
> Many idioms have a figurative meaning that is an extension of their literal meaning. For example, "Any port in a storm" could logically apply to ships. And by expension, it comes to mean a safe haven in any emergency situation.

Workshop

This workshop gives you the opportunity to practice answering conversations questions that use idioms. Read Script 4 and indicate your answers by circling the letter of the response in your book. Check your answers against the key below.

NOTE
> These questions reference Script 4 in Appendix A. Visit www.cambridgereview.com for audio transcripts.

Drill

Question 1

    (A) Harry didn't bring the sodas.
    (B) The woman wasn't thirsty.
    (C) Harry brought the sodas only a minute ago.
    (D) Harry was almost late bringing the sodas.

Question 2

    (A) Change his major to art.
    (B) Try to find a new topic.
    (C) Resubmit the old outline.
    (D) Drop Professor Smith's course.

Question 3

    (A) She doesn't like the man any more.
    (B) She hasn't been well recently.
    (C) The student lounge is too far away.
    (D) She has been very busy.

Question 4

    (A) He attended a sports event.
    (B) He enjoyed the party.
    (C) The woman shouldn't worry about him.
    (D) Two o'clock is not very late.

Question 5

    (A) She prefers to go to Rutgers instead of Princeton.
    (B) The man should consider applying to Princeton.
    (C) It is more likely that she will go to Rutgers.
    (D) The man would prefer to go to Princeton.

Question 6

    (A) Take a course in Roman Culture instead of Latin.
    (B) Take a second major in Classics.
    (C) Take a course in Roman Culture as well as Latin.
    (D) Ask the Classics Department to teach a course in Latin.

Question 7

    (A) She is tired and wants to go to bed.
    (B) She doesn't want the responsibility of class president.
    (C) She wants to think about the decision before answering.
    (D) She thinks that the committee is not sincere.

Question 8

    (A) The children were trying to frighten their parents.
    (B) The children have been found unharmed.
    (C) The sounds of children were heard nearby.
    (D) The news report was inconclusive.

Question 9

    (A) Telephone a restaurant for food to be delivered.
    (B) Make dinner using ingredients in the kitchen.
    (C) Ask the man to go to the grocery store.
    (D) Use an electric mixer to make dinner.

18

Question 10

   (A) Helen has not been feeling well.

   (B) Helen has dropped out of school.

   (C) The weather has been very bad.

   (D) Helen was in class, but the woman didn't see her.

Question 11

   (A) She doesn't want the man to go home.

   (B) She plans to listen the radio.

   (C) She ignores the talking around her.

   (D) She likes a lot of noise when she studies.

Question 12

   (A) Keep working after the semester ends.

   (B) Relax after the semester is over.

   (C) Stop work before the semester ends.

   (D) Ask the woman to help him with his work.

Question 13

   (A) It's raining very hard.

   (B) No one has come into the building recently.

   (C) Everyone has left for the day.

   (D) In a few minutes, people will start arriving.

Question 14

   (A) He prefers to forget he knows William Rogers.

   (B) William Rogers is a good friend of his.

   (C) William Rogers is at the front door.

   (D) He doesn't remember a William Rogers.

Question 15

   (A) He doesn't care if he pays his bills.

   (B) He's been in training for a race.

   (C) He's been looking for a job.

   (D) She will help him pay his bills.

Question 16

   (A) Brooks has already found an apartment.

   (B) Brooks cannot move into her apartment.

   (C) Brooks has not asked to move into her apartment.

   (D) The man can move into her apartment.

Question 17

   (A) He paid less for the jacket than the woman might think.

   (B) He plans to return the jacket because he doesn't like it.

   (C) He would sell the jacket to someone else if he could.

   (D) The jacket doesn't belong to him.

Question 18

   (A) She plans to tell Alex about the party privately.

   (B) She can't attend the party because people will be smoking.

   (C) She doesn't know Alex but will come anyway.

   (D) She won't mention the surprise party to anyone else.

Question 19

   (A) George does not have to worry about running out of money.

   (B) Everyone knows that George comes from a wealthy family.

(C) George doesn't have a lot of money to spend.

(D) George's family is very wealthy.

Question 20

(A) He felt out of place at the party.

(B) He doesn't like his sister's friends.

(C) He gave his sister a fish for her birthday.

(D) Fish was the main course served at the party.

Question 21

(A) The suggestion is exactly what she would like to do.

(B) Her doctor told her that she should not work so hard.

(C) She is studying to become a doctor.

(D) She wants a friend who is a doctor to come with her.

Question 22

(A) He may get the scholarship provided the interview goes well.

(B) His grades and letter are so strong he doesn't have to go for an interview.

(C) The scholarship depends entirely on explaining what one will do with the money.

(D) The interview is really just a formality that won't last long.

Question 23

(A) Rube would be willing to tutor the man for a fee.

(B) Rube worked on legislation regarding the mining of precious metals.

(C) Rube probably knows a lot about what goes on behind the scenes.

(D) Rube can show the man where to dig a little deeper to find the information.

Question 24

(A) He has already gotten paid.

(B) He plans to look at merchandise but not buy.

(C) He needs to buy some windows.

(D) He plans to look out the window of his apartment.

Question 25

(A) She doesn't have any of the cream pastries.

(B) The fruits on the cream pastries are not fresh.

(C) The cheesecake is fresher than the pastries.

(D) The cream pastries are out in the kitchen.

18

Review

1. D	8. B	15. C	22. A
2. B	9. B	16. B	23. C
3. D	10. A	17. A	24. B
4. B	11. C	18. D	25. A
5. C	12. B	19. C	
6. A	13. A	20. A	
7. C	14. D	21. A	

Q & A Session

Q: Why would the TOEFL test idioms?

A: Your facility with idioms is a pretty good measure of your overall command of the language. People whose skills are very basic will only know a few idioms; people whose skills are advanced will know many idioms.

Q: Do all conversations use idioms?

A: No, but many do. Remember that you worked out your basic strategy in Hour 15: focus on the second statement. Use your knowledge of idioms to refine that strategy and make it even more effective.

Q: How can I learn more about idioms?

A: First, you can go back to your English course materials. You'll find that your notes contain idioms, and your books probably have a long list of them as well. Second, at a bookstore, you can probably find a book in your native language that specifically concentrates on English idioms. Third, you should listen to the way contemporary English is spoken. Television shows, movies, and newsbroadcasts will be helpful in building "idiom power."

This Hour's Review

1. Idioms are a good measure of your command of English, and that's why the TOEFL uses them.

2. Your list of common English idioms, when coupled with ones you've already learned from your studies, will give you a good base of idioms from which to work. You can expand this base by doing further reading in English.

3. If you don't know the meaning of an idiom, try to figure it out from the context. In any event, avoid an answer choice that looks like a literal translation of the idiom.

HOUR 19

Teach Yourself Listening (III)

What You'll Do This Hour

- Get All the Inside Info on Talks
- Learn how to Listen to Talks
- Learn Methods for Answering Questions
- Workshop
- Q & A Session

Your Goals for This Hour

Talks are longer Listening exercises. Although they may also involve verbal exchanges between two people, the exchanges are extended and more involved than conversations. A Talk may also be a single person speaking on a topic, like a professor giving a lecture. A Talk can also be a professor leading a seminar discussion. In this hour, you'll develop an Action Plan especially for Talks. Your goals for this hour are:

- Get all the inside info on Talks
- Learn how to listen to Talks
- Learn methods for answering questions
- Get answers to frequently asked questions

Get All the Inside Info on Talks

Most talks now try to simulate a classroom experience. Typically, a Talk will feature a professor giving a class on a subject that you might study at the university, such as philosophy or biology or geology. The Talk may feature visuals such outlines, timelines, schematics, photographs, and virtually anything else that a professor might bring to class to help teach a subject.

Then, the questions ask about the lecture: what did the professor say, what was the significance of some detail mentioned in the lecture, what conclusion are you supposed to draw from an illustration?

In essence, then, the Talk is a classroom simulation, and you're the student. You listen to the lecture or discussion, and then you're tested on the material. Very much like school.

When described like this, the new Talks form seems to make a lot of sense. It's a little curious, then, that even as the TOEFL is working so hard to bring realism to the test, it fails in one very important respect: *you can't take notes!* The rules clearly state that you are not supposed to have any writing instrument or paper during this part of the exam, and you are expressly forbidden from taking notes to help you answer questions.

Would you go to class and *not* take notes? Obviously not. That would defeat the whole purpose of going to class in the first place. But that's how the TOEFL works. (Apparently, they are concerned that to allow note-taking would open the door to a new kind cheating whereby some people would take the exam, write down the questions and answers, and then pass those questions and answers on to people who have not yet taken the TOEFL.)

There are three important features of Talks to keep in mind:

1. Talks are extended verbal exchanges, lectures, or seminar discussions.
2. Increasingly, Talks are designed to simulate the classroom experience and include visual aids and illustrations.
3. You can't take notes on the Talks.

These three key elements dictate how you should approach this kind of question. Your Action Plan is presented in the following two parts.

> The Action Plan for Talks is a lot like the Action Plan for Reading that you developed in Hours 11 and 12. And that makes sense. After all, a professor's lecture is a lot like a chapter in a textbook—except that you listen to one and read the other.

Learn How to Listen to Talks

With Talks, you're the student who is listening to a lecture. After the lecture, there will be a test and you'll have to answer questions. But you can't take notes during the class. So what should you do? Here's how to listen to Talks:

1. Listen carefully to the narrator's introductory remarks.

2. Try to determine as quickly as possible the main point of the lecture.

3. Pay careful attention to any examples, visual aids, or illustrations.

The first step is to listen carefully to the narrator's introduction. The introduction will explain who is speaking, something about the setting, and, in general terms, the topic of the Talk. Here's an example:

Narrator: Next you will hear part of a lecture on anthropology. The professor is discussing the role of the shaman in primitive cultures. Listen to the first part of the lecture.

The narrator's remarks give you a point of reference: you're in an anthropology class, and the professor is going to explain the role of the shaman in primitive cultures.

The second step is to listen to the lecture. Since you won't be able to take notes while you listen, you'll have to concentrate and learn everything you can the first time through. As you listen, ask yourself, "What is the main theme that the lecture is developing?"

The main theme is important for two reasons. First, you need to understand the main theme of the lecture in order to understand the significance all of the other points made. Second, you're almost guaranteed to have a question that asks you to identify the main point of the lecture.

And pay careful attention to details. These are also likely to be the basis for one or more questions.

19

To illustrate the second step, we'll use the lecture introduced by the narrator above. Read through the lecture, looking for the key elements. They are discussed for you below. (For now, you'll be reading rather than listening to the lecture, but in the Workshop later, you'll be listening.)

Primitive humans believed that everything around them—trees, streams, and even rocks—contained spirits. Even the sophisticated Greeks believed in wood nymphs.

When humans first settled into primitive shelters, they became interested in the spirits of the sky and the earth and especially in how to prevent them from causing harm to themselves. This concern gave rise to the shaman, a term that originated among the Mongol peoples of eastern Siberia and may be related to their word for ascetic. The shaman is a magician, medium, or healer who owes his powers to mystical communion with the spirit world. The shaman protects humans from destructive spirits.

Cave paintings, carved bones, and other artifacts indicate that shamanism was widespread 20,000 years ago. Surviving forms are seen even today among Siberians, Polynesians, Eskimos, and American Indians. The close resemblance in many shaman rituals raises the question of whether practices arose spontaneously in several regions or whether they were spread by prehistoric migrations.

Occasionally, it was believed that shamans inherited their vocation, but more often it was thought that they were called by spirits. The calling, an event that could occur anytime between birth and manhood, would be signaled by some powerful sign such as lightning. Novice shamans were subjected to severe trials, and their final ordination was marked by dramatic visions, trances, convulsions, or seizures.

The shaman dealt mostly with illnesses that were believed to arise from a disturbance of the spirit. A shaman might also practice herbal therapy, but most often that was left to a medicine man or other tribal member of lower standing. Through divination or consultation with spirits, the shaman would make his diagnosis, usually a spirit loss. The shaman would travel through the underworld to locate the spirit and persuade it to return.

The topic of this Talk is shamanism. The professor begins by talking about the origins of the practice. Then the professor discusses some of the most important elements of shamanism. Here are the kinds of questions you might be asked, along with possible correct answers:

Question	Possible Correct Answer
What is the main topic?	The origins of shamanism
According to the professor, the word *shaman* originated with what people?	Mongols of eastern Siberia
Why does the professor mention cave paintings and carved bones?	To show that shamanism was widespread
What can be inferred about the theory that shamanism was spread by prehistoric migrations?	The evidence is inconclusive.

These questions may not seem that hard, but remember that you got to *read* the Talk. On the TOEFL, you have to *listen* to the Talk, and you only get to hear it once.

Also, the right answers suggested in the table aren't surrounded by wrong answers. The addition of wrong answers makes things a little trickier because you not only have to have a pretty good idea of what the right answer is, you also need some idea of why the wrong answers are wrong. And that is the topic of the next section.

Learn Methods for Answering Questions

There are really only four different types of questions that you might be asked about a Talk:

- What is the main idea?
- What did the speaker say?
- Why did the speaker say something?
- What can you infer?

These are illustrated by the four questions in the preceding table.

NOTE Your computerized TOEFL will include some "gimmick" questions where you have to point and click to move words or phrases around to match them up with other concepts in a table or to put ideas into sequence. But the questions still belong to one of the four categories.

19

Now let's look at some samples that have wrong answer choices as well. First, here's a question that asks about the main idea of the Talk:

What is the main topic?

    (A) The origins of shamanism.

    (B) The practice of herbal therapy.

    (C) The training of shamans.

    (D) Shamanism in modern cultures.

The correct answer is **(A)**. But what's wrong with the other choices? (B) is an idea mentioned in the fifth paragraph, but only in passing. (C) is an idea mentioned in the fourth paragraph, but it is not the main theme of the Talk. And (D) is mentioned in passing in the third paragraph. So (A) is not only correct, but (B), (C), and (D) are wrong because they are small parts of the Talk and not the main point.

TIP

If a question uses a phrase like "main idea" or "purpose," the correct answer summarizes the overall point of the Talk. Any choice that refers to just part of the Talk is wrong.

And here is an example of a question that asks about what was specifically said by the speaker:

According to the professor, the word *shaman* originated with what people?

    (A) Greeks

    (B) Mongols

    (C) Polynesians

    (D) American Indians

The answer is given specifically in the third paragraph. Notice, however, that the other three groups of people are mentioned in the Talk. But those are wrong answers because they don't answer the question asked. That is, the term *shaman* did not originate with the Greeks, or the Polynesians, or the American Indians, even though those cultures are mentioned in the Talk.

CAUTION

Don't pick an answer choice just because it's mentioned in the Talk. Make sure that it is an answer to the question asked.

The third type of question based on Talks is one that asks about the significance of a detail or an illustration. Here's an example:

Why does the professor mention cave paintings and carved bones?

> (A) To show how shamans were trained.
>
> (B) To show how shamans diagnose spirit loss.
>
> (C) To show that shamanism is an ancient practice.
>
> (D) To show that shamanism was widespread.

The correct answer is **(D)**. The speaker mentions cave paintings and carved bones in the third paragraph and says that they "indicated that shamanism was widespread." The other choices are ideas mentioned by the professor, but they are not the reason for introducing the paintings and the bones. (C) is a particularly close call because the professor does use the phrase "20,000 years ago" in that sentence. But the purpose of the artifacts is to show that the practice of shamanism was widespread at that time, not to prove that it is an ancient practice.

CAUTION

> Don't pick the first answer that looks right. Read all of the choices before making your selection. One word can make the difference between a right answer and a wrong one.

And finally, here is an example of the fourth type of question:

What can be inferred about the theory that shamanism was spread by prehistoric migrations?

> (A) The theory has been definitely proved.
>
> (B) Evidence for the theory is inconclusive.
>
> (C) Scholars don't take theory seriously.
>
> (D) The theory has be been rejected.

The correct answer is **(B)**. The professor doesn't specifically say what the status of the theory is, but you can infer that there is some evidence for it and some evidence against it. This situation is best described by (B).

TIP

> Sometimes it's easier to eliminate wrong answers than to find the right answer. If you can eliminate all the *wrong* answers, then the one that's left is the *right* answer.

19

The discussion of question types and the right answer and wrong answers can be summarized in the following Action Plan:

 Look for the appropriate right answer, given the wording of the question:

1. **For a "main idea" question, it's the thesis of the Talk and not a minor point or a detail.**

2. **For a "what was said" question, it's a point mentioned in the Talk that is an answer to the question asked.**

3. **For a "why was this mentioned" question, it's an explanation of why a point was mentioned.**

4. **For a logical inference question, it's an idea that can be inferred from the Talk.**

Now it's time for you to practice these strategies.

NOTE These questions reference Script 5 in Appendix A. Visit www.cambridgereview.com for audio transcripts.

Workshop

This workshop will let you practice the Action Plan for Talks. Read Script 5 and answer the questions.

Indicate your answer choice by circling the letter of your choice in your book. After you finish the Drill portion of the Workshop, review your work.

Drill

Directions: Read Script 5 and answer the following questions.

1. What is the professor's main point?

   (A) Elephants are survivors from the Pleistocene glaciation.

   (B) Serious factors threaten the Asian elephant with extinction.

   (C) Asia has a large population, much of which is poor.

   (D) Elephants should not be hunted for their tusks.

2. Why have Asian elephants not been hunted for ivory?

   (A) The population is extremely small.

   (B) Many do not have tusks.

(C) The population is fragmented.

(D) Humans have traditionally revered them.

3. What is the greatest threat to Asian elephants?

(A) Ivory poachers

(B) African elephants

(C) Tigers

(D) Human expansion

4. Why is the Periyar Tiger Reserve notable?

(A) Tigers there are no longer endangered.

(B) The elephant herd includes very few males.

(C) It is lacking in forest cover.

(D) It is home to a herd of African elephants.

5. What will the professor probably discuss next?

(A) Efforts to protect the African elephant

(B) Proposals to save the Asian elephant

(C) Conditions in zoos and circuses

(D) Methods of clearing more land for agriculture

6. What is the main topic?

(A) The three-part structure of the human brain

(B) The brain functions of lower mammals

(C) The evolution of humans from primates

(D) The ability of humans to reason

7. In what order does the professor discuss the topics?

	FIRST	SECOND	THIRD
(A)	Reptilian Brain	Mammalian Brain	Neocortex
(B)	Reptilian Brain	Neocortex	Mammalian Brain
(C)	Mammalian Brain	Reptilian Brain	Neocortex
(D)	Mammalian Brain	Neocortex	Reptilian Brain

8. Which of the following correctly matches the function with the brain part?

(A) Mammalian Brain — Path Finding
Neocortex — Speech
Reptilian Brain — Pain Avoidance

(B) Mammalian Brain — Speech
Neocortex — Pain Avoidance
Reptilian Brain — Path Finding

(C) Mammalian Brain — Path Finding
Neocortex — Pain Avoidance
Reptilian Brain — Speech

(D) Mammalian Brain — Pain Avoidance
Neocortex — Speech
Reptilian Brain — Path Finding

9. What does the professor compare the human brain to?

(A) A reference book

(B) An archaeological site

(C) A philosophy text

(D) A layer cake

10. What can be inferred about lower mammals?

(A) They lack the reptilian component.

(B) They do not exhibit innate behaviors.

(C) They don't have a neocortex layer.

(D) They don't react to pleasure and pain.

19

11. What is the topic of the lecture?

    (A) Rural poverty in America
    (B) Poverty in urban United States
    (C) Traditions in farming communities
    (D) Farm-to-city population migration

12. What does the professor mean by "inherit one's occupation"?

    (A) Receive farmland when relatives die
    (B) Go into the kind of work one's parents did
    (C) Care for elderly family members who can't work
    (D) Give up a farming job for work in the city

13. Why does the author mention poverty in the large cities?

    (A) To explain why rural families have many children
    (B) To demonstrate that farm workers earn more than city workers
    (C) To show that migration does not eliminate poverty
    (D) To refute the idea that rural poverty is significant

14. According the professor, why are large farm families no longer economically justified?

    (A) Because too many generations live in the same household
    (B) Because the young adults have migrated to the city
    (C) Because farmer workers are now paid higher wages
    (D) Because children are no longer needed for farm labor

15. According to the professor, what two factors encourage large rural families?

    I.   Availability of jobs.
    II. Plentiful food, clothing, and housing.
    III. A tradition of large families.
    IV. Religious beliefs favoring large families.

    (A) I and II
    (B) I and III
    (C) II and IV
    (D) III and IV

16. What is the main topic of the lecture?

    (A) An early observation of a supernova
    (B) Procedures for observing stars
    (C) A history of astronomy
    (D) An important personality in science

17. Sixteenth-century observers compared the nova to what object?

    (A) The planet Venus
    (B) Tycho's silver nose
    (C) An earlier nova
    (D) Observable stars

18. According to the professor, why had the star not been noticed before it became a supernova?

    (A) Astronomers were not looking in the right direction.
    (B) The star was so far away its light was dim.
    (C) Sixteenth-century observers believed that it did not exist.
    (D) Observers were interested only in stars with fixed positions.

19. Why was the fixed position of the super-
    nova important to Tycho Brahe?

    (A) It made it easier to observe the
        nova.
    (B) It proved the changing light was a
        star.
    (C) It made it possible to locate Venus.
    (D) It reinforced his faith in the
        permanence of stars.

20. Why was the observation of the supernova
    significant?

    (A) It proved that stars were not
        unchangeable.
    (B) It showed that some stars could not
        be seen.
    (C) It demonstrated that stars are more
        distant than planets.
    (D) It was evidence for the theory that
        stars are planets.

Answer Key

1. B	6. B	11. A	16. A
2. B	7. B	12. B	17. A
3. D	8. B	13. C	18. B
4. B	9. B	14. D	19. B
5. B	10. C	15. D	20. A

Q & A Session

Q: Where can I get a look at the "gimmick" questions that were mentioned?

A: You'll need access to a computer plus some TOEFL software. You can download
some samples directly from the TOEFL site: www.toefl.org. Just look for a link to
sample questions. You can get more extensive preparation on the computer by using
the Cambridge Review software that came with this book (if you bought the edition
that includes software). Otherwise, you can order the software directly from
www.cambridgereview.com or by calling 1-800-HIGHER ED.

Q: What about getting practice on Talks with diagrams and photos?

A: You can download some samples from the TOEFL Web site or use the Cambridge
software.

Q: What happens if I try to take notes on the Talks and get caught?

A: It's not entirely clear, because the consequences may depend upon the exact
circumstances and on the informal policies of your testing center. But one thing is
certain: nothing good is going to happen if you get caught cheating. So don't do it.

19

This Hour's Review

1. Talks are long Listening exercises. Many of them try to simulate the classroom experience: you're the student, you listen to the professor, you take a test—but you can't take notes.

2. Start by listening to the narrator's introduction of the Talk, then pay careful attention. Try to determine the main point of the talk, and be particularly interested in any tables, diagrams, or other visuals.

3. The questions will fall into one of four categories. And you now know what to look for in terms of the right answer and how to eliminate wrong answers.

HOUR 20

Take the Listening WarmUp

What You'll Do This Hour

- Review Your Action Plan for Listening
- Take the Listening WarmUp
- Evaluate Your Performance
- Q & A Session

Your Goals for This Hour

Today, you'll do a quick review of everything you've learned about Listening. Then you'll take the Listening WarmUp and evaluate your performance. After that, you'll review your work by comparing it to the scripts of the WarmUp.

Your goals for today are:

- Review your Action Plan for listening
- Take the Listening WarmUp
- Score the WarmUp and evaluate your performance
- Review your work

Review Your Action Plan for Listening

The TOEFL uses the two different kinds of Listening questions. Here are your Action Plans for both types:

 For Conversations:

1. **Listen to the conversation.**

    A. Ignore the visual on the monitor.

    B. Listen to what the first speaker says.

    C. Concentrate on what the second speaker says.

    D. Ignore what the narrator says.

2. **Use your knowledge of English to pick the correct answer.**

3. **Eliminate as many choices as possible before you guess:**

    A. Eliminate all answer choices that use the literal meaning of an idiom.

    B. Eliminate answer choices that have strong *negative* emotions.

    C. Eliminate answer choices that are completely unrealistic.

4. **Guess.**

    A. Choose an answer that refers to an ordinary experience.

    B. Choose an answer that is consistent with your experience.

For Talks:

1. **Listen carefully to the narrator's introductory remarks.**

2. **Try to determine as quickly as possible the main point of the lecture.**

3. **Pay careful attention to any examples, visual aids, or illustrations.**

4. **Look for the appropriate right answer, given the wording of the question:**

- For a "main idea" question, it's the thesis of the Talk and not a minor point or a detail.

- For a "what was said" question, it's a point mentioned in the Talk that is an answer to the question asked.

- For a "why was this mentioned" question, it's an explanation of why a point was mentioned.

- For a logical inference question, it's an idea that can be inferred from the Talk.

Now you're ready to take the Listening WarmUp.

Take the Listening WarmUp

DIRECTIONS: The Listening Comprehension component of the TOEFL consists of two different kinds of listening exercises: Short Conversations (Part A) and Talks (Part B).

The audio is in the CD audio portion as follows:

Script 1 = track 1
Script 3 = track 2
Script 4 = track 3
Script 5 = track 4
Script 6 = track 5

Script 2 is used in our computer program.

You can start these tracks by inserting the CD into your CD Player and selecting the appropriate track number.

Part A: Short Conversations

In a short conversation, you will listen to brief conversations between two people. Then you will hear a third person ask a question about what was said or implied by the speakers in the conversations.

The topics of short conversations concern student life. They might be about living arrangements, scheduling recreational activities, completing homework assignments, and similar topics. The speakers have many different reasons for speaking with each other, such as seeking advice, asking for information, or arranging schedules.

Some questions may ask you to select a paraphrase of what a speaker has said. Other questions may ask you to draw a further inference from the conversation.

20

Part A: Short Conversations

Short Conversations

In this part, you will hear short conversations between two people. After each conversation, you will hear a question about the conversation. The conversations and questions *will not* be repeated. After you hear a question, read the answers and choose the best one.

Example:

You'll hear:

Man: I missed the weather on the radio this morning.

Woman: The forecast wasn't certain, but I decided to carry an umbrella with me anyway.

Narrator: What does the woman imply?

      (A) The forecast said it might rain.

      (B) No forecast was broadcast that morning.

      (C) Weather is reported in the evening.

      (D) The umbrella belongs to the man.

Sample Answer: **(A)**

You learn from the dialogue that the man did not hear the morning weather forecast. The woman, however, did; and, based upon that information, she decided to carry an umbrella. You can infer, therefore, that the forecast mentioned the possibility of rain.

NOTE These questions reference Script 6 in Appendix A. Visit www.cambridgereview.com for audio transcripts.

Question 1

(A) He will have 25 students this semester.
(B) He is a difficult grader.
(C) He teaches only introductory physics.
(D) The most recent semester was his last.

Question 2

(A) The time is early evening.
(B) It is likely to rain.
(C) The house is nearby.
(D) Items in the house were just washed.

Question 3

(A) The dinner was not worth $20.
(B) The man should not leave a tip.
(C) Two dollars is sufficient.
(D) The tip should be more than $2.

Question 4

(A) The man does not like movies.
(B) The woman does not like music.
(C) The movie has been canceled.
(D) The man has other plans.

Question 5

(A) The man is not likely to receive a grant.
(B) The man will probably receive a grant.
(C) The man will certainly receive a grant.
(D) The man has already received a grant.

Question 6

(A) The woman's landlord will not allow Martha's dog.
(B) Martha recently got a small dog.
(C) The woman does not want Martha to share the apartment.
(D) The man has a large dog.

Question 7

(A) Confident
(B) Unconcerned
(C) Relieved
(D) Anxious

Question 8

(A) A sporting goods store
(B) A gymnasium
(C) A public library
(D) A tennis match

Question 9

(A) The man is in charge of the newspaper.
(B) The woman does not like her advisor.
(C) The woman is very busy.
(D) The man recently saw his advisor.

Question 10

(A) The noise in the car is not important.
(B) The woman's car may need repairs.
(C) The woman should not go to Chicago.
(D) The woman can repair the car herself.

20

Question 11

    (A) The plant was not intended as a birthday present.

    (B) The man's bookcase is overcrowded with other items.

    (C) The plant may not be getting enough light.

    (D) The man has not been giving the plant enough water.

Question 12

    (A) Trains are a good alternative to cars.

    (B) Cars are more efficient than trains.

    (C) Trains are less expensive than cars.

    (D) Trains slow down car traffic.

Question 13

    (A) She will be using the microscope for a long time.

    (B) The microscope belongs to Jane.

    (C) The man should ask Jane about using the microscope.

    (D) The microscope is not working properly.

Question 14

    (A) The professor chooses teaching assistants who are well-known.

    (B) Being a teaching assistant has advantages and disadvantages.

    (C) The professor chooses several teaching assistants each semester.

    (D) Most teaching assistants usually do not become famous.

Part B: Talks and Longer Conversations

In this part, you will hear longer exchanges. After each exchange you will be given two or three questions. Read the answer choices and choose the best one.

Question 15

    (A) A can of soup

    (B) A homemade pie

    (C) Some apples

    (D) A pie from the bakery

Question 16

    (A) Cooking

    (B) Chess

    (C) Business

    (D) Philosophy

Question 17

    I. Getting the apples at the store.

    II. Cutting up and seasoning the apples.

    III. Making the pie crust.

    IV. Baking the assembled pie.

    (A) I and II

    (B) I and IV

    (C) II and III

    (D) II and IV

Question 18

    (A) The *Star Trek* special effects were not very convincing.

    (B) The *Star Trek* special effects were costly to produce.

    (C) Special effects were central to the *Star Trek* plot.

    (D) The *Star Trek* special effects were on a par with movies.

Question 19

    I. It used characters from Star Trek.
   II. It predated the Star Trek series.
  III. It dealt with questions of morality.
  IV. It employed clumsy special effects.

  (A) I and II
  (B) I and IV
  (C) II and III
  (D) II and IV
  (E) III and IV

Question 20

  (A) He cannot explain why.
  (B) The special effects are very good.
  (C) It reminds him of the *Flash Gordon* series.
  (D) The series was made on a limited budget.

Question 21

  (A) Return to the pasture to see if the soil is contaminated.
  (B) Go to the campus infirmary for a tetanus shot.
  (C) Purchase his own copy of the *First Aid Encyclopedia.*
  (D) Wash the affected area and treat it with disinfectant.

Question 22

  (A) He was bicycling in the country.
  (B) The wire fencing was near animals.
  (C) Tetanus is a potentially serious disease.
  (D) A shot will guard against tetanus.

Question 23

  (A) He did not disinfect the scratch.
  (B) The scratch is very painful.
  (C) The scratch may leave a scar.
  (D) Tetanus is potentially serious.

Question 24

  (A) Infancy
  (B) Adolescence
  (C) Early adulthood
  (D) Middle age

Question 25

  (A) Physical changes in early adolescence.
  (B) Emotional challenges of young adulthood.
  (C) Intellectual changes during early adolescence.
  (D) Physical change during early adolescence.

Question 26

  (A) They claim many victims.
  (B) They are insignificant.
  (C) They flow from physical changes.
  (D) They are often exaggerated.

Question 27

  (A) 2 to 5 years
  (B) 7 to 10 years
  (C) 12 to 15 years
  (D) 17 to 20 years
  (E) 22 to 25 years

Question 28

  (A) By thinking about moral values
  (B) By being told by an authority figure
  (C) By discussing ethics with other children
  (D) By seeking to become a member of a group

Question 29

  (A) Porous rock
  (B) Nonporous rock
  (C) Precipitation
  (D) Groundwater

20

Question 30

(A)

THE VISUALIZATION	THE EARTH
I Plastic-covered bottom sponge.	A Porous rock layer.
II Water poured on top.	B Nonporous bedrock..
III Top sponge.	C Precipitation.

(B)

THE VISUALIZATION	THE EARTH
I Plastic-covered bottom sponge.	B Porous rock layer.
II Water poured on top.	C Precipitation.
III Top sponge.	A Non-porous bedrock.

(C)

THE VISUALIZATION	THE EARTH
I Plastic-covered bottom sponge.	B Non-porous bedrock.
II Water poured on top.	C Precipitation.
III Top sponge.	A Porous rock layer.

(D)

THE VISUALIZATION	THE EARTH
I Plastic-covered bottom sponge.	C Precipitation.
II Water poured on top.	A Porous rock layer.
III Top sponge.	B Non-porous bedrock.

Question 31

(A) Ground water emptying into a body of surface water

(B) Ground water flowing through a porous rock layer

(C) Precipitation seeping into the ground

(D) Precipitation flowing over the surface into a river or lake

Question 32

(A) Plastic wrap

(B) Porous rock layers

(C) Nonporous bedrock

(D) Surface-water bodies

Question 33

(A) Playwright

(B) Professor

(C) Musician

(D) Physician

Question 34

(A) Finns

(B) Swedes

(C) Germans

(D) Nomads

Question 35

(A) A magician

(B) A warrior

(C) A damsel

(D) An artist

Question 36

(A) Whatever value it may have is derived from earlier Nordic and Germanic works.

(B) Its humble origins make it unworthy of academic study.

(C) It is a genuine work of literature that inspires Finnish people.

(D) Its value as a literary work has been grossly overstated.

Question 37

    (A) Red

    (B) Brown

    (C) Yellow

    (D) Green

Question 38

    (A) Simple-shaped

    (B) Dandelion-shaped

    (C) Elongated cluster

    (D) Daisy-shaped

Question 39

    (A) It includes details that help to confirm or disinfirm the identification of a specimen.

    (B) It provides more accurate photographic depictions of the various species.

    (C) It offers an encyclopedic treatment of all wild flowers.

    (D) It includes step-by-step procedures for cultivating wild flowers.

Question 40

    (A) Because students need to devote more time to their observations

    (B) Because a specimen may not look exactly like the photograph in the *Guide*

    (C) Because there may be discrepancies between the photographs and the descriptive information in the *Guide*

    (D) Because certain colors and flower shapes are less common than others

Evaluate Your Performance

Use the answer key to check your work. Then total the number of questions you answered correctly and evaluate your performance using the graph below.

Answer Key

1. B	11. C	21. B	31. A
2. B	12. A	22. B	32. C
3. D	13. C	23. D	33. D
4. D	14. B	24. A	34. B
5. B	15. D	25. C	35. D
6. A	16. D	26. D	36. C
7. D	17. D	27. C	37. C
8. A	18. A	28. B	38. C
9. C	19. D	29. D	39. A
10. B	20. A	30. B	40. B

20

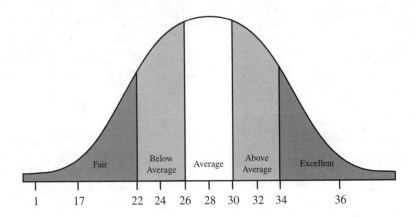

1   17   22 24 26 28 30 32 34   36

Fair   Below Average   Average   Above Average   Excellent

Q & A Session

Q: When I take the TOEFL on the computer should I answer all the questions?

A: Yes. You need to answer one question before you go on to the next. Also, your overall score will be higher if you complete all questions that are assigned, even if you have to hurry a bit.

Q: Does the time the speakers are talking count against me?

A: No, the time needed for listening is not factored into the total time you're given.

Q: Won't some students have an advantage if they get Talks on topics they're familiar with?

A: Theoretically, yes; but practically, no. Even when a topic is chosen from an area like biology or history or sociology, the Talk is usually about some obscure aspect of the topic.

Part V

The Writing Test

Hour

Hour 21

Take the Essay PreTest

What You'll Do This Hour

- What is the Writing/TWE?
- The Essay PreTest
- Sample Response

Your Goals for This Hour

Today, you'll take the Essay PreTest. Here are your goals for this hour:

- Learn what the Writing/TWE is
- Write an essay
- Compare your work with a sample essay

What Is the Writing/TWE?

The Writing element of the Structure/Writing component of the computer-based TOEFL and the TWE supplement to the paper-and-pencil–based test are essentially the same exercise: you have 30 minutes to write an essay on an assigned topic. In either case, the essay is graded on a holistic basis by two readers, each of whom assigns it a score on a scale of 0 to 6. (0 is the minimum, given only to papers that are illegible or off-topic; 6 is the maximum.) The primary difference between the Writing section of the computer-based TOEFL and the TWE of the pencil-and-paper–based version is that the Writing score is incorporated with the score on the Structure component of the computer-based version to produce a composite score. But the preparation for the Essay is the same in both.

If you're taking the computer-based TOEFL, you'll be given the option of handwriting your answer or using the keyboard and the computer's word-processing capability to input your answer. If you're taking the paper-and-pencil–based TOEFL, then you will not have the option of typing your essay; you will have to write it on paper.

The Essay is graded on a scale of 0 to 6, as follows:

Excellent	6
Very Good	5
Good	4
Average	3
Below Average	2
Poor	1
Illegible or Off-Topic	0

The reported score is the *average* of the scores assigned by the two graders who read your essay. The possible essay scores are: 6.0, 5.5, 5.0, 4.5, 4.0, 3.5, 3.0, 2.5, 2.0, 1.5, 1.0, 1 or 0.

If you are taking the paper-and-pencil version of the test, you will see a separate essay score on your score report. If you are taking the computer-based version, you'll not only receive an essay grade, but your essay grade and score on the Structure part will be combined into a single number called the Structure/Writing score, with the two scores weighted equally.

The graders who read your essay have been trained to apply a set of criteria developed especially for the TOEFL essay. Two graders are used for each essay to minimize the possibility of a gross mistake in grading. The descriptions they use to assign grades are very instructive. Compare the descriptions of an "Excellent" essay to a "Below Average" essay:

EXCELLENT	BELOW AVERAGE
Addresses all aspects of the writing assignment	Addresses some or few of the aspects of the writing assignment
Well organized	Poorly organized
Uses details and examples to support and illustrate ideas	Little or no detail to support or illustrate generalizations
Consistent facility with language and expression	Meaning sometimes not clear; frequent errors in structure and usage
Syntactic variety and appropriate word choice	Ineffective expression; accumulation of errors

We'll return to this table in Hour 22 when we talk about what you should write, but for now, one thing is very important: right or wrong is not part of the grading process. In other words, the content of your essay is not important; the organization and execution are.

This last point is reinforced by the topic used for the essay. Here are some sample topics that may be used on your essay test:*

It has been said, "Not everything that is learned is contained in books." Compare and contrast knowledge gained from experience with knowledge gained from books. In your opinion, which source is more important? Why?

Do you agree or disagree with the following statement?

Universities should give the same amount of money to their students' sports activities as they give to their university libraries.
Use specific reasons and examples to support your opinion.

Every generation of people is different in important ways. How is your generation different from your parents' generation? Use specific reasons and examples to explain your answer.

*"Writing Topics" in *TOEFL: Information Bulletin*, (Educational Testing Service: 1998), p. 35 *et seq.*

NOTE   You can see more examples of topics by visiting the TOEFL Web site: www.toefl.org

21

There is no right or wrong answer to these questions, so you won't be graded so much on what you say—for example, "I agree" or "I disagree"—as on how you say it.

In this hour, you will write a sample essay under timed conditions. Then you'll be able to compare your essay to one that is rated as "above average."

Take The Essay PreTest

Directions: You have 30-minutes to write an essay on the following topic. Write only on the topic assigned.

If you could change one important thing about your country, what would you change? Use reasons and specific examples to support your answer.

_____

_____

_____

_____

_____

_____

_____

_____

_____

_____

_____

_____

_____

21

Sample Response

If I could change one important thing about my country it would be to have a mandatory service requirement. I mean that everyone who is able would be required to serve their country for a one- or two-year period. People would be given a choice about what kind of service they would do. You could choose the military, but you wouldn't have to. You could be assigned to work in a poor area in the city or in a rural area. And you could be a carpenter, or a teacher, or whatever. I think that this requirement would be good for three reasons.

First, required service would be good for the people who do it. I have seen many people come back from military service who went in as children but became adults. I think this is because they were treated like adults and asked to do adult things. Also, they learned to work well with other people on a team, and they even learned some valuable skills.

Second, the service would be good for the people who are served. Just think about the different things people could do. One group of people could restore run-down housing in a poor neighborhood and make a place for people to live. Some other people could work in a farm area and help people raise crops. Some other people could be teachers and work in schools. And everyone who was served would benefit.

Third, the service would make being a citizen more valuable. We too often take our citizenship for granted. A lot of people don't even bother to vote. Perhaps that's because if it's free people don't think that it's worth very much. If people had to "buy" their citizenship with their time, they would think that it was more important.

For these three reasons I would like to see required service in my country.

21

HOUR 22

Teach Yourself All About the Writing Section

What You'll Do This Hour

- What to Say
- How to Say It
- Q & A Session

Your Goals for This Hour

Today, you'll teach yourself how to get a top score on the Writing section. Here are your goals for this hour:

- Get all the inside info on the Writing section
- Learn what to say

- Learn how to say it
- Get answers to frequently asked questions

What to Say

Nothing strikes more fear into the hearts of students around the world than hearing a teacher say, "Now, you will have to write an essay on a surprise topic." And, in one way, that is what the essay part of the TOEFL does. You don't know what topic you're going to be asked to write on, and there is no body of material you can study that will give you the content you need for a response. For example, you won't be asked to explain how a nuclear reaction works or anything like that.

On the other hand, the topic will not exactly be a surprise. In the first place, if you read through the list of sample topics in the TOEFL *Bulletin* or at the TOEFL Web site, you'll start to notice some repetition. But even more important, the topics all share one common feature: they don't test any subject matter! There's no right or wrong answer, so whatever you write is okay, so long as it's relevant to the topic you're given.

NOTE   Essay topics don't test any specific subject; they don't have a right or wrong answer.

Does that mean that you won't have anything to say? Not at all. In fact, somewhat paradoxically, there's so much you could say that you may feel as though you don't have anything to say. Take this topic as an example:

Do you think books teach more than experience?

The topic is so open-ended that, at first, you may not be able to think of anything to say. But this is not because you don't have anything to say; rather, it's because you have too much to say!

TIP   Start by writing down six to ten ideas as they come to mind.

So your first task is to define more clearly what you want to say. Begin by jotting down a few thoughts about the topic. These are very preliminary thoughts; they are not yet answers to the essay prompt. But putting your thoughts down on paper starts the process of converting that vague *feeling* about the topic into an *idea* about the topic. You can't express a feeling in writing; you have to express an idea.

The next step is to use your preliminary ideas to formulate an answer to the question asked. Your answer must be responsive and it must be specific.

Now let's do a little experiment. Pretend that this is an essay topic:

> What's your favorite geometric shape—a triangle, a rectangle, a square, a circle, or some other figure? State your position. Provide reasons to support your position.

At first, you may think that this should be an easy topic to answer because you don't have to know anything; but as you start to think about it, you'll find that it's really very hard. Why should such a simple (and silly) topic be hard? Because there's no good reason to prefer one shape over another. Triangles, rectangles, squares, circles, and other shapes are all good shapes—it just depends on what you need. A circle is a perfectly good shape for an automobile tire, a rectangle makes a lousy tire; a rectangle is a great shape for a soccer field; an irregular polygon with acute angles would make the game impossible.

So which shape do you like the best? It doesn't matter. Just start by jotting down some ideas:

> Rectangles have four corners, good for soccer fields.
>
> Circles have no corners, great for tires.
>
> Rectangles good for apartments, places for cabinets, closets, furniture, etc.
>
> Circular tables versus rectangular ones? Family dinners versus business meetings?
>
> Rectangles good for photographs, paintings, windows (except for ships).

These are all interesting observations, but they are not yet a response to the prompt. Your response has to be a specific position:

> I prefer . . . because . . .

For example:

> I prefer rectangles because they make good soccer fields, they make it easy to put furniture like couches and TVs into your apartment, and they make good meeting tables because the boss can sit at the head of the table.

Is that silly? Of course it is, but if you ask a silly question, you get a silly answer. And that's one of the main things about the TOEFL Writing component. They're not completely silly, but the prompt is not about a real subject so it's really tough in 30 minutes to write anything very intelligent. So forget about writing something intelligent, and give them what they want: a response to their question with some reasons for your position.

Make sure you answer the questions asked. Make sure your answer is complete. If the question asks, "Do you agree or disagree?" be sure to take a position. If the question asks, "What's your favorite food?" you must clearly state which is your favorite. It may seem silly, but that's what you have to do.

TIP

Give them what they want. The Writing section uses a particular kind of prompt, and essays are graded by using preestablished criteria. You get a top score by fitting your essay into their mold.

How to Say It

What you say is not very important—so long as it is a response to the question asked. How you say it is very important.

Let's take another look at the criteria for an excellent essay. The table mentions "well organized" and "uses details." These are very important. First, your essay must be well-organized. And the way to make sure that it is well-organized is to do the organization in advance. Here is the outline for your essay:

Introduction: State Position

Paragraph 1: First reason for position

Paragraph 2: Second reason for position

Paragraph 3: Third reason for position

Conclusion: Summarize position

This organization will work for any topic. Let's take the sample topic mentioned in Hour 21:

It has been said, "Not everything that is learned is contained in books." Compare and contrast knowledge gained from experience with knowledge gained from books. In your opinion, which source is more important? Why?

And for working purposes, let's use these three ideas:

Practical details are often missing from books.

Traditional wisdom is not in books.

Cutting-edge developments may not yet be in books.

And we'll agree with the statement. Our essay becomes:

I agree with the statement for three reasons.

One, practical details are often missing from books.

Two, traditional wisdom is not in books.

Three, cutting-edge developments may not yet be in books.

So, not everything is found in books.

So far, we've actually written about one-fourth of the essay. Now we need to develop the ideas, and the best way to develop ideas is to use examples. Here are some suggestions:

One, practical details are often missing from books. I once bought a book on motorcycle repair to learn how to adjust the engine. I read the chapter and tried to do what they said. But they didn't say that I needed a special tool called an "impact driver" just to get the cover off the engine.

Two, traditional wisdom is not in books. My grandfather once removed a growth from my friend's arm by using a bean. He cut the bean in half, put blood from the growth on one half and burned it, then buried the other half. I can't explain why the growth went away, but it did. And you won't find that in a book.

Three, cutting-edge developments may not yet be in books. Professionals have meetings and conferences to discuss important new ideas because they are not yet in books. When a cure for cancer is found, doctors will first hear about it from colleagues over the phone or at a meeting, long before it's written down in a book.

Those are just our suggestions; you'll have ideas of your own. Now, if we combine everything into an essay we get:

I agree with the statement that not everything is in books for three reasons. One, details may be known that are not in books; two, traditional wisdom isn't written down; three, the newest developments are too new to be in books.

One, practical details are often missing from books. I once bought a book on motorcycle repair to learn how to adjust the engine. I read the chapter and tried to do what they said. But they didn't say that I needed a special tool called an "impact driver" just to get the cover off the engine. My friend, who also owned a motorcycle, told me about it. Without my friend's help, the book was useless.

Two, traditional wisdom is not in books. My grandfather once removed a growth from my friend's arm by using a bean. He cut the bean in half, put blood from the growth on one half and burned it, then buried the other half. I can't explain why the growth went away, but it did. And you won't find that in a book.

22

Three, cutting-edge developments may not yet be in books. Professionals have meetings and conferences to discuss important new ideas because they are not yet in books. When a cure for cancer is found, doctors will first hear about it from colleagues over the phone or at a meeting, long before it's written down in a book.

Books are important, but they don't have everything that is known. They are a good way of teaching people, but they can't be the only way of teaching people.

And that's a good essay.

Q & A Session

Q: **Are the essay topics that I study in this book the same ones that will be used on my TOEFL?**

A: No, but they are very similar. If you can write an essay on the topics in this book, then you can write an essay on similar topics on your TOEFL.

Q: **Can I really write my essay before I get to the test?**

A: In a way, yes. Practice using the outline form that we developed. Memorize it. Then, all you'll have to do is write it down when the essay section starts and fill in the details for the question that you're asked.

This Hour's Review

1. Both versions of the TOEFL offer an essay part. It's required for the computer-based version. It's required for only some administrations of the paper-and-pencil–based versions.

2. Essays are graded on a scale of 0 to 6 by readers who are told specifically what to look for. The readers are well aware that you are writing under time pressure and will treat your essay as a "first draft."

3. The key to getting a top score is making sure that your essay is well-organized. Once you have an outline, the essay is almost just "fill-in-the-blanks." The sentences that make your main points are the structure of the essay, and the rest of what you write just fills in with details.

Hour 23

Take the Essay WarmUp

What You'll Do This Hour

- The Essay PreTest
- Sample Essay Response

Your Goals for This Hour

Today, you'll take the Essay WarmUp. Here are your goals for this hour:

- Write an essay
- Compare your work with a sample essay

In this hour, you will write a sample essay under timed conditions. Then you'll be able to compare your essay to one that is rated as "above average."

DIRECTIONS: You have 30 minutes to write an essay on the following topic. Write only on the topic assigned.

Some people prefer to live in the city. Other people prefer to live in the country. Which do you prefer and why?

_____

_____

_____

_____

_____

_____

_____

_____

_____

_____

_____

_____

_____

_____

_____

_____

_____

_____

_____

_____

_____

15

_____

_____

_____

_____

_____

_____

_____

_____

_____

_____

_____

_____

_____

_____

_____

_____

_____

_____

_____

_____

_____

Sample Responses

Weak Essay

This is an example of a "weak" essay.

I think the city is a place where some people prefer to live. When some lives in the city. There are things to do. What's more They will have friends and a job. However, living in the city is hard. Costs are great and airpollution is there. Plus, they are more crowded.

Notice that this "weak" essay lacks any fundamental structure or organization. It's really just a few ideas strung together with no indication to the reader of their significance. The transitional words like "however" and "plus" seems to suggest an organization, but if you look carefully, you'll see that there is no development of ideas.

Strong Essay

This is an example of a "strong" essay.

I prefer to live in the city for three reasons. First, I am near my job. Second, I am near my friends. Third, I am near a lot of activity.

First, I prefer to live in the city because I am near my job. My job requires me to work at odd times. On some days I have to work until midnight, but on some days I get off at 4:00 pm. Somedays I have to go to work at 6 in the morning, but somedays I can wait until after lunch. Because I can walk or ride my bicycle to my job I don't care when I have to be there.

Second, I prefer to live in the city because I am near my friends. I have one best friend who lives in my apartment building. Even though we both work hard, it's easy for us to be together sometimes. I may see him in the elevator and we will go to dinner. If I lived in the country, that could not happen. Also I have three or maybe four other friends I like to see every few days. We can make a date to see a movie or go to a restaurant. If one person isn't there, it's not a big deal. They can be late or not come at all.

Third, I prefer to live in the city because there is so much going on. My friends and I like going to dance clubs (when I have the time.) We know a lot of the local bands and follow them around. One band that we knew, "The Hard Rocks," became very famous and have even been on television and in a movie. It's fun because we knew them when they were just getting started.

So for all these reason I like the city. I like to visit the country where my parents live, and it's nice to relax there. But soon I get bored and want to get back to work, see my friends, and do things in the city.

The writer begins by announcing his/her conclusion and then saying what will follow—a kind of road map for the reader. Then the essay presents and develops each of the three ideas.

Two important things to note here. One, the "First" tells the reader that this is the first point mentioned above, so the reader can follow the line of thought. Two, the first sentence is the main point of the paragraph; the other sentences develop the idea that the writer lives near his/her job.

Again, the writer begins by signaling that this is the "second" main point in the essay. And the other sentences develop the idea of being near friends. Notice also the use of examples: the elevator, dinner, a movie. Examples like this help a reader to understand the point being made.

And the "third" tells the reader that this is the third point mentioned in the first paragraph. And the other sentences talk about "what's going on" in the city. Again, the "Hard Rocks" example is very interesting.

This short conclusion summarizes the essay for the reader. A conclusion is not essential, but it is a nice point.

Part VI

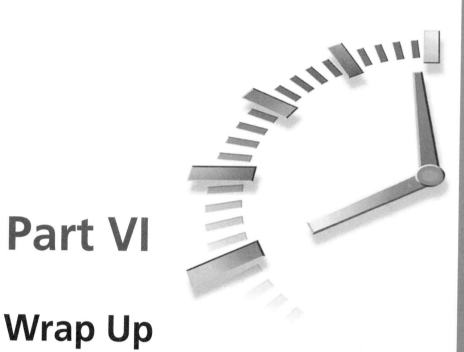

Wrap Up

HOUR 24

Getting Ready for the Big Day

What You'll Do This Hour

- The Test Day
- Review the Important Points You've Learned
- A Final Word

Your Goals for This Hour

Congratulations, this is graduation day. Your goals for today are

- Prepare mentally for the Test Day
- Review the important points you've learned in this book

The Test Day

There's no doubt about it. The TOEFL is a big day. So you want to be ready to peak. In order to do that, your long-term preparation and your short-term preparation have to come together at that moment.

You've invested a lot in your long-term preparation. Your short-term preparation is also important: how you feel physically and mentally on that day can affect your score. So here is an Action Plan to implement, beginning a couple of days beforehand and taking you right through the test.

1. **Two or three days before the test, stop working on the TOEFL (except for a quick review).**
2. **The day before the test, attend to all of the administrative details.**
3. **The night before the test, relax and get some sleep.**
4. **The day of the test, arrive early and settle in.**
5. **During the test, concentrate on what you're doing and maintain a positive attitude.**

Let's talk about each of the steps.

Step 1: Two or three days before the test, stop working on the TOEFL (except for a quick review).

Your mind needs a break and some time to absorb everything, and learning one more thing about the TOEFL at the last minute isn't going to help you.

Ideally, you also want to take some time off from your other studies, but that may not be feasible. Still, if you can, plan to take care of other responsibilities, such as an important paper, well in advance of your TOEFL. That way, those responsibilities won't be hanging over your head

So the last couple of days before the test, there's nothing else terribly important that you absolutely have to do. You can, if you wish, spend an hour or two just reviewing the important points you've covered in this book. (We've included a list of them in this chapter for easy reference.)

Don't keep studying right up until the time of the test. The TOEFL tests knowledge acquired over time. With the help of this book you've reviewed what you already knew and focused that knowledge directly on the TOEFL. "Cramming" one more fact isn't going to help.

Step 2: The day before the test, make sure that you have taken care of all the administrative details.

The TOEFL has very strict rules about who will be admitted to take the test and who will not. The rules include acceptable and unacceptable forms of identification. All of these details must be taken care of well in advance, even weeks in advance of the test. Fortunately, all procedures are set forth in the TOEFL Information Bulletin that you use to register for the test. Make sure that you pay careful attention.

You may have to travel to another location to take your TOEFL and sit in an environment you're not familiar with. You may be taking the test at a time that doesn't fit your usual schedules. All of these things can add up to a tremendous psychological burden.

You can minimize the burden by planning in advance and having everything ready to go:

- **Know where you're going and how to get there.** If you're not familiar with the testing center, plan your route in advance. And make sure you know precisely where the testing center is if it is in a complex of buildings, for example, where on campus.

- **Pack your bag.** Put together everything you're going to need, including the necessary I.D., your admission ticket, #2 pencils plus a small sharpener—if you're taking the paper-and-pencil version. Include whatever personal items you think you might need such as tissues, medicine, extra clothing, and a snack. (You won't be allowed to eat in the testing room, but you may need to eat before or immediately after the test; and you'll find that whatever vending machines are around run out of things quickly.)

Step 3: The night before the test, relax and get some sleep.

This should go without saying, but it can't hurt to say it anyway. You won't be doing yourself a favor if you stay up late the night before. Go to bed at a reasonable hour and get up a little early to give yourself some extra time to get to the testing center.

Step 4: The day of the test, arrive early, and settle in.

Plan to get to the testing center early. This will give you a time cushion against unforeseen events like a construction detour, a late-running train, a traffic accident, and so on. (Even if you've planned your route carefully and think you know which entrances and parking areas are available, you can just about bet that someone will have decided that would be a good day to close off half the campus for a major road repair.) Once there, you can stand around, sit around, read the paper, eat your donut, or do something until the administrators start processing you. From that point on, everything is pretty much out of your control: which room you go in, where you sit, what you can and cannot have on your desk, and so on.

24

Step 5: Concentrate on what you're doing and maintain a positive attitude.

Once testing has begun, you have to maintain your concentration. You'll find that now and again your mind begins to wander off the task. That's normal. Just take a few seconds to compose yourself and put yourself back on track.

TIP | When your mind begins to wander (and it will), take a few seconds to compose yourself and get back to work.

Review the Important Points You've Learned

The day before your test, it would be a good idea to review the most important points you've learned in this book. If any of the following points is not clear to you, return to the Hour in which the material appears and refresh your memory.

Sentence Structure

Remember that there are two types of Sentence Structure questions. In Type I (the one with the blank), you have to pick the answer that correctly completes the sentence. In Type II, you have to find the underlined part that contains the error.

The following checklist of commonly tested errors will help you find the right answers:

- Nouns (Hour 4)

Does the noun have the correct form—either singular or plural?

Is a modifier incorrectly used where there should be a noun?

- Verbs (Hour 4)

Does the verb agree with its subject?

Do the verb tenses reflect the logic of the sentence?

Is the proper infinitive or gerund form used?

Are similar verb elements in parallel form?

- Pronouns (Hour 5)

Does the pronoun agree with its referent (antecedent)?

Does "which" or "that" refer to people?

Is "what" used in place of a relative pronoun?

Is "which" used in an essential clause?

- Modifiers (Hour 5)

Are adjectives and adverbs properly formed?

Are adjectives properly positioned in front of the noun?

Is the correct article used?

Is an essential article missing?

- Sentences (Hour 5)

Does the sentence have a main (conjugated) verb?

Are participles correctly used as modifiers?

Reading (Hour 10)

Remember that you probably won't be familiar with the reading topics, but everything you need to know to answer the question will be in the passage. Your Action Plan for reading is

1. **Read the first sentence of each paragraph and the last sentence of the selection.**
2. **Track the development.**
3. **Read through details.**
4. **Summarize the development.**

There are five types of questions: (Hour 11)

- **Thesis:** Look for the answer that summarizes the main idea or theme of the selection.
- **Specific detail:** Look for the answer somewhere in the text of the selection.
- **Development:** Look for the answer that explains "why" the author mentioned some idea.
- **Implication:** The answer is not written in the text but can be inferred from the text.
- **Vocabulary-in-context:** Look for the meaning the word has in the passage.

Listening

There are two types of Listening Comprehension: short conversations and talks.

Here is your Action Plan for short conversations: (Hour 17)

24

1. **Ignore the visual on the monitor.**
2. **Listen to what the first speaker says.**
3. **Concentrate on what the second speaker says.**
4. **Ignore what the narrator says.**

Here is your Action Plan for Talks: (Hour 19)

Look for the appropriate right answer, given the wording of the question:

1. **For a "main idea" question, it's the thesis of the Talk and not a minor point or a detail.**
2. **For a "what was said" question, it's a point mentioned in the Talk that is an answer to the question asked.**
3. **For a "why was this mentioned" question, it's an explanation of why a point was mentioned.**
4. **For a logical inference question, it's an idea that can be inferred from the Talk.**

The Essay (Hour 22)

Your essay will be graded on organization, development (use of examples and details), and command of standard written English. Here is how you approach it:

1. **Jot down some ideas. Examples are good.**
2. **Formulate an answer to the response.**
3. **Outline your essay, using your ideas.**
4. **Write your essay.**

A Final Word

Now you're thoroughly prepared for the TOEFL. You've studied all the kinds of questions used on the test, and you've practiced a lot. There is just one final bit of advice:

Maintain a positive attitude.

You've done a lot of work to get ready for this test. (Even if you've cut a few corners, you're still way ahead of the curve.) You're ready for your best performance.

Good Luck!

APPENDIX A

Listening Comprehension Scripts

SCRIPT 1

Question 1

[*man*] I called last night, but you didn't answer.

[*woman*] My phone was out of order. The telephone repair service came this morning, and now it's working again.

[*narrator*] What does the woman imply?

Question 2

[*woman*] The sporting goods store is having a huge sale on ski equipment. Do you want to go?

[*man*] No thanks. Last fall, I bought all new equipment.

[*narrator*] What does the man mean?

Question 3

[*man*] I can't find my calculus book. Did I lend it to you?

[*woman*] Hah! I haven't taken a math course since junior high school.

[*narrator*] What does the woman mean?

Questions 4–5

[*man*] I'm looking for an apartment, but I haven't had any luck yet.

[*woman*] Have you tried the bulletin board at the Housing Office? Students often post notices there when they're looking for a roommate.

[*man*] Not yet. But I really would like to live alone for a couple of semesters while I write my thesis.

[*woman*] That could be expensive because rents are pretty high.

[*man*] Yes, but living by myself may be the only way I'll ever finish my thesis.

[*narrator*] What are the man and woman talking about?

[*narrator*] What does the man imply?

Questions 6–10

[*narrator*] Next you will hear a professor lecturing to a class on ancient civilizations.

A central tenet of the belief system of the ancient Egyptians was the conflict between Horus, the god of light, and Set, the god of darkness. They believed that this struggle accounted for the seasons. During the unfruitful winter, Set ruled; during the fertile summer, Horus ruled. A belief in the duality of nature was characteristic of many other ancient cultures as well.

The ancient Egyptians also believed that their own actions influenced the outcome of the struggle between the power of light and the power of darkness. During the spring-time, when the outcome of the struggle seemed to the ancient mind to be in doubt, they participated in the conflict by engaging in mock combat over a round object suggestive of an egg, the symbol of ferility.

Eventually, the concrete meaning of the mock battle receded into memory and only the ritual survived. The mock combat became stylized play according to rules; the symbol of fertility became simply a ball; and the forces of dark and light became teams. In other words, the life-and-death struggle became a game.

Question 6

What is the main focus of the passage?

Question 7

According to the professor, who was Set?

Question 8

Why did the mock combat take place in the spring?

Question 9

According to the professor, what did the ball originally symbolize?

Question 10

Why did the ancient Egyptians stage mock combat?

A

SCRIPT 2

Question 1

[*woman*] I hate to bother you, but your television is really loud.

[*man*] Sorry, I didn't realize that you could hear it next door.

[*narrator*] What will the man probably do?

Question 2

[*man*] Look at the cost of these long-distance calls.

[*woman*] We really can't afford that much every month.

[*narrator*] What are the speakers talking about?

Question 3

[*man*] The light in the dining room doesn't work.

[*woman*] The bulb is probably burned out. I'll buy one tomorrow.

[*narrator*] What does the woman imply?

Question 4

[*woman*] We plan to go to a jazz club this evening. Would you like to come with us?

[*man*] No thanks. I wouldn't be caught dead in a jazz club.

[*narrator*] What does the man mean?

Question 5

[*man*] Do you want to go on a trip with us to New York City on spring break? It's only four hundred dollars per person.

[*woman*] Four hundred dollars! Do you think I'm made of money?

[*narrator*] What does the woman imply?

Question 6

[*man*] Congratulations on your recent promotion to Vice President at your company. I'll bet you're really happy.

[*woman*] To tell you the truth, it's a mixed blessing. The pay is better, but the hours are longer. I have a lot of responsibility that I didn't have before.

[*narrator*] What does the woman imply?

Question 7

[*woman*] These blisters are really hurting my feet.

[*man*] The next time we go, you might want to wear good shoes that are especially made for hiking.

[*narrator*] What can be inferred from the conversation?

Question 8

[*man*] Thank you for making dinner this evening.

[*woman*] Well, I knew that you were going to have a very hard day and probably wouldn't feel like cooking when you finally got home.

[*narrator*] What does the woman imply about the man?

Question 9

[*man*] Professor Johnson suggested that I take a course in elementary statistics before I enroll in the advanced seminar on economics next semester.

[*woman*] That's probably not a bad idea.

[*narrator*] What does the woman mean?

Question 10

[*woman*] I thought you were going to hang the drapes in the living room today.

[*man*] No, I want to do the ceiling first so that paint doesn't drip on anything.

[*narrator*] What does the man intend to do?

Question 11

[*man*] I spoke with Professor Adams today, and she will be offering a course in Medieval English this semester.

[*woman*] Oh, so she decided to give the course after all.

[*narrator*] What can be inferred about Professor Adams?

Question 12

[*woman*] I'd like a reservation on the 11:30 shuttle flight from New York to Washington, D.C.

[*man*] Oh, just show up at the ticket counter 30 minutes before then. If the plane fills up, a second plane will be put into service for the overflow.

[*narrator*] What does the man mean?

A

Question 13

[*woman*] John is in such a panic. He plans to stay up all night finishing the footnotes on his term paper for Sociology.

[*man*] But he's known that the paper was due tomorrow since the beginning of the semester. Professor Williams said that on the very first day.

[*narrator*] What does the man imply about John?

Question 14

[*man*] Will you be using the copier for very long?

[*woman*] Yes, this is quite a long article. However, there are two other copy machines in the basement.

[*narrator*] What will the man probably do?

Questions 15–17

[*man*] Hi Mary, have you got a minute?

[*woman*] Sure Bob, what can I do for you?

[*man*] I'm supposed to go to Boston this weekend for a wedding. It's my cousin who's getting married. But I don't know whether I should take the bus or the train. What do you think?

[*woman*] Well, I personally prefer the train. The seats are roomier, and the tracks make for a smoother ride. Plus, you can get up from your seat to stretch your legs or go to the refreshment car for a snack and a cold drink. But the train is more expensive, and the bus runs more frequently.

[*man*] Yes, the schedule would be important because I have to get back early enough on Sunday to prepare my assignments for Monday's classes. Thanks for your help, Mary.

Question 18–20

[*student*] Good afternoon. I need help in locating some materials for an assignment in a course on American Government.

[*librarian*] Perhaps if you tell me what kind of material you need, I can be of assistance.

[*student*] I am supposed to become familiar with the hearings that are conducted by Congressional committees on whether proposed legislation should be enacted into law.

My teacher says that we can choose any topic and that transcripts of the hearings are published by the U.S. Government.

[*librarian*] That is correct—by the U.S. Government Printing Office to be precise. The Government Printing Office then gives these books to college and public libraries that have been designated as depositories for the information. Our library is a partial depository, which means that we get many but not all of the government publications.

[*student*] How will I know what's available?

[*librarian*] Just use the computer to search under the heading ?Government Documents.? Pick a topic that interests you, say, health care, or education, or foreign affairs, and then choose a specific piece of proposed legislation. Push the >PRINT< command and bring the printout back to me. I'll get you the book from the stacks.

Questions 21–23

[*student*] Hello Professor Farivar. Have you got moment?

[*professor*] Sure. I'm sorry, but I don't believe that I know your name.

[*student*] We haven't met before. My name is Tim Potter, and I'm a senior. Next semester you're offering a graduate level course entitled Post-1989 Afghanistan. I was wondering whether I might get special permission to enroll?

[*professor*] Well, the course will be fairly demanding. We'll be studying the collapse of the Kabul government, the border dispute with Iran, and the rise to power of the Taliban. Tell me a little about your familiarity with these topics.

[*student*] I'm majoring in International Affairs, and I've taken two courses in the politics of the region; but most of what I know I've learned from my roommate who is from Afghanistan.

[*professor*] Hmmm, that's pretty good, but let me suggest this. Here's a list of relevant topics. Why don't you review them, and come back next week. Don't worry. It won't be an oral exam or anything. Just an informal discussion to help me get to know you better.

[*student*] That would be great! See you next week.

Questions 24–27

[*narrator*] A professor in an introductory course in geology is discussing the causes and effects of flooding. Listen to the first part of the lecture.

[*professor*] A flood is an overflow of water that inundates lands that are normally not covered by water. A flood occurs, for example, when a stream or river overflows its banks.

A

Small streams are subject to flash floods—that is, to very rapid increases in run off that may last only a few minutes. On larger streams, floods usually last from several hours to a few days. And a series of storms might keep a river above flood stage for several weeks.

Floods can occur at any time, but weather patterns have a strong influence on when and where floods happen. Cyclones, or storms that bring moisture inland from the ocean, cause floods in the spring in the western United States. Thunderstorms are relatively small but intense storms that cause flash floods in smaller streams in the summer in the South-west. Frontal storms at the edge of large, moist air masses moving across the country cause floods in the northern and eastern parts of the United States during the winter.

The magnitude of a flood is described by a term called recurrence interval, which is based upon long-term study of flow records for a stream. A five-year flood is one that would occur, on the average, once every five years. Although a 100-year flood is expected to happen only once in a century, it is important to remember that there is a 1 percent chance that a flood of that size could happen during any given year.

Of course, the frequency and magnitude of floods can be altered if changes are made in a stream or river's drainage basin. Harvesting timber or changing land use from farms to housing can cause the runoff to increase, resulting in an increase in the magnitude of flooding.

On the other hand, dams can protect against flooding by storing storm runoff. Although the same volume of water must eventually move downstream, the peak flow can be reduced by temporarily storing water and then releasing it when water levels have fallen.

Questions 28–31

[*narrator*] Next you will hear a Professor of Sociology lecturing to a class on the criminal behavior of gang members.

[*professor*] During the past decade, the problem of gang-related crime has become a significant policy issue in the United States. According to recent estimates, more than 16,000 gangs are active in this country, with at least half a million members who commit more than 600,000 crimes each year.

Gang membership leads to criminal behavior. The study mentioned in your textbook reported that 80 percent of individual gang members said that they had stolen cars but only 10 percent of at-risk youths who were not gang members had. Gang members were also more involved with selling drugs.

The study reports similar contrasts for violent crimes. About 40 percent of gang members had participated in a drive-by shooting, compared with 2 percent of at-risk youths. Gang members were far likelier to own guns, and the guns they owned were of larger caliber.

Most gang members join for security and a sense of belonging. As for security, research demonstrates that the benefits of avoiding gang membership far outweigh those of joining. For example, gang members are five times as likely to suffer a violent death than at-risk youths who are not gang members. As for the sense of belonging, creative prevention that fosters feelings of belonging in the community as a whole might dissuade many of these youths from joining gangs.

Question 32–34

[*narrator*] Next you will hear a professor lecturing to a biology class. The lecture concerns research that helps to explain the workings of circadian rhythms—the internal clocks that some organisms possess that allow them to react to day and night.

[*professor*] It has long been known that certain organisms react to the two most predictable events on Earth—day and night. To learn more about circadian rhythms, researchers are studying certain bacteria, the simplest organisms known to have such internal clocks.

Circadian rhythms are the result of complex chemical reactions that control the timing of events in certain cells. Researchers noticed that whenever the circadian clock was working, the cells made proteins that caused the cells to glow with a predictable pattern throughout the day. This made it easy for researchers to know when the circadian clocks were working, since the bacteria blinked off and on like tiny light bulbs.

On further investigation, the researchers found a cluster of genes that they named kaiABC, after the Japanese word for cycle, "kai." The researchers found that concentrations of chemicals associated with kaiABC increase during daytime and decrease during night-time.

Identifying the mechanisms in the simplest creatures known to have circadian clocks is likely to affect our thinking about how all biological clocks, even our own, function. We can theorize about how the circadian rhythms first evolved, that is, how bacteria first learned how to tell time.

Questions 35–37

[*narrator*] Next you will hear a professor of economics and finance lecturing about the history of the New York Stock Exchange.

[*professor*] The financial revival that began in the United States about 100 years ago, in 1897 to be exact, ushered in a new and quite remarkable epoch in the history of the New York Stock Exchange. The supply of capital available in the United States for investment purposes suddenly seemed unlimited—largely because of the nation's immensely profitable harvests at a time of European famine, but also on account of a wholly unprecedented increase in general export trade of manufactured goods.

This increase in capital was utilized by promoters for all kinds of businesses, and the shares of publicly held companies were actively traded on the New York Stock Exchange. During this period, records of every kind were shattered. Whereas, a few years earlier, transactions of 200,000 shares in a day had been regarded as extraordinary, during this period scarcely a day passed in which the volume did not exceed one million shares. And all the time prices were rising.

The driving force was the purchase of stock companies by other companies which pledged their credit to raise the funds needed to make such purchases. The movement culminated in the famous Northern Pacific Corner of May 9, 1901, when the efforts of two rival groups of capitalists to acquire railroad property forced the price of shares to $1,000—ten times the $100 of just three weeks earlier. The entire financial public was soon caught up in the speculation.

But by 1903, it became clear that the large syndicates formed to underwrite the huge stock acquisitions were unable to support prices, and a severe and general decline on the Stock Exchange followed.

Questions 38–40

[*narrator*] Next you will hear a professor of anthropology leading a seminar discussion on techniques for researching folklore.

[*professor*] This semester you will be doing some fieldwork. Before you begin, however, it is important for you to have a firm understanding of the object of your research. Who can define folklore? Yes, Bill.

[*Bill*] The term folklore was coined in 1846 by William J. Thomas. It is the expression of the traditional shared culture of various groups.

[*professor*] That's a good start. What do we mean by traditional shared culture? Monica.

[*Monica*] The shared culture can be familial, ethnic, occupational, religious, or regional. And it is expressed in a wide range of creative and symbolic forms, such as language, drama, architecture, music, dance, and handicraft.

[*professor*] But then what distinguishes folklore from what is often called fine art? After all, T.S. Eliot wrote plays, George Ballanchine choreographed ballets, and Henry Moore sculpted figures.

[*Bill*] Aren't folklore and folk art distinguished from fine art by education?

[*professor*] Yes, generally folklore is learned orally, by imitation, or in performance, and it is perpetuated without formal instruction or institutional direction. Initially, the desire to collect folklore derived largely from the fear that these aspects of cultural expression, which had no institutional center, were disappearing.

[*Monica*] But aren't we being educated here at the university to study folklore?

[*professor*] That's correct. Your fieldwork requires firsthand observation, recording, or documenting what we see and hear in a particular setting, whether that be a rural farming community or a city neighborhood, a local fish market, or a grandmother's living room. This raw material may one day find its way into a library or museum to be used to produce an essay, a book, or an exhibit.

What you study is folklore, but what you produce is scholarship.

A

SCRIPT 3

Question 1

[*man*] I'm so tired, but I really want to see the movie that comes on at midnight.

[*woman*] You'd better forget about it. We have to get up early tomorrw; and, anyway, it'll be on another night.

[*narrator*] What does the woman suggest the man must do?

Question 2

[*woman*] The copy center opens at 10:00 in the morning.

[*man*] Oh no. I need to make a copy of my report before my 9:00 class.

[*narrator*] What does the man mean?

Question 3

[*man*] The five-kilometer run is this weekend. Are you ready?

[*woman*] Almost. The new running shoes I want are going on sale tomorrow.

[*narrator*] What does the woman imply?

Question 4

[*woman*] Josh says that he really likes classical music.

[*man*] But you don't ever see him at any of the concerts.

[*narrator*] What does the man imply about Josh?

Question 5

[*man*] Excuse me. Could I read that newspaper when you're finished with it?

[*woman*] I'm sorry, but Mary asked me first.

[*narrator*] What does the woman mean?

Question 6

[*woman*] I'm afraid there is some mistake. I didn't order a hamburger.

[*man*] Sorry. I see that you are having the vegetarian special. I'll be right back with your meal.

[*narrator*] What can be inferred about the man?

Question 7

[*man*] We haven't seen you at the coffee house in a couple of weeks. Where have you been?

[*woman*] I didn't think that I'd ever finish my economics term paper.

[*narrator*] What does the woman mean?

Question 8

[*woman*] Remember that we're meeting the others for lunch at 1:00, so we need to leave by noon.

[*man*] I've got some errands to run, so I'll meet you at the restaurant.

[*narrator*] What does the man mean?

Question 9

[*woman*] Can you please stop whistling to yourself? I can't concentrate on my book.

[*man*] Why didn't you say something earlier?

[*narrator*] What does the man mean?

Question 10

[*man*] It was really great to hear all of the nice things people said about Dr. Roberts at his retirement dinner.

[*woman*] It wasn't surprising. He's always been popular with colleagues and students.

[*narrator*] What does the woman mean?

Question 11

[*woman*] Would you be be the guest speaker at the next meeting of the Issues Group?

[*man*] I wish you'd asked me earlier. Just yesterday I agreed to be on a panel in Chicago that day.

[*narrator*] What does the man imply?

Question 12

[*man*] I didn't get up this morning until 9 o'clock.

[*woman*] Are you feeling okay? You usually get up at the crack of dawn.

[*narrator*] What does the woman imply?

A

Question 13

[*man*] I can't go through another summer in the city without air conditioning.

[*woman*] Really? My apartment stays quite cool with just a window fan.

[*narrator*] What does the woman imply?

Question 14

[*woman*] Did you hear that Peter won $50 in the lottery last week?

[*man*] I never win anything. I don't even know why I play.

[*narrator*] What does the man mean?

Question 15

[*woman*] Do want me to return this book to the library when I go today?

[*man*] I still need to get a couple of things out of it.

[*narrator*] What does the man imply?

Question 16

[*woman*] This traffic is terrible. We'll never get to the game at this rate.

[*man*] Things should start moving just as soon as we get past this intersection.

[*narrator*] What does the man imply?

Question 17

[*woman*] Did you see the dog show on television? The papillion won best in show.

[*man*] I'm not really an animal lover.

[*narrator*] What does the man imply?

Question 18

[*man*] The weather forecast calls for snow and sleet tomorrow morning. Do you think classes will be cancelled?

[*woman*] We'll have to listen to the radio when we get up.

[*narrator*] What does the woman imply?

Question 19

[*woman*] Do you think Bill knows Jan's new address?

[*man*] No, you'll probably have to ask Miriam.

[*narrator*] What does the man imply?

Question 20

[*man*] Pardon me, but do you know when the next bus leaves?

[*woman*] I'm sorry but I don't. You could ask at the information window.

[*narrator*] What does the woman mean?

Question 21

[*woman*] John and I are going to use the three-day weekend to go camping. How about you?

[*man*] Now that I finally have some extra time, I'm going to do some chores around the house.

[*narrator*] What does the man imply?

Question 22

[*man*] It's really difficult to hear the discussion on this tape recording. And I used a microphone.

[*woman*] Maybe you didn't have the microphone close enough to the table.

[*narrator*] What does the woman mean?

Question 23

[*woman*] I thought you said that you really liked that sweater coat. And that it was on sale, too.

[*man*] I'd have bought one if they'd had it in my size.

[*narrator*] What does the man imply?

Question 24

[*man*] Has anyone seen Sue recently?

[*woman*] Check the library. I think she's decided to take up residence there.

[*narrator*] What does the woman mean?

A

Question 25

[*man*] I can't believe that Professor Daniels assigned another 50 pages to read by tomorrow. Doesn't she know that Biology is not the only course on campus?

[*woman*] I know what you mean. I'll be up most of the night.

[*narrator*] What does the woman imply?

SCRIPT 4

Question 1

[*woman*] I wasn't at the meeting last night. Did Harry get there with the sodas?

[*man*] Just at the last minute. Everyone was starting to get thirsty.

[*narrator*] What does the man imply?

Question 2

[*man*] Professor Smith didn't like the outline for my term paper. He said that the topic is too broad.

[*woman*] Well, it's back to the old drawing board for you.

[*narrator*] What does the woman suggest the man should do?

Question 3

[*man*] We've missed you down at the student lounge. Where have you been?

[*woman*] I've hardly had time to breathe since the semester began.

[*narrator*] What does the woman mean?

Question 4

[*woman*] I didn't hear you come in last night. How was the party?

[*man*] I didn't get in until after 2 o'clock, but I had a ball.

[*narrator*] What does the man mean?

Question 5

[*man*] I hear that you've applied to graduate school. Where do you plan to enroll?

[*woman*] I'd like to get into Princeton, but in all probability I won't be accepted there. So it looks like Rutgers instead.

[*narrator*] What does the woman imply?

Question 6

[*woman*] I really don't want to have to take another semester of Latin.

[*man*] Well, in lieu of Latin, you could take the course in the Classics Department on Roman Culture.

[*narrator*] What does the man suggest the woman do?

A

Question 7

[*man*] The committee appointed me to ask you if you'd consider running for class president. We think you'd do an excellent job.

[*woman*] I'm flattered, but class president is a big responsibility. Let me sleep on it, okay?

[*narrator*] What does the woman mean?

Question 8

[*woman*] Did they hear anything about those two children who were reported missing?

[*man*] Yes, the evening news reported that they had been found safe and sound, though they gave their parents quite a scare.

[*narrator*] What does the man imply?

Question 9

[*man*] I'm hungry. Why don't we go out for something to eat?

[*woman*] We don't have to do that. There's food in the kitchen. I'll just whip up something quick.

[*narrator*] What will the woman do?

Question 10

[*woman*] Helen wasn't in class today. Have you seen her?

[*man*] She's been under the weather recently, but she should be back soon.

[*narrator*] What does the man imply?

Question 11

[*man*] I'm going home to study where it's quiet. I can't concentrate with everyone talking.

[*woman*] Oh, I just tune out the noise.

[*narrator*] What does the woman mean?

Question 12

[*woman*] I've noticed that you've been working very hard recently.

[*man*] Yes, and at the end of the semester, I'm going to take some time off.

[*narrator*] What will the man do?

Question 13

[*man*] The weather forecast called for thunderstorms. Has it started raining yet?

[*woman*] Well, everyone coming into the building for the past few minutes has been soaked to the skin.

[*narrator*] What does the woman imply?

Question 14

[*woman*] I just met someone named William Rogers who said he might know you.

[*man*] William Rogers? No, the name doesn't ring a bell.

[*narrator*] What does the man mean?

Question 15

[*man*] Victor told me that he was having trouble paying his bills this semester and needed a job.

[*woman*] Well, he's been pounding the pavement for the last two weeks but still hasn't found anything.

[*narrator*] What does the woman imply about Victor?

A

Question 16

[*man*] I heard that Brooks is looking for a place to live. Could he move into your apartment?

[*woman*] That would be out of the question.

[*narrator*] What does the woman mean?

Question 17

[*woman*] That's a very nice-looking jacket that you're wearing. Was it expensive?

[*man*] Well, I got it on sale.

[*narrator*] What does the man mean?

Question 18

[*man*] We're planning a surprise party for Alex's birthday. Can you come?

[*woman*] Sure. And I won't breathe a word of it to anyone.

[*narrator*] What does the woman mean?

Question 19

[*woman*] I heard that George comes from a very wealthy family. He must have a lot of money to spend.

[*man*] I don't know who told you that, but George can hardly make ends meet.

[*narrator*] What does the man imply?

Question 20

[*woman*] Did you go to your younger sister's birthday party yesterday?

[*man*] Yes, and I felt like a fish out of water. I was the only person who was over the age of 18.

[*narrator*] What does the man mean?

Question 21

[*man*] After the test, we're all planning to go out for something to eat and listen to some music. Can you come?

[*woman*] Sure thing. In fact, that's just what the doctor ordered.

[*narrator*] What does the woman mean?

Question 22

[*woman*] Liz told me that you were one of three people being considered for a scholarship.

[*man*] Yes. I submitted my transcript and a letter explaining why I want the money. Now it looks like everything hinges on the interview.

[*narrator*] What does the man imply?

Question 23

[*man*] I'm writing a paper on the legislative process, but I can't seem to find a lot about the behind the scenes maneuvering that goes on.

[*woman*] Talk to Rube. He worked for two summers as a legislative intern. I'm sure that he's a goldmine of information.

[*narrator*] What does the woman mean?

Question 24

[*woman*] You said that you're going shopping this afternoon, but I thought that you don't get paid until tomorrow.

[*man*] I said that I'm going window shopping this afternoon. Tomorrow I may buy something.

[*narrator*] What does the man mean?

Question 25

[*man*] I'd like a half dozen of those cream pastries—you know, the ones with the sliced fruit on top.

[*woman*] I'm sorry but we're fresh out of them. But we have some nice cheesecake.

[*narrator*] What does the woman mean?

A

SCRIPT 5

[*narrator*] Next you will hear a professor of zoology lecturing to a class about the severe environmental pressures threatening some animal species. Listen to a part of the lecture.

[*professor*] From the appearance of a small tapir-like mammal in what is now Egypt 45 million years ago, elephants evolved a number of species which at one time inhabited every continent. By the end of the Pleistocene glaciation about 10,000 years ago, however, only two species survived—the Asian elephant and the African elephant. Now, the Asian elephant is an endangered species.

The position of the Asian elephant is somewhat paradoxical. It is the elephant usually seen in zoos and circuses; yet, while the story of the dramatic decline of the African elephant, primarily from large-scale poaching, is well known, the African elephant is still ten times more numerous than the Asian species, which now numbers only 35,000 to 45,000 animals.

The dramatic decline of Asian elephant numbers is primarily due to the fact that it shares its habitat with the largest and poorest human population in the world. Massive conversion of forest cover to agriculture and villages has fragmented elephant habitat and populations. There are only about ten populations with over 1,000 elephants. The remaining populations are small, with less than 100 elephants each.

Also population growth has inevitably led to increasing conflict with humans. People once revered the elephant and tolerated the occasional crop raiding and destruction; now they strike back, often with lethal results.

Asian elephants have not traditionally been threatened by poaching for the ivory trade, perhaps because females are tuskless and only 60 percent of the males carry tusks. However, poaching for ivory is on the upswing, especially in southern India. In one outstanding example, out of 1,000 elephants in the Periyar Tiger Reserve, only five adult males are left, and only two of those are tuskers.

Question 1

What is the professor's main point?

Question 2

Why have Asian elephants not been hunted for ivory?

Question 3

What is the greatest threat to Asian elephants?

Question 4

Why is the Periyar Tiger Reserve notable?

Question 5

What will the professor probably discuss next?

[*narrator*] Next you will hear a professor teaching a class in psychology. The professor is talking about the structure and function of the human brain.

The human brain is like an archaeological site, preserving within its layers the basic brain structures of its evolutionary predecessors, the reptiles and the lower mammals. The oldest part of the human brain is the reptilian brain, which is found in the lower center. It resembles the brain of reptiles (the ancestors of mammals) and serves many of the same functions in humans that it serves in reptiles. It regulates a large number of innate behaviors such as path finding, hunting, and reproduction.

During the course of evolution, a new formation of brain cells developed in lower mammals giving them a second brain. The ancient mammalian brain introduced the desires and emotions that motivate mammals to seek pleasure and avoid pain.

The brains of many mammals stopped evolving at this point, but the human brain continued to develop and added a third layer called the neocortex. This new brain gives humans the capability of rational thought. It is because of the neocortex that we are able to engage in verbal communication, to read and write, to empathize with others, and to contemplate our own existence.

A

Question 6

What is the main topic?

Question 7

In what order does the professor discuss the topics?

Question 8

Which of the following correctly matches the function with the brain part?

(A)

Mammalian Brain	Path Finding
Neocortex	Speech
Reptilian Brain	Pain Avoidance

Question 9

What does the professor compare the human brain to?

Question 10

What can be inferred about lower mammals?

[*narrator*] Next you will hear a professor lecturing to a sociology class. The professor is discussing the problem of rural poverty in America.

There are two main factors that make it difficult to escape from rural poverty in America. First, there is a tendency to inherit one's occupation. If a person's parents work in agriculture, the chances are good that that person will also work in agriculture; and the income levels of many farmers and farmworkers are very low. Nor is migration to a city any guarantee of escaping poverty, as the presence of millions of poverty-ridden people who moved from rural areas and who now live in large cities demonstrates.

The other main problem is the size of low-income families in rural America. At one time, economic factors favored large families in rural areas. Before machines and modern technology, the farm family needed children as workers. But now, even though economic conditions have changed, tradition and religious beliefs continue to encourage large families. Although the birth rate in the United States as a whole has steadily declined since the 1950s, it remains high in rural areas. As a result, scarce resources have to be stretched to feed, house, and clothe children. The problem is compounded because low-income rural households often include several generations, and older members are no longer economically productive. Then, when the young adults of these families migrate to the cities in search of jobs, those who are left behind have an even greater burden to bear.

Question 11

What is the topic of the lecture?

Question 12

What does the professor mean by "inherit one's occupation"?

Question 13

Why does the author mention poverty in the large cities?

Question 14

According to the professor, why are large farm families no longer economically justified?

Question 15

According to the professor, what two factors encourage large rural families?

[*narrator*] Next you will hear a professor of astrophysics talking to a class about some of the earliest recorded observations of supernovas.

To the sixteenth-century mind, the idea of an exploding star was an absurdity. It was contrary to the order of nature since stars were thought to belong to a celestial world that was free from change or corruption. The stars were symbols of the eternal and the unchangeable, part of a system of permanence standing above the changing and corruptible world below.

Then, in 1572, a star brighter than the planet Venus was noticed throughout the world. This New Star, or nova, shattered the belief in the incorruptibility of the stars. The thinker most responsible for this rearrangement of the cosmic landscape was Tycho Brahe, an astronomer known for his acid tongue and for the silver nose that he wore to replace the one he lost in a duel.

During a period of 18 months, Tycho made accurate measurements of the star and noted that although the star declined steadily in brightness until it became invisible, its position remained fixed. Today, we use the word supernova to describe this kind of object that is not a new star at all. The star that Tycho observed had been there for tens of millions of years, invisible to the naked eye because it was more than 6,000 light years away. It became visible at the end rather than at the beginning of its evolution because it ended in a cataclysmic explosion.

Question 16

What is the main topic of the lecture?

Question 17

Sixteenth-century observers compared the nova to what object?

Question 18

According to the professor, why had the star not been noticed before it became a supernova?

Question 19

Why was the fixed position of the supernova important to Tycho Brahe?

Question 20

Why was the observation of the supernova significant?

SCRIPT 6

Question 1

[*woman*] Have you heard anything about the new professor?

[*man*] Just that he gave only one A last semester in a class of 25 students in introductory physics.

[*narrator*] What can be inferred about the new professor?

Question 2

[*woman*] The sky is becoming quite cloudy.

[*man*] I hope you remembered to close the windows in the house, otherwise everything might get wet.

[*narrator*] What can be inferred from the conversation?

Question 3

[*man*] The check for dinner totals $20. Is $2 a large enough tip?

[*woman*] It's customary to leave 15% of the check total for tip.

[*narrator*] What does the woman imply?

Question 4

[*woman*] Would you like to take in the movie tonight at the Student Center?

[*man*] Perhaps another time. I have a ticket to the concert being given by the Music Arts Program this evening.

[*narrator*] What can be inferred from the conversation?

Question 5

[*man*] I'm applying for one of the Senior Research Grants. What are my chances?

[*woman*] Twenty-three other students have applied, and there are only three grants. But your *curriculum vitae* looks like one of the top five.

[*narrator*] What does the woman imply?

Question 6

[*woman*] It looks like Martha won't be sharing my apartment after all.

[*man*] That's too bad. I thought that your landlord said that it was okay to have a small dog.

[*narrator*] What can be inferred from the conversation?

Question 7

[*man*] You don't seem yourself today. You keep fidgeting in your chair and looking at the clock.

[*woman*] Oh, the final Biology grades are being posted at 1 o'clock.

[*narrator*] How does the woman feel?

Question 8

[*woman*] Can you tell me where to find a tennis racket?

[*man*] Yes, they're on the second floor, next to the ski equipment.

[*narrator*] Where is this conversation probably taking place?

Question 9

[*man*] Did you see your academic advisor today?

[*woman*] No, I had to cancel again because there was another crisis at the newspaper.

[*narrator*] What can be inferred from the conversation?

Question 10

[*woman*] A couple of days ago my car started making a funny noise.

[*man*] You'd better have a mechanic check it out before you go to Chicago next week.

[*narrator*] What does the man imply?

Question 11

[*man*] I don't understand it. The plant that you gave me for my birthday isn't doing well, even though I water every day.

[*woman*] Why don't you try putting it on the window ledge instead of the bookcase?

[*narrator*] What does the woman imply?

Question 12

[*woman*] The commuter train was jam-packed this morning. It took me nearly 45 minutes to get to school.

[*man*] On the other hand, if everyone drove their cars into the city, we'd all still be sitting in traffic.

[*narrator*] What does the man imply?

A

Question 13

[*man*] Can I use the microscope when you're finished with it?

[*woman*] You'll have to work that out with Jane. She asked first.

[*narrator*] What does the woman imply?

Question 14

[*woman*] I heard that Professor Carsworth chose you to be his teaching assistant next semseter. You must be very pleased.

[*man*] On the balance, yes. It is a quite an honor to work with someone so well known, but it will be a lot of work.

[*narrator*] What does the man imply?

Questions 15–17

[*woman*] I just remembered that the Chess Club is having a pot-luck supper tonight, and I'm supposed to bring a pie. The bakery's closed now. What should I do?

[*man*] You can bake a pie.

[*woman*] Bake a pie? I have trouble heating up a can of soup. How do you expect me to bake a pie?

[*man*] I'll show you how. We've got some apples in the refrigerator, and everything else is in the kitchen cupboard. I'll make the pie crust.

[*woman*] What do I do?

[*man*] Cut the apples into bite-size pieces and sprinkle them with sugar and a little cinnamon—until they have a taste that you like. I'll put the crust in a pie dish. Then you dump in the apples and bake the whole thing in the oven for about 45 minutes.

[*woman*] Well, you sure sound like you know what you're doing.

[*man*] It's so easy that you may drop out of the doctorate program in philosophy and become a pastry chef instead.

Question 15

What did the woman originally plan to take to the supper?

Question 16

What is the woman studying?

Question 17

The woman is responsible for which of the following?

Questions 18–20

[*narrator*] The following conversation takes place in the student cafeteria at a college.

[*man*] Last night I watched an episode from the original *Star Trek* series. The special effects were really crude. The bridge looked like it was made from cardboard boxes with blinking holiday lights for the control panels.

[*woman*] Well, the original series was made in the 1960s for television. Special effects were still in their infancy, and a weekly television program didn't have the huge budget of today's movies.

In fact, I recently saw an episode of *Flash Gordon*, a sci-fi series from the 1950s, in which the characters are supposed to be under water on another planet, so the camera filmed the actors through an aquarium full of tropical fish.

[*man*] Even so, there was something I liked about the *Star Trek* episode—though I can't quite put my finger on it.

[*woman*] Perhaps you sensed that the episode was a morality play. I remember reading that the writers were less interested in special effects than in using the futuristic setting to explore ethical issues.

A

Question 18

The man and the woman agree about what point?

Question 19

The woman mentions which of the following about the *Flash Gordon* series?

Question 20

Why does the man like the *Star Trek* episode?

Questions 21–23

[*man*] Boy, this scratch really hurts.

[*woman*] How did you get it?

[*man*] We were biking on a country road and stopped to watch some cows grazing in a pasture, and I got tangled up in some wire fencing. When I got home, I washed the scratch and put some disinfectant on it.

[*woman*] You really should go to the campus infirmary and get a tetanus shot.

[*man*] Why?

[*woman*] Here's what the *First Aid Encyclopedia* says about tetanus:

Tetanus, also known as lockjaw, is a potentially serious disease of the nervous system caused by bacterial poison. You get tetanus by having a cut or scratch that becomes infected. Tetanus bacteria are most commonly found in and around areas contaminated with animal feces.

[*man*] Okay, you've convinced me.

Question 21

What will the man probably do?

Question 22

Why does the woman think the man may have been exposed to tetanus bacteria?

Question 23

Why is it important for the man to get a tetanus shot?

Questions 24–28

[*narrator*] Next you will hear a professor lecturing to a class on developmental psychology.

[*professor*] Early adolescence is the second most rapid time of growth and change in human development. Only infancy exceeds early adolescence in the rapidity of growth.

Physically, young adolescents are experiencing a growth spurt and the onset of puberty. They have special health and nutritional needs related to these physical changes.

More important, however, are the emotional and social changes. Young adolescents are looking for both a sense of uniqueness and and a sense of belonging, both separation and commitment, and both future goals and personal past. For the first time in their lives, they have awakened to a sense of personal destiny; and, on the other hand, for the first time in their lives, they see themselves as belonging to a particular generation.

Intellectually, young adolescents are exploring values and ideas in a new way. They are beginning to form abstractions, to generalize, and to think about thinking itself. This intellectual development enables them to shift away from an authoritarian and childlike sense of right and wrong to a more open and complex approach to value formation. And they begin to struggle with conflicting concepts like individual rights and the overriding social good.

Because this is a critical time in human development, there is a tendency to be apprehensive about the outcome. It is important to remember, however, that the great majority steers its way safely through the various dangers of a demanding period of life.

Question 24

What is the most rapid time of growth and change in human development?

Question 25

What is the focus of the lecture?

Question 26

What is the author's attitude toward the problems of adolescence?

Question 27

What is the age group referred to by the phrase "early adolscence"?

Question 28

Before early adolescence, how does a child usually learn right from wrong?

Questions 29–32

A

[*narrator*] Next you will hear a professor lecturing to a geology class.

[*professor*] What is ground water? Ground water is precipitation (rain, snow, etc.) that seeps down through the soil until it reaches rock material that is saturated with water.

A couple of important factors are responsible for the existence of ground water. On the one hand, there is gravity. Water on the surface will try to seep into the ground below it. On the other hand, beneath our feet are layers of rock, some of which are relatively porous, through which water can flow, others of which are dense and relatively impervious to water.

Gravity can't pull water all the way to the center of the Earth because deep in the bedrock are rock layers made of dense material, such as granite, or material that water has a hard time penetrating, such as clay. These layers may be underneath porous rock layers and, thus, act as a confining layer to retard the downward movement of water. Since it is more difficult for the water to go any deeper, it tends to pool in the porous layers and flow in a more horizontal direction underneath the ground until it reaches an exposed surface—water body, like a river or a lake.

Visualize it this way. Get two sponges. Cover one with plastic wrap and lay the other on top of it. Pour water on top of the sandwich and it will seep through the top sponge downward until it hits the plastic wrap. The top sponge will become saturated, and water will start flowing sideways and come out at the edges of the sponge. The top sponge is like the porous rock layers beneath the Earth's surface, while the plastic covered bottom sponge is like the impervious bedrock through which water cannot flow easily.

Question 29

What is the lecture primarily about?

Question 30

Match the features of the professor's visualization to the actual features of the Earth.

Question 31

It can be inferred that the water flowing from the side of the sponge in the professor's visualization is most like what?

Question 32

What stops precipitation from seeping deeper and deeper into the Earth?

Questions 33–36

[*narrator*] Next you will hear a professor lecturing to a class on World Literature.

[*professor*] The Finnish epic, *Kalevala*, is probably the best known Finnish literary work throughout the world. It was first published over 150 years ago by Elias Lönnrot, but its fantastic adventures with damsels, warriors, and magicians had been preserved for centuries by traditional singers in isolated villages on the Finnish-Russian fontier.

A medical doctor by profession and an avid folklore collector by avocation, Lönnrot logged many miles on foot in the early 1830s writing down as many variants as he could find of the songs about these Finnish folk heros; and, in 1835, he published the *Kalevala* as an epic—the Finnish counterpart to the Nordic *Edda* and the Germanic *Nibelungelied*.

For Finnland, the publication of the songs served as a major stimulus to the building and fostering of a distinct national identity. Until then, the Finnish language had been held in rather low esteem, because Finland's educated, urban elite had embraced, for the most part, the language, culture, and traditions of the governing Swedes. Through Lönnrot's *Kalevala*, the intelligentsia began to awaken to the richness of the Finnish heritage.

For the Finnish people, much under the influence of the general Romantic trends of the times, the *Kalevala* presented a past of which they could be proud. It became requried reading in secondary schools; and playwrights, composers, and other artists were soon using its themes. Although it took some time, the *Kalevala* helped to kindle national aspirations that eventually culminated in the establishment of an independent Finland.

Question 33

What was the profession of Elias Lönnrot?

Question 34

What ethnic group governed Finland at the time the *Kalevala* was published?

Question 35

Which of the following would LEAST likely have appeared in the *Kalevala*?

Question 36

What is the professor's attitude toward the *Kalevala*?

Questions 37–40

[*narrator*] Next you will hear a professor talking to a biology class. The students are about to go on a field trip to learn how to identify wild flowers.

[*professor*] We're going to spend this afternoon out in the field looking at wild flowers. We'll be using the Audobon Society's *Field Guide to North American Wildflowers*. I hope you all have your copies of the *Guide*.

You'll notice that the *Guide* is divided into two major parts: color photographs and descriptive information. You'll be using the color photographs to make a tentative identification of any species you find. Then you'll use the detailed descriptive information to confirm or disconfirm the tentative identification and to learn more about the species.

The photographs are divided into basic colors. Yellow, white, pink, and blue are the most common colors, though you might find a red, brown, or even a green flower. Within each color set, the photographs are categorized according to flower shape: simple-shaped, daisy- and dandelion-shaped, and odd-shaped, with a few other, less-common varieties such as rounded clusters and elongated clusters.

When you find a specimen, note its color and shape and consult the corresponding pages in the photograph section of the *Guide*. When you think that you have identified the specimen by its photo, then read the detailed information provided in the descriptive part of the book. There you learn about the range of the specimen, its habitat, more particulars regarding its flower and leaf structures, and other facts such as the months in which it is likely to bloom.

A word of advice. Identification is complicated by the fact that the appearance of a flowering plant may change as it grows to maturity. Thus, you may need to work back and forth from the specimen, to the photographs, to the descriptive information. Still, if you apply yourself diligently, you should be able to identify at least a dozen different species before our trip is over.

Question 37

What is the most common of the following flower colors?

Question 38

What is the *least* common of the following flower shapes?

Question 39

Why is the descriptive information of the *Guide* important?

Question 40

Why does the professor warn that a flower plant may change as it matures?

APPENDIX B

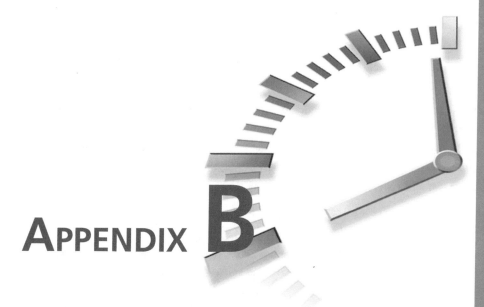

Common English Idioms

Familiarize yourself with common English idioms by consulting the following list.

Back out   Break an agreement, withdraw from a commitment. *Kevin promised he would tutor me in Spanish, but now he's trying to back out.*

Back to back   Following one right after the other. *What a hard day; I had physics and chemistry back-to-back.*

Back to the drawing board   Starting over again. *The professor did not like my proposal for a term paper, so I guess it's back to the drawing board.*

Back to the salt mines   Back to hard work. *I enjoyed dinner, but now it's back to the salt mines; I've got 75 more pages to read tonight.*

Be that as it may   Even granting what you say to be true. *Perhaps we won't have to do another lab project; but be that as it may, the course still requires a lot of work.*

Beat one's head against the wall   Waste time trying to do something impossible, suggests frustration. *I feel like I'm beating my head against the wall; I don't think I'll ever understand probability theory.*

Before you know it   Almost immediately, very quick because time will pass very fast. *It's already Thanksgiving, and before you know it the semester will be over.*

Beg to differ   Respectfully disagree. *I beg to differ; I think that Buchanan was a greater president.*

Begin to see the light   Start to understand something. *The equations in organic chemistry are really tough, but I think I'm beginning to see the light.*

Best laid plans of mice and men   The most carefully thought-out plans. *I thought I would be through with all of my assignments by now, but it will take another two hours; the best laid plans of mice and men, you know.*

Better late than never   Better to do something late than never at all. *The papers were due last week, but Eleanor turned hers in today; but I guess it's better late than never.*

Bit off more than one can chew   Over confident, to take on more than one can handle. *This semester I bit off more than I can chew; chemistry and two math courses are just too much.*

Bite the bullet   To do something painful or undesirable. *I don't really want to take biology, but it's a required course; so I guess I'll just bite the bullet, and take it next semester.*

Blessing in disguise   Something unfortunate that turns out to be for the good. *I got closed out of Dr. Johnson's math class last semester, but that turned out to be a blessing in disguise because I had to take Dr. Adam's course, which I really like.*

Blows something   To ruin something, to waste a chance. *Carl got a B; he could have had an A, but he blew it when he didn't get his term paper in on time.*

Boiled down do something   To come down to, in the final analysis. *I'll get either an A or a B; it all boils down to how I did on the exam.*

Bored stiff   Find something very uninteresting. *I thought I would enjoy astronomy, but I'm bored stiff in that class.*

Bored to death   See **bored stiff**.

Bound and determined   Committed to doing something. *Mike is bound and determined to finish that report before Tuesday.*

Breath of fresh air   Literally, air that is not stale; figuratively, a new or imaginative approach. *After that study session, I need a breath of fresh air; I think I'll walk over to the cafeteria.*

Breathe easy   Relax after a stressful period. *As soon as this semester is over, I'll be able to breathe easy.*

Bright and early   Very early. *We've got a long drive, so please be ready bright and early.*

Brush up on   Review. *I think I'll brush up on my French before we go to Paris.*

Buckle down   Get serious, get down to business. *Harry had better buckle down this semester; his average is not all that good.*

Burn bridges   Sever ties. *I said "yes" even though I don't want to sit on the committee, because I don't want to burn any bridges.*

Burn out   Become very tired. *I'm glad this semester is nearly over because I'm burned out.*

Burn the candle at both ends   Work very hard; stay out very late. *I'm worried that Peter hasn't been getting enough sleep; he's been burning the candle at both ends.*

Burn the midnight oil   Work very late. *With exams scheduled for next week, I'll be burning the midnight oil for sure.*

Business as usual   As expected; routine. *It's been business as usual; two weekly quizzes, a term paper, and a mid-term.*

Call it a day/night   To stop or to quit work. *It's 11:00, so I'm going to call it a day; I have to get up early in the morning.*

Catch something   See or attend. *Did you catch the concert the other night? I heard it was really good.*

Catch on to something   To figure out, to finally understand. *It took three months, but I finally caught on to algebra.*

Changed horses in midstream   Make an important change in the middle of some process. *During my junior year, I was thinking of changing my major from history to philosophy, but I didn't want to change horses in midstream.*

Chip in   Pay a part of, contribute money for. *Since Dan is driving his car to Boston, we'll all chip in for the gas.*

Clear sailing   An easy path; projecting easy progress. *Once I get past my history final, it'll be easy sailing right through to graduation.*

Come full circle   Return to an original position. *I've come full circle; at first I really enjoyed history, then I didn't, but now I do again.*

Come in handy   To be useful or convenient. *Thanks for giving me your old dictionary; it'll come in handy.*

Come to a standstill   Stop; arrive at impasse. *We've come to a standstill; the vote is tied at 3-3.*

B

Come to an end   To be over, to be finished. *The meeting finally came to an end at midnight.*

Come to/cross one's mind   To come to mind; to become a conscious thought. *The idea of becoming a lawyer had never crossed my mind until last semester, but next year I'll be starting law school.*

Come up   Something unexpected occurs. *I wanted to go to San Francisco this weekend, but now I can't; something came up.*

Cover a lot of ground   Go over a lot of information or material. *We covered a lot of ground the last two weeks of this semester, two chapters on the last day.*

Crack a book   Literally, to open a book; figuratively, to study. *Laura always seems to get straight As, but you never see her crack a book.*

Cross a bridge when one comes to it   To deal with the problem if and when it arises. *My adviser says I may have to take a course in symbolic logic, but that's a really tough course; I'll cross that bridge when I come to it.*

Cross one's fingers   Literally, to overlap one's fingers out of superstition; figuratively, to hope for the best. *Paul's worried that he may not have passed algebra, but I'll keep my fingers crossed for him.*

Cry over spilled milk   To regret something that nothing can be done about. *Last semester was a disaster for me, but I guess there's no reason to cry over spilled milk; I'll just have to do better next semester.*

Cut and dried   Predetermined, routine, uninteresting. *You shouldn't worry too much about the lab final; everything covered on it is pretty much cut and dried.*

Cut class   Fail to attend class without proper authorization. *I'm worried about Bob, he's been cutting classes recently; I'm afraid his professors will begin to notice.*

Die is cast   The decision has been made. *Prof. Beard may not like the approach I took in my paper, but the die is cast; I'll have to live with the consequences.*

Dirt cheap   Extremely cheap. *Term papers are dirt cheap; I'm surprised more students don't buy them instead of writing their own.*

Do an about face   Change one's position. *Arnold wasn't going on the class trip to Phoenix, but he did at about face; yesterday he said he would be going after all.*

Do something on the run   To do something while one is on the move, without stopping. *I can't have dinner with you because I'm just too busy; I'll have to grab a sandwich on the run.*

Don't hold your breath   Don't expect for something to happen. *I asked the dean's assistant whether I might be one of the winners, and she said don't hold your breath; so I guess I'm out of the running.*

Down in the dumps   Depressed. *Let's take Mary out to dinner to try to cheer her up; she's been down the dumps ever since she learned that she got a B in English.*

Down to the wire   In doubt until the last moment. *Both Ellen and Linda are very well qualified; the election will be close and go down to the wire.*

Downhill from here   Easy the rest of the way. *My hardest finals are already over, so it will be downhill from here.*

Draw a blank   Fail to remember. *When I got to the last question on road doctrine, I drew a blank; I wrote down something, but I don't think it was correct.*

Draw to a close   Come to an end. *Well, our college careers are drawing to a close, and I think we've had a great time.*

Dream come true   Extremely satisfactory, beyond expectations. *The new apartment is very spacious and has fantastic views of the city skyline; it's like a dream come true.*

Drive someone crazy/up the wall   Literally, make someone insane; figuratively, to get on someone's nerves. *My new roommate is a music major; her constant practicing is driving me up the wall.*

Drop in the bucket   A tiny bit; so small as to not make a difference. *I found a job working three hours a week, but the money I would earn is just a drop in the bucket.*

Drop the ball   To make a mistake; to fail to discharge one's responsibility. *The study group was counting on John to have notes for week 3, but he dropped the ball; someone else will have to report on that chapter.*

Eagle eye   Watchful; very attentive. *Old Prof. Robbins has an eagle eye for plagiarism; last year, he caught three students who had bought term papers.*

Easier said than done   A task more difficult to do than to describe. *Today in class, Prof. Michaels said that we should submit outlines by Monday, but that's easier said than done.*

Eat and run   To eat a meal quickly and leave immediately. *I hate to eat and run, but I have to get back to the library.*

Eat one's words   Confess that one was wrong. *I was absolutely certain that Monroe was the fourth president, but I have to eat my words; it turns out that Monroe was the fifth president.*

B

Everything but the kitchen sink   Everything imaginable except something like the kitchen sink which doesn't really belong. *Adele brought two suitcases just for the weekend; she had everything in there but the kitchen sink.*

Fall into place   To come together; to become organized. *Now that I'm a senior, everything seems to be falling into place; I know what I want to do next year and what I want for a career.*

Fall through   Not happen. *I wanted to study in Ireland next semester, but that fell through.*

Feather in one's cap   An award or honor; something to be proud of. *Getting the only A on the history final was quite a feather in Steve's cap.*

Feel out of place   Feel uncomfortable. *I don't think I'll go to the party at Clara's house; I always feel out of place there.*

Fighting chance   A good possibility of success, provided a good effort is made. *Our team is in second-place with only two games to go, but they have a fighting chance of finishing in first.*

First come, first served   Serving those who arrive first, in order. *The library is giving away some old books, but it's first come, first served, so you'd better get there early.*

Flat broke   Completely without money. *I'm flat broke; I can't even afford to buy a sandwich.*

Follow up on   Attend to details. *The committee likes the idea of sponsoring a park cleanup and asked me to follow up with the city park agency.*

For the moment/for the time being   For the present; for now. *I'm not entirely happy with my living arrangements, but for the time being they will have to do; next semester I'll find a different apartment.*

Fresh out   Completely used up. *There were some sodas in the refrigerator, but it seems we're fresh out now.*

From the horse's mouth   Coming from someone who knows. *It looks like Dean Roberts will be retiring next semester; that information comes straight from the horse's mouth.*

Get a break   To benefit from some good luck. *I got a break last week when Prof. Johnson was sick; I had not yet finished my paper.*

Get a handle on something   Understand; manage. *I can't seem to get a handle on statistics, I guess I'll have to get a tutor.*

Get around to doing something   To do something after a long delay. *I finally got around to answering the letter from Amy; she only wrote me three months ago.*

Get busy/get cracking   Start to work; start working harder. *You'd better get cracking on your lab project; there's only one more week in the semester.*

Get hold of someone   To contact; to reach; to speak with. *I can't get hold of Larry. Has anyone seen him recently?*

Get in touch with someone   To communicate with someone. *Has anyone seen Fred recently; I can't get in touch with him at his phone number.*

Get one's feet wet   To have a new experience; to begin a new project. *I'm just getting my feet wet down at the police department, but I think I'm really going to enjoy my internship this semester.*

Get one's second wind   To catch one's breath. *About 10 o'clock I got my second wind and was able to keep studying until midnight.*

Get rolling   Get started. *We didn't get rolling until about three so we didn't finish up until six.*

Get out of the wrong side of the bed   Be in a bad mood. *Al must have gotten out of the wrong side of the bed this morning; he just snarled when I said good morning.*

Give someone a rain check   An event that has been canceled but rescheduled for later; figuratively, to tell someone that an invitation remains open. *I'd like to have dinner with you, but I just have too much to do; can I have a rain check?*

Go a long way toward doing something   Accomplish quite a lot toward a specific objective. *The money we made from the charity auction will go a long way toward buying the plaque that we want to put in the library.*

Go along for the ride   Accompany someone for the purpose of watching rather than participating in an activity. *I don't really want to bungee jump, but I'll go along for the ride and watch you.*

Go along with   Agree with; agree to do something; perhaps not wholeheartedly. *I'll go along with the majority on the proposal to extend the library hours, but I can't support the plan to hire a new security officer.*

Go bad   To turn; to become rotten. *Something in the refrigerator smells awful; I think the milk has gone bad.*

Go 50-50   Share the cost equally. *I agree that we need a new television set for the apartment, so we'll go 50-50 on the cost.*

Go out of one's way   Make an extra effort. *Bob went out of his way to make sure that we had a cake for the party; he called six different bakeries before he found one that was open.*

B

Go through the motions   To do something insincerely. *Since Jane learned that she won't be returning next semester, she's just been going through the motions.*

Go to the trouble of   Make an effort. *Don't go to the trouble of cooking tonight; we'll eat out.*

Go window shopping   Literally, look at the display in a store window; figuratively, to look at merchandise without intention of buying. *I really can't afford a new winter coat, but I think I'll go window shopping.*

Gold mine of information   A reference or someone who has a lot of information. *Evan's grandfather was a hippie during the 1960s, and he's a gold mine of information about the anti-war movement.*

Half a loaf is better than none   Having something is better than having nothing. *I tried to get both Saturday and Sunday off work, but I have to work Saturday; I guess half a loaf is better than none.*

Hand it to someone   Give someone credit. *You have to hand it to Jerri; she really worked hard on the grant proposal, and she got everything she asked for.*

Hardly have time to breathe   To be very busy. *With the part-time job and my academic overload, I hardly have time to breathe.*

Have a ball   Enjoy something immensely. *We really had a ball at the party last night; thank you very much for inviting us.*

Have a change of heart   To change one's attitude or mind. *John was going to stop seeing Mary, but he had a change of heart; now it looks as though they'll get married.*

Have a close call/close shave   Narrowly avoid harm or bad consequences. *We had a close call in the car this morning; a truck pulled out in front of us, and we nearly hit it.*

Have a good command of   Understand clearly. *Seth has a good command of the rules of football; you can ask him anything about sports and he'll know the answer.*

Have a green thumb   Have the ability to grow plants well. *My roommate has a green thumb; our apartment is full of plants.*

Have a rough time   To live through a difficult period. *Since John's mother died, he's been having a rough time; I know his grades will suffer this semester.*

Have a shot at something   Have a chance to succeed. *Dan has a shot at becoming class president; a lot of people already like him, and more and more people are getting to know him.*

Have a weakness for   To be very fond of. *I have a weakness for doughnuts; this morning I ate 3 with my coffee.*

Have come a long way   To have accomplished much. *Candy has come a long way since she got to the University; when she first arrived, she could hardly speak English, and now she's fluent.*

Have one's hands full   Be very busy. *I have my hands full this semester, working 10 hours per week at the library and taking an extra course.*

Have something to go   To buy food for takeout. *I don't have time to sit down to eat, so I'll just get some Chinese food to go.*

Have the time of one's life   To have a very good time; to enjoy immensely. *I had the time of my life at the party last night; thank you very much for inviting me.*

Hinge on something   To depend upon something. *I think I have a good chance of getting into medical school, but everything hinges upon the interview and my recommendations.*

Hit a snag   Encounter an unexpected problem. *Our plans to go skiing this weekend hit a snag; the weather report says there's no snow.*

Hit the books   Study. *I've got to hit the books; the big test is only three days away.*

Hit the hay/sack   Go to bed; get some sleep. *It's very late, and I have to get up in the morning; so I'm going to hit the hay.*

Hit the spot   Refreshing. *On a very hot day, a glass of cool lemonade really hits the spot.*

Hitch/thumb a ride   To ask for a ride; to get a ride with someone. *If you're going to Philadelphia this weekend, I'd like to hitch a ride with you; I'm going to visit my brother.*

Hold up   To endure; to manage. *I think Nancy's holding up very well; it's been a very difficult semester for her.*

Hop, skip, and a jump   A short distance. *Our apartment is just a hop, skip, and a jump from the museum; it will take you no more than five minutes to get here.*

If push comes to shove   Under the worst possible circumstances. *I haven't found a new apartment yet; but if push comes to shove, I can always sleep on Pat's couch for a couple of weeks.*

In a fog   Preoccupied; not paying attention. *Ingrid has been studying too hard; she's really in a fog.*

In all probability   Very likely; almost certainly. *I don't think my scores on the placement test were very good; and in all probability, I'll have to take freshman math.*

In case of something   In the event of; as a contingency. *In case I don't get back by midnight, please leave the front porch light on.*

B

In full swing   In progress; underway. *We hit traffic; by the time we got there, the meeting was in full swing.*

In lieu of something   In place of something; instead of something. *In lieu of the required math course, I can take a course in symbolic logic in the philosophy department.*

In mint condition   In perfect condition. *Frank's new car is three years old, but it looks like it's in mint condition.*

In one ear and out the other   Unheard; not heeded. *I doubt that George will change; I explained that everyone else wants the apartment to be cleaner, but with George it's in one ear and out the other.*

In one's mind's eye   In one's memory; in one's imagination. *I can see the town square in my mind's eye, and the courthouse is right next to the bus station.*

In one's spare time   During one's extra time; during time not reserved for something else. *Sam is a full-time student, but in her spare time she likes to paint.*

In practice   In reality as opposed to theory. *The college requires you to pay your tuition by the beginning of the semester, but in practice you can pay as late as three weeks after the semester begins.*

In round numbers   Approximately. *How much is the dinner check? In round numbers $18.*

In short supply   Scarce; difficult to find. *I wanted to serve asparagus for dinner, but they're in short supply right now; so we may have broccoli.*

In stock   Readily available. *I called the sporting goods store, and they have parkas in stock; so you shouldn't have any trouble finding a warm coat that fits you.*

In the hole   In debt; owing money. *I'd like to take a vacation, but I'm two hundred dollars in the hole because my car broke down.*

In the near future   Immediately ahead; foreseeable. *I don't think I'll be going home in the near future, but maybe this summer I can afford the plane fare.*

In the running   In contention; having a chance to win. *Two hundred people applied for the position, and all but ten have been rejected; Jacob is still in the running.*

In the same boat as   In a position similar to. *Kurt and I are in the same boat; we both have to take at least one course during summer semester.*

In the works   Being done; in progress. *The administration says that a new parking lot is in the works; but I doubt that it will be finished before I graduate.*

It's about time!   Almost too late; a long time coming. *It's about time! I submitted that request over three weeks ago.*

Join the club!   To recognize that someone is a similar situation. *You haven't finished your paper either? Join the club! I guess we'll all be up all night.*

Just what the doctor ordered   Exactly what is needed; suitable; appropriate. *Thank you for inviting me to go bike riding; after a long day in the library, it's just what the doctor ordered.*

Keep on one's toes   Stay alert; be watchful. *Thanks for the warning about pickpockets; I'll stay on my toes.*

Keep someone or something in mind   Think about someone or something. *I don't need an assistant right now, but I'll keep you in mind in case I do in the future.*

Keep something to one's self   Keep something a secret. *The news about Karen is not public information; I'll keep it to myself.*

Killed time   To waste time. *My order won't be ready for an hour, so I'll kill some time walking in the park.*

Killed two birds with one stone   To solve two problems with one solution. *I'll listen to the tape of the lecture while I jog; that way, I can kill two birds with one stone.*

Know something backwards and forwards   To know something very well. *I studied for three days, and I know the material backwards and forwards; I'll be very disappointed if I don't get a good grade on the exam.*

Knuckle down   Get to work. *Because of the wedding, I'm behind schedule; I'll have to knuckle down and really work hard if I hope to get the project done on time.*

Lay down the law   To state the rules firmly. *Too many papers were being submitted late, so Friday I laid down the law to the class: no more extensions.*

Lay someone off   Fire someone; dismiss an employee. *I got laid off from my job at the newspaper on Friday; Monday I'll start looking for something else.*

Learn to live with something   To adapt to something uncomfortable or unpleasant. *I don't like the library's new policy on book returns, but I can live with it; I'll just have to make sure I get my books back on time.*

Leave no stone unturned   To be thorough; to consider all possibilities. *Someone at this college must speak Romanian; I'll ask everyone; I'll leave no stone unturned.*

Leave something on   Fail to turn off. *When you get home, will you check the air conditioner in my room? I think I left it on.*

B

Leave something open   To leave a date or time open. *We need to get together to discuss the upcoming meeting; I'll leave Wednesday open for you.*

Let someone down   Disappoint someone; fail to deliver on a promise. *I know that the others are counting on me, and I won't let them down; the cake will be ready by six.*

Let something slide   To neglect something. *I know I should check the last citation, but I'll let it slide; I don't think anyone really reads all the footnotes.*

Like a fish out of water   Completely out of place; very awkward. *Everyone was speaking French, but I don't speak French; I felt like a fish out of water.*

Live and let live   To avoid interfering with another's business. *I don't care that Nancy smokes; so long as it's not in my house; my philosophy is live and let live.*

Look forward to something   To anticipate something with pleasure. *I'm looking forward to the class reunion; I have such fond memories of college.*

Loose sleep over   To worry excessively. *I got Cs on all the mid-terms, but I'm not going to lose any sleep over it.*

Make a big deal about   Make something very significant or important. *The committee rejected my dissertation proposal, but I'm not going to make a big deal of it; I'll just work on it some more.*

Make a fuss over   To worry about something; bother about something. *Please tell your wife not to make a fuss over my coming to dinner; I like good home cooking.*

Make a living   Earn money to live on. *I would have more time to study if I didn't have to make a living.*

Make an exception for   To create an exception to a rule. *I don't usually have wine with lunch, but in this case I'll make an exception.*

Make ends meet   To manage to live on a certain amount of money. *Even with my scholarship and my part-time job, it's hard to make ends meet; I'm going to have to go to the college for an emergency loan.*

Make do   To do as well as possible under the circumstances. *I want to buy a new car, but I'll have to make do with the old one for another year.*

Make oneself at home   To make oneself comfortable as though one were at home. *Please come in and make yourself at home; the others won't be here for awhile.*

Make up one's mind   Decide. I could go to Miami or to St. Petersburg; *I haven't made up my mind which yet.*

Make someone's mouth water   To make someone hungry. *This looks like a really good restaurant; just reading the menu makes my mouth water.*

Make time   To schedule time for someone or something. *I'm really busy, but I'll make time to stop by the library to pick up the book for you.*

Meet someone halfway   To compromise. *We still don't like the idea of an additional student activities fee, but we'll meet the administration halfway on this demand.*

Mend one's ways   To correct one's behavior. *I was really disappointed in my mid-term grade; I guess I'll have to mend my ways and study harder.*

Mind one's own business   To ignore things that don't concern one. *Mike and Sally seem to be having personal problems, but I'm going to mind my own business and say nothing.*

Money burning a hole in someone's pocket   A strong urge to spend money. *I can hardly wait to get to New York City and go to the stores; this money is burning a hole in my pocket.*

Move on to something else   To leave behind something and go on to something new. *College is almost over, and I'm ready to move on to something new; I begin my new job next Monday.*

Mull something over   To think about something. *I'll mull over what you said, but I can't make you any promises.*

Never fear   Have confidence; don't worry. *Never fear; I'll pick you up in time to make your flight.*

No hard feelings   Bearing no anger or resentment. *Sure we lost the game; but no hard feelings. We'll drive to the party together.*

Nose about   To investigate; to check into something. *I don't know the answer to your question; but I'll nose about the library to see what I can turn up.*

Not believe one's eyes   An exaggeration. To be so surprised or shocked as not to believe what one sees. *I couldn't believe my eyes, but there it was: an orange Volkswagen in the center of the quad.*

Not breathe a word of something   To say nothing. *I understand that this information is very sensitive; I won't breathe a word of it to anyone.*

Not to sleep a wink   Not to sleep at all. *I was so worried that I might miss the bus this morning that I didn't sleep a wink.*

Nothing to it   Easily done. *The trick with the string looks complicated, but there's nothing to it.*

B

Off duty   Not working at the moment. *When I go off-duty at 4 o'clock, I'll call the restaurant.*

Off the record   Unofficial; not for attribution. *Officially I'm not able to comment on that question; but off the record, I'll tell you that the dean supports the idea.*

Off to a running start   Off to a good beginning. *I'm off to a running start this semester; I've already gotten As on two pop quizzes.*

On a diet   Trying to lose weight by eating selectively. *I'd like to have dessert, but I'm on a diet.*

On one's best behavior   Being as polite or proper as possible. *I promise you that when Mary's parents visit, I'll be on my best behavior.*

On one's mind   Thinking about. *Prof. Johnson's remarks about Feuerbach have been on my mind for some time, and I'm thinking about them as a possible term paper topic.*

On one's way   Already en route. *I'll be on my way in five minutes, and I should be there before noon.*

On sale   Offered for a special price. *The shoes were on sale, so I bought two pairs.*

On second thought   Having reconsidered. *On second thought, I think I will have coffee after all.*

On the dot   Precisely, exactly. *We'll be arriving at three o'clock on the dot.*

On the double   Twice as fast; very fast. *Maria's having the baby, and we have to get there on the double.*

On the horizon   To happen sometime in the future. *It's not official yet, but Dean Smith's retirement is on the horizon.*

On the house   Given away for free by a merchant as a gesture of good will. *The waiter apologized for the delay and told us that the beverages were on the house.*

On the spur of the moment   Spontaneously; suddenly. *We hadn't planned to go to the movies, but on the spur of the moment we decided to go see* Shakespeare in Love.

On the verge of doing something   About to do something fairly important. *Gerry has been dating Ann for three years, and he's on the verge of asking her to marry him.*

One's work is cut out for one   A difficult task has been defined. *With an overload this semester, I've really got my work cut out for me.*

Out like a light   Unconscious; or as though unconscious. *I was so tired after the trip to the beach, that when my head hit the pillow, I was out like a light.*

Out of commission   No longer working. *I can't drive us to school this morning; my car is out of commission.*

Out of gas   Having no fuel. *We ran out of gas on the Turnpike, and I had to walk to the nearest exit.*

Out of luck   Without good luck. *I know you wanted chocolate ice cream, but you're out of luck; you'll have to eat strawberry.*

Out of order   Not working. *This pay phone seems to be out of order; I'll try the next one.*

Out of reach   Not close enough to be reached or touched. *Please put the cookies on the counter where they will be out of reach of the children.*

Out of season   Not available. *Cantaloupes are out of season, so I substituted honeydew melon instead.*

Out of service   Inoperable; not working. *The elevators are out of service, so we'll have to walk to the third floor.*

Out of shape/out of condition   Not in good physical condition. *I enjoyed the walking tour of the city, but we'll have to take a taxi back to the hotel because I'm out of condition.*

Out of stock   Not immediately available for sale. *We went to the hardware store to buy the new wrench we saw advertised on television, but they are temporarily out of stock.*

Out of the question   Not possible; not permitted; not even open to debate. *Paying more than five hundred dollars per month rent is out of the question; we'll just have to keep looking for an apartment.*

Out of town   Away from home. *No, I'm sorry Fred is not available to speak with you; he's out of town for the weekend.*

Out of work   Not working; not employed. *Michael's been out of work since October; I don't know how he pays his bills.*

Over the hump   Having passed the most difficult part. *Now that I've finished my required courses, I'm over the hump; I can enjoy the rest of college.*

Pass   Decline. *Thank you for the offer of the ride, but I think I'll pass. I enjoy walking.*

Pass the hat   Ask for contributions. *Albert's birthday is coming up, and I think I'll pass the hat. We'll buy him a nice birthday present.*

Pick someone's brains   To go to someone for information. *Ted knows a lot about applying for financial aid; I think I'll pick his brains before I do my applications.*

B

Pick up the tab/check   Pay the bill. *You've been so kind to have us for the weekend; I want to pick up the check for dinner.*

Piece of cake   Easily accomplished. *Don't take Dr. John's course; take Prof. Smith's. It's a piece of cake, and he's an easy grader.*

Pitch in   To help out. *If we all pitch in, we can have this apartment cleaned out in no time.*

Plug something in   Insert the plug of an appliance into an electrical outlet. *Look, the television's not broken; you just need to plug it in.*

Polish something off   To finish up. *There's a little more orange juice in the refrigerator; I'll just polish it off and throw the container away.*

Pound the pavement   Look extensively for a job. *I've been pounding the pavement for two weeks, but I haven't gotten any offers; if nothing turns up soon, I'm going to have to drop out of school.*

Pressed for time   Very busy. *Sorry, I can't stop to chat; I'm pressed for time. I've got to be in the city in half an hour.*

Presence of mind   Composed; ability to act sensibly in an emergency. *After the collision, we were all pretty shaken, but John had the presence of mind to turn off the ignition.*

Pull through   To recover from an illness. *Tina was really sick for a while, but she pulled through and is much better now.*

Put in an appearance   To show up at briefly. *I don't really want to go the dance, but I'll put in an appearance, just so that people can see my face.*

Put something on hold   To postpone something. *I've had to put my business school plans on hold for a year; I need to work for a while to pay off my student loans.*

Put up with something   To endure; to suffer. *I can't put up with Peter's incessant chattering anymore; I'm going out for a walk.*

Quiet as a mouse   Very quiet; silent. *Barbara's big test is tomorrow, so please be as quiet as a mouse so she can study.*

Race against time   In a hurry; rushing to meet a deadline. *It's a race against time; the manuscript has to be at the printer no later than 1:00.*

Raise one's sights   To set higher goals. *I was just going to apply to the state university, but my adviser said to raise my sights. So now I'm also applying to some Ivy League schools.*

Resign oneself to something   To accept something reluctantly. *I had wanted to go to Mexico during spring break, but I've resigned myself to staying in town.*

Ring a bell   Seem familiar. *No, I do not know an Albert Devonworth; the name does not ring a bell.*

Roll out the red carpet   To give special treatment. *Irene's boyfriend will be visiting this weekend, and I'm going to roll out the red carpet: cheese and crackers, champagne, and later a nice dinner.*

Run a fever   Have a temperature above normal. *Sy is running a fever; and if it gets any higher, I'm going to take him to the emergency room.*

Run an errand   Make a short trip to do some business. *I've got to go to the bank and run some other errands, but I'll be back in an hour or so.*

Run out of gas   Exhaust the fuel supply. *We ran out of gas at three in the morning and had to wait until 7 o'clock for the service station to open.*

Safe and sound   Out of danger; unharmed. *We were concerned when we found the empty canoe, but later the campers were found safe and sound.*

Set the table   To place plates, glasses and utensils on the table before a meal. *Martha will set the table while I finish cooking.*

Sew something up   To secure; to make certain. *I asked about the scholarship this morning, and the secretary says I've got it all sewed up.*

Sight for sore eyes   A welcome sight. *I haven't seen you in three months; you're a sight for sore eyes.*

Sign on the dotted line   To execute a contract or other important document. *It's official; we bought the house this morning; we signed on the dotted line down at the lawyer's office.*

Sit tight   To wait patiently. *No, I'm not going to call the admissions office; I'm going to sit tight until they notify me one way or the other.*

Sleep in   To sleep late in the morning. *Tomorrow's a holiday, so I plan to sleep in.*

Sleep on something   To think about something overnight. *I like the idea, but I want to sleep on it. I'll give you my answer tomorrow.*

Slip one's mind   To forget about something. *I know I was supposed to pick up milk on my way home, but it slipped my mind.*

Slip up   To make a mistake. *I know the surprise party was supposed to be a secret, but I slipped up and mentioned it to Fred.*

Small hours of the night/wee hours of the night   The hours immediately following midnight. *I finally got the paper done, but I was up until the wee hours of the night.*

So far, so good   Everything going well so far. *How are my my classes? So far so good. I like them all.*

Soaked to the skin   Very wet. *We got caught in a rain storm on the way to the concert, and now we're soaked to the skin.*

Speak one's mind   To speak frankly. *I know that I was critical of the university's policy, but I always like to speak my mind.*

Split up   To separate; to leave one another. *Let's split up now and everyone look for Frank; we'll meet back here at 2:00.*

Spread oneself too thin   To take too much responsibility. *I've spread myself too thin this semester; I'm working ten hours per week plus I'm taking an extra class.*

Start from scratch   To start from the beginning. *Somewhere, I lost the first draft of my paper, so I'll have to start from scratch.*

Stay in touch with   Maintain contact with on an intermittent basis. *We'll be graduating soon, but let's all stay in touch with each other.*

Step on the gas/step on it   Go fast. *Driver, step on it! The concert begins in 10 minutes.*

Stock up on something   Build up a supply of something. *The college bookstore is having a sale on supplies, so I'll stock up on paper, pens, and printer cartridges.*

Straighten up   Tidy up; to make neat. *While you're out, I'm going to straighten up the living room because company is coming over tonight.*

Stroke of luck   Piece or bit of luck. *It was a stroke of luck that I caught Prof. Smith just she was leaving her office.*

Swallow one's pride   To admit one was wrong; to accept humiliation. *I guess I'll swallow my pride and ask for an extension because I don't see how I can finish this paper in time.*

Take a crack at something   To try something. *I've never played golf before, but I'll take a crack at it.*

Take an interest in something   To become interested in something. *I've taken an interest in economics, and I'm even thinking about majoring in it.*

Take five   Take a brief rest. *We've been working pretty hard; everybody take five.*

Take off   To leave. *I've got to take off now because I have a dinner engagement.*

Take off from work   To take time away from one's job. *I plan to take off from work tomorrow, so that I can go to the dentist.*

Take one's time   Do in a leisurely fashion. *I want to take my time with this project and make sure that it's done right.*

Take something lying down   To accept without argument or resistance. *I'm not going to take the professor's decision lying down; I plan to appeal to the university council.*

Take something up with someone   To discuss with someone. *Several of us in the class want to do some additional reading for credit; were going to take it up with Prof. Smith tomorrow.*

Take time off   To stop working for a while. *As soon as the semester is over, I'm going to take some time off to visit my friend in California.*

Talk something over   To discuss with. *I'd like to have Angel move into the apartment; I'm going to talk it over with my roommates.*

Tear one's hair out   To be frustrated or angry. *I still haven't heard from the financial aid committee, and I'm ready to tear my hair out.*

That makes two of us   The same is true for me; includes me. *So, you're going to write on the Age of Reason; that makes two of us.*

The more the merrier   More people are always welcome. *Art wants to go with us to dinner? That's great! The more the merrier!*

Throw a party for someone   To have a party for someone. *Marsha's going home to Israel, so were going to throw a party for her.*

Thumbs down   Disapproval of. *I suggested that we try the new Vietnamese restaurant, but that idea received a thumbs down from Bob.*

Tied up   To be busy. *I'd like to come visit you in Kansas City, but I'm tied up until the end of the month.*

Tone something down   To make something less extreme. *I think that the speech may be too aggressive for some people; I'd tone it down a bit.*

Touch and go   Uncertain; not settled. *We may have enough votes to approve the waste disposal project, but it's touch and go at this point.*

Train of thought   Sequence of ideas; thinking. *I lost my train of thought when the phone rang, and now I can't seem to find it.*

Try one's hand at something   To try something new. *I'd like to try my hand at photography when I get a chance.*

Tune something out   To ignore. *The television noise doesn't bother me, I just tune it out.*

B

Turn in   To go to bed. *I think I'll turn in because I have to get up early in the morning.*

Turn over a new leaf   To start anew with the intention of correcting past errors. *After he got a C in political science last semester, Tom resolved to turn over a new leaf and to attend every class.*

Turn someone or something down   To reject; to refuse. *The committee turned down my proposal; they suggested that I needed to spend more time researching some of the finer points of the thesis.*

Under the weather   Not feeling well; ill. *I'm not going to class today because I'm under the weather; perhaps I'll feel better later in the week.*

Until all hours   Until very late. *My roommate has been out until all hours every night this week. I don't see how she gets up to go to class.*

Wait and see attitude   Willing to wait to see what happens. *The new grading policy is interesting, but I think I'll take a wait-and-see attitude before I make up my mind.*

Wear out one's welcome   To stay too long; to visit too often. *The dinner was delicious, but I don't want to wear out my welcome, so I'll be going home now.*

Whip something up   To prepare something from available ingredients; to improvise. *We don't have to go out to eat; I can just whip something up in the kitchen.*

Wild-goose chase   A futile errand or pursuit. *It turned out that Dickens never wrote such a novel; the trip to the library was a wild-goose chase.*

Within a stone's throw   Nearby; close to. *Please come see us; our apartment is just a stone's throw from the college.*

You bet!   Surely; certainly. *You bet I'll be there; I wouldn't miss it!*